R.D.'s True Crime Library

Pilar Publishing of California
pilarpublishing@yahoo.com

Paperback Edition
ISBN: 97983954044374

Also From Pilar Publishing of California

By Franklin Alfred Kirby Edwards
Diary of Agent 355
In Search of André and Arnold
Return of the Templars
◊
By R.D. Byron-Smith
True Stories I Never Told My Kids
Dinner with a Killer
Two Ladies in Minsk
The Lost 11 Days of Agatha Christie

Courtroom Misfits ©2024 Pilar Publishing of California. All rights reserved. No part of this book may be used or reproduced in any manner whatsoever without written permission from the publisher except in case of brief quotations embodied in critical articles or reviews. Manuscript follows the Associated Press Stylebook.

COURTROOM MISFITS

Fifty Years of Judges Behaving Badly in America

Ronnie Dale Smith

Table of Contents

Introduction..10
Chapter One...18
Chapter Two..34
Chapter Three..52
Chapter Four...74
Chapter Five..89
Chapter Six..102
Chapter Seven..128
Chapter Eight...142
Chapter Nine..153
Chapter Ten...172
Chapter Eleven...210
Chapter Twelve...233
Chapter Thirteen...253
Chapter Fourteen..264
Afterword..286

"Honesty is a minimum qualification expected of every judge." — *California Commission on Judicial Performance.*

Introduction

    Many funny, dim-witted and even scary people have sat on the judicial bench over the past half century. Yet the miscreants who occupy these pages do not represent the majority of bright, hardworking judges in America; far from it. It is indeed this minority of wrongdoers who make the honest judges look all the better.

    Origins of this book stem from witnessing thousands of court proceedings as a newspaper reporter, from death penalty trials to the United States Supreme Court pondering Rubik's Cube legal complexities – even a case in which a parishioner sued his pastor for violating the Seventh Commandment against adultery, although the judge ruled he couldn't follow "biblical law" in his court.

    Altruistically I'd like to say my intention is to aid judges from making the mistakes of others, but that's poppycock because most sitting judges already know the rights and wrongs of ethical behavior. I wrote the book because these cases of misconduct are interesting. Like a pack of cigarettes this book comes with a user warning. Covering 50 years of jurisprudence, from the 1970s to the 2020s, it must be stated that much has changed in America during this time, especially in the culture and what is acceptable and what is not. The following documented words and deeds by judges touch extremes, and include racial and gay slurs and misogynist remarks, which will offend some readers. The book lists a full array of judges who tried to crack funny in court, and instead ran afoul of their ethics because they offended someone, and the judges were punished for it. Some of their antics are hilarious and others pathetic, ranging from a California judge who allowed an attorney to sing a strange song to a jury that had nothing to do with the case to a New York judge exercising his sexual proclivities with an extremely naive young woman on his desk in chambers. In between these bizarre extremes, scores of colorful tales of real judges are laid out in fully documented prose.

    For sure, however, by its nature and in turns, this book can be utterly funny and gut-wrenchingly disturbing because some cases involve judges doing things as bad as the criminals they sentence.

By its nature as well, the work doesn't portray what happens in courtrooms on a daily basis because it details unethical behavior and judicial misconduct by a tiny minority of the nation's jurists, many of whom were fired for their wrongdoing. A deeply disturbing trend also surfaced in researching the book: repeat offenders. American discipline records tended to show the same judges being punished for misconduct over and over again. A judge would be reprimanded for rude courtroom conduct and three years later be punished again for the same offense. A few years afterward the same judge would commit new misconduct and would be, finally, fired by his state judicial misconduct commission.

Recidivist – a word judges themselves don't like to hear a criminal called in their courtrooms.

A few relevant questions must be asked.

Who disciplines judges? All states have official watchdog agencies that investigate wrongdoing by judges. Whether called a commission, an inquiry board or a council, they operate similarly. They accept complaints filed by litigants and others – even fellow judges – and, after screening them, hand the credible gripes to a panel of investigators, usually three judges, for a closer look-see. After an investigation which can take months and involve dozens of witnesses, the investigators recommend a judge's punishment to the full commission, which can have as many as 28 members, some of them non-lawyers. The commission reviews evidence, which normally includes the judge's defense against the alleged misconduct, and votes on whether to recommend discipline to the state's Supreme Court to carry out. Punishments or sanctions range from a private letter telling a judge not to repeat the misconduct to his out-right firing. Unlike in California, where its powerful Commission on Judicial Performance can dismiss judges itself, most states give firing power only to their respective Supreme Courts.

It's far from a perfect system. Court advocates complain judicial commissions go too easy on judges. They lambaste them for being too opaque in disclosures about discipline cases. Still it is not unreasonable to argue that without these "flawed" judicial watchdogs many errant judges might well have gone right on doing unsavory things. In their own way these commissions act as deterrents to judicial misbehavior. Nationwide since the 1960s thousands of judges have been punished publicly and privately for misconduct.

Judicial discipline cases stem from violations of a state's ethics code for judges. Violations range from a judge committing a crime to making racially charged remarks from the bench. All states have judicial ethics codes and most have been modeled after California's, as it was the first to establish a commission to discipline judges in 1960. Its judicial code has six canons: (1) A judge shall uphold the integrity and independence of the judiciary. (2) A judge shall avoid impropriety and the appearance of impropriety in all of the judge's activities. (3) A judge shall perform the duties of judicial office impartially, competently, and diligently. (4) A judge shall so conduct the judge's quasi-judicial and extrajudicial activities as to minimize the risk of conflict with judicial obligations. (5) A judge or candidate for judicial office shall not engage in political or campaign activity that is inconsistent with the independence, integrity, or impartiality of the judiciary. (6) [A judge shall] comply with the Code of Judicial Ethics.

Every misconduct case brought against a judge by California's commission, and indeed every other state commission, falls within one of these canons. It's amazing how commissions ably shoehorn the facts of every case into a violation of a canon. For instance, a judge who "started rubbing" a woman's breasts violated Canon 2 – a "judge shall avoid impropriety" in "all of [his] activities." I can see a commission claiming that a judge who murders has violated Canon 1 – failure to "uphold" the court's integrity. Remarkably by their vagueness, the canons possess what law doesn't cotton to, much: ambiguity. In a case in which a judge in Texas argued that the state's code of conduct was overbroad, the state's highest court ruled in 1998: "Vagueness and overbreadth doctrines are generally used to challenge the validity of laws defining criminal conduct . . . [But] a greater degree of flexibility is permitted with respect to judicial discipline than is allowed in criminal statutes." Thusly vagueness makes the code extremely effective and amply pliable. Discipline commissions also follow legal precedents from their respective Supreme Courts. Such rulings come from appeals by judges who believed they were unfairly disciplined. From these precedents, "guidelines" for considering punishments have been laid down. Factors both in aggravation and mitigation include the nature of the misconduct; existence of prior discipline; whether a judge shows remorse; a judge's integrity and veracity; likelihood of future misconduct; and, the overall impact of a judge's misconduct on the justice system. Reading like a defendant's bill of rights, it doesn't take a legal scholar to see that such "guidelines" militate against a judge being punished. Nevertheless it isn't surprising that the most severe unethical laps by judges result in the harshest punishment.

Many judges featured in these pages no longer serve because they were either removed on the recommendations of their state commissions or retired voluntarily because they were under investigation for misconduct and suspected they'd be booted out anyway. Other judges in this book still sit on their respective state court benches, administering justice after being scolded publicly for both minor and serious misbehavior. A common tenant of every discipline commission is this: when discipline is levied it is done to "protect" the public from a judge ever repeating the unethical behavior rather than to "punish" him for doing it in the first place. That is the spin every discipline board puts on it. Sometimes this stated goal allows commissions to go easy on judges, especially if they confess an abundance of remorse for their misconduct. Expressing remorse is a tactic every defense attorney knows because it can lead to a lesser sentence for his convicted client, and judges are no different. Commissions also give deference to judges who speedily settle discipline cases. The Arizona Commission on Judicial Conduct states that when a judge acts "quickly" to settle a discipline case it "avoids subjecting his victims to a lengthy, embarrassing disciplinary process," especially in sexual harassment claims. In other words, cooperation reaps reward. On the other hand attorneys of the State Bar of Arizona state that when a judge cooperates and makes a deal early to end his case it "enables him to minimize" disclosure of facts against him and "spares him the embarrassment of a formal hearing." Obviously it also spares the court system itself heightened embarrassment.

The legal standard of proof in finding a judge "guilty" of violating ethics codes isn't what jurors must follow in criminal cases, which is "guilt beyond a reasonable doubt." Civil courts apply a less rigorous standard which is called "clear and convincing." This is the standard used in discipline cases against judges. It simply means there must be "clear and convincing" evidence that a judge's misbehavior violated the ethics code. Not really a difficult concept to grasp, the California Supreme Court defines it this way: "Clear and convincing evidence is sufficiently strong to command the unhesitating assent of every reasonable mind." This lower standard of evidence makes it easier to find a judge "guilty" of misconduct.

The subtitle of this book is *Fifty Years of Judges Behaving Badly in America's Courts*. It begs the question. What happened in the 190 years before that? Not much. Before the decade of the 1960s, errant judges were voted out of office for wrongdoing when enough people became aware of it. Some jurists were fired by state Supreme Courts for committing crimes. Yet when it came to violations of judicial ethics, judges were largely immune from punishment. That's because there was nobody to complain to. That's why as a result of a public vote in 1960, California became the first state to establish an independent commission to investigate ethical lapses by its judges. The original Commission on Judicial Qualifications had nine members consisting of five judges, two attorneys and two non-lawyer, lay-persons to investigate judicial misconduct. Over the years the commission not only got a new name – Commission of Judicial Performance – but it also gained power, including sanctioning judges for alcohol and illicit drug use, the ability to open investigative hearings to the public and require public statements in cases as long as the judge being disciplined agreed, or "when the charges involved moral turpitude, corruption or dishonesty and when to do so would be in the pursuit of public confidence and in the interests of justice." Despite reforms to the California judicial discipline agency over three decades, by the mid-1990s voters called for further reform after it was disclosed that of 7,185 complaints against state judges over a 27-year span, only 25 complaints resulted in punishment. That one-third of a percent "conviction" rate was alarmingly dismal. Reformers cried foul, and wanted the power to remove judges taken from the hands of the state Supreme Court and, after expanding the commission, giving it authority to remove bad judges. In 1994 voters passed significant changes to the commission, including making investigative hearings open to the public, giving the commission power to fire judges itself and to adopt its own rules in governing judge misconduct. Significantly the reform added four non-lawyer members to a new eleven-member commission. Today the California Commission on Judicial Performance, along with the New York State Commission on Judicial Conduct, remains the gold standard for the rest of the nation.

Judicial commissions adapt to changing times. California's, for example, shows a fresh sensitivity in punishing judges for improper gender and racial remarks. This mirrors society's empowerment of women, and even more so to profound demographic changes in the Golden State, where in 2020, whites dropped to 35 percent of the population, compared to 40 percent in 2010. Because of this, California's court system "established access and fairness" as its top goal in recent years. This book's mission is not to dissect inadequacies of judge discipline commissions. Nonetheless, not all state commissions are created equal. For instance, it wasn't until 2017 that Georgia lawmakers brought the state's Judicial Qualifications Commission, created in 1972, into the twenty-first century after state voters rebelled and eliminated the highly secretive body in favor of a new one, with some members who are not lawyers or judges. In the Georgia reforms, although complaints remain secret, once discipline is administered records are subject to public disclosure. Other state commissions vary widely on the amount of detail made public. On a sliding scale of transparency, Wyoming ranks a miserable one, while New York ranks a solid ten and provides an abundance of intricate detail. But far too many judicial commissions refuse to release investigative materials, and instead issue sparce press releases when a judge is disciplined. As referenced, the Wyoming Commission on Judicial Conduct and Ethics is highly secretive. This is from the body's 2022 Annual Report: "Except in limited circumstances specified by statute and rule, all complaints, papers and testimony received or maintained by the Commission on Judicial Conduct and Ethics are confidential and cannot be disclosed. Any violation of the confidentiality provision constitutes an act of contempt and is punishable as such. A recommendation for public discipline, filed by the Commission with the Wyoming Supreme Court, loses its confidential character upon its filing, subject to the procedures, rules or orders of the Court. However, the record which is the basis of the recommendation remains confidential unless otherwise ordered by the Court." Other states stingy on information include Vermont and Idaho. Are these commissions, even weak ones, vital? Absolutely. Unavoidably it is to these commissions where the public turns to learn whether the courts are adequately self-policing. To be sure, in the national justice system the workings of these judicial discipline agencies isn't very well known, and it is the author's hope that this book will shed light on the esoteric world of judge discipline, particularly the kinds of words and deeds requiring it.

    What are judges disciplined for, normally?

Obviously judges are punished for breaking the law, which can be as minor as shoplifting to felonies as serious as arson, possession of child pornography and lying to the FBI – all cases covered in these pages. More often, judges get disciplined for technical legal things, like failure to file an election campaign report or for talking to one litigant in a case without the other litigant present. These "technical" violations, though numerous nationwide, aren't very interesting. This book focuses on more interesting cases, from mistreating jurors to judges driving drunk, from slapping a 9-year-old with contempt of court to judges acting whacky. Like the jurist who turned her courtroom into a television show and a judge who muscled her way into the trial of pop music icon Michael Jackson. Other cases involve judges threatening murder and having sex with defendants appearing before them. Commonly discipline commissions investigate instances of judges losing their cool. Even if a judge gets hot enough to pull out his hair, he isn't supposed to lose his temper and run afoul of ethics rules requiring him to be patient and courteous. In one case, for instance, a judge was censured for becoming "embroiled" in a case when he poked a prosecutor in the chest and said, "Buddy boy, you're not going to get away with this . . . I'm going to see that you lose this case big." Judges even get in trouble for what they say and do off the bench. Later I detail a classic: a judge striking out with his ethics commission for yelling at an ump at his kid's baseball game. I'm sure there's a few armchair lawyers asking about a judge's right to free speech, about now. Isn't he free to say what he wants in his private life? Supreme Courts nationwide agree with Texas's, which ruled "judges do not have full First Amendment rights," noting their "right to free speech may not be as broad as that of other citizens." Another way to put is when a judge signs up for the job, he forfeits rights. Sometimes judges have been punished for misconduct which most juries would never have convicted them of. Like the Florida judge whose mother was "wiped out" by Wall Street fraud impresario Bernie Madoff, who scammed 5,000 people out of $64 billion. To help her, the judge represented his mother in a mortgage case, which is against Florida's judicial ethics code. He was punished for his "unethical" conduct. But, come on, what son wouldn't have helped his poor mom who'd been scammed out of her lifesavings?

Judges are like the rest of us. They put their pants on one leg at a time, and they have families and nurture their children. They barbecue in the back yard. They drive to the mall and shop, and attend baseball games. And, like the rest of us, they screw up, even in funny ways. Undeniably some discipline cases will raise a chuckle. Like the Connecticut Superior Court judge suspended for two weeks in 1992 for slapping a $1,000 arrest warrant on a chicken farmer who littered a small town street by "dripping chicken manure . . . out of his truck." Connecticut's Judicial Review Council punished the judge because the maximum fine for littering was $250, and because he had a history of suing the poultry farmer, showing bias. Judges also seem to like spinning clichéd pearls of wisdom from the bench, such as a California judge disciplined for telling a defendant, "No, you've been hanging out with dogs and wondering why you get fleas." Other times judges can't resist cracking a joke. During a criminal trial a defense attorney asked a witness: "Did you hear anything that lady said as she was entering?" The judge found it vague, and couldn't hold back, quipping, "Like did she belch . . . ?" Or like the Alaskan judge whose courtroom was cold in 2005, and he wrote a note to a female courthouse employee wearing a tight-fitting sweater that stated, "Your Hillbilly thermometers are distracting." Yeah, for these jokes the judges got minor punishments.

 Source material for this book is drawn from public records available at state judicial discipline commissions nationwide, and from court decisions as well as other public sources. Official records by their limited nature rarely tell the whole story of an event, or a case of judicial discipline. Because of lack of space or other reasons, commission staffers cannot include every shred of information in public filings. Therefore, a book which relies on such reports is inherently flawed. Additionally, state Supreme Courts that remove judges from office pick and choose facts, tending to support their decisions. As a consequence, it follows, that a book based on court decisions omits facts. To provide balance, when a judge's denial of misconduct or defense against the charges appeared in records, it is included in the narrative of each discipline case.

Chapter One

This chapter might well be titled "judicial tech wrecks" because the internet has brought down many judges for misconduct, from posting about trials they're presiding over to electronically sending nude photos of themselves. The American Bar Association was so concerned about the rise of judges using social media that it issued a declaration, "Formal Opinion 462" in 2013. The subject was the use by judges of social media like Facebook and other electronic forums. State discipline commissions such as Arkansas's have recognized the spread of jurists taking to the web, and have adopted rules saying "judges must at all times act in a manner that promotes public confidence in the independence, integrity, and impartiality of the judiciary" in all activities, even postings on social media sites. In 2021, the Tennessee Supreme Court told judges and attorneys that when they used social media sites like Facebook, they "must realize they are handling live ammunition."

The granddaddy case of judicial misconduct on social media goes to Arkansas Circuit Judge Michael A. Maggio, who had been a judge for 13 years when he was fired by the state's Supreme Court in 2014 for his postings on a sports fan web forum for Louisiana State University. It ranks as one of the ugliest cases of judicial misconduct on the internet, and as readers will see, one of the most ironic.

In 2012 the judge presided over adoptions for the Circuit Court in Conway, Faulkner County, Arkansas. On a day he wasn't on the bench another judge filled in for him and handled the adoption of a child for a woman, and afterward, the other judge filled him in on what had happened. Between the judges, the information was meant to remain confidential because adoptions were not subject to public disclosure. On January 17th, 2012 and using the name "geauxjudge" – geaux is a French word meaning go and is used by fans of the LSU Tigers – Judge Maggio disclosed private information about an adoption by writing: "Re: [Actress] Charlize Theron adopt a baby today? I . . . have a friend who is the judge that did her adoption today. It was a single parent adoption. I offered to be the baby daddy. He said she came dressed with long brown wig, oversized clothes, trying [to] camouflage her appearance. They took pixs but can't be published because closed proceeding. He said she did have an entourage . . . / know CSB [Cool Story, Bro]. Just when you hear it on TMZ."

To his post someone asked on the forum: "Did she get herself a black baby?"

Geauxjudge: "Yep."

Question: "Are you a judge as well?"

Geauxjudge: "Yes."

On March 4th, 2012 press reports carried some of the judge's posts from the LSU web site. By noon of the same day the Arkansas Judicial Discipline and Disability Commission announced it had an "on-going investigation" into the "subject matter" of the press reports.

Judge Maggio admitted that after the press coverage he "attempted to delete or edit postings" he had made. For example, on the subject of "would you wear shorts to a strip club," the judge's post of March 3rd, 2014 was deleted. In the days after press coverage of the judge's indiscretion of posting information about single mother and movie star Charlize Theron's adoption, she broke silence about having adopted her son, Jackson. Under Arkansas law adoptions are "closed," meaning confidential.

The adoption story made worldwide headlines.

While the commission stopped short of saying the judge exploited his position by disclosing the actress' adoption of a black child, there was "at least a measure of exploitation when a judge uses confidential information to brag about having the scoop on a noteworthy news item contained in a sealed case file. In fact, the judge used the common internet acronym CSB which means Cool Story, Bro," used when internet posters show off "inside knowledge," the records stated.

In justifying his removal from the bench, the commission also stated that, "Judges hold confidential information about people who are vulnerable and are given the protection of confidentiality under the law. This is certainly true for most juvenile proceedings as well as closed adoptions . . . In this case, you [Judge Maggio] violated the trust of an adopting mother. The case was on your docket and you were informed about the adoption. You had no valid reason to broadcast the information. This resulted in a violation of the faith the people placed in your hands upon taking the oath of your office. It cast doubt on whether information in closed proceedings is ever truly confidential."

It wasn't only for his internet posting about the actress that he was fired, however. The judge had been posting messages on the LSU fan forum since 2005, and on other sites, and many of these messages were also part of the discipline case against him. In listing many of his posts in the official record, the Arkansas Judicial Discipline and Disability Commission wrote: "All of the inappropriate comments by Maggio will not be reiterated. However, others included improper jokes and posts about sex with bi-polar women, suggesting a gift of "lube, beer and blow" (when asked about potential ideas for a wedding present), a non-consensual "rodeo sex" reference, incest references, how sex with teachers is like trophy hunting for teenage boys and how women make divorce decisions on "emotions" rather than business sense."

Here is a sampling of posts the judge admitted making from his telephone and from computers at home and in his office, and which were included in commission documents.

November 4th, 2008: "I have bunch of public intox[ication] cases in 20 minutes and just can't wait to slam the gavel!"

August 12th, 2009, commenting on a divorce case in which the husband is not sexually satisfied: "This case is still pending. I send them to mediation . . . No need to drag the kids into court if can be avoided. I will say I get tired of hearing how the husband works all the time (uhh no kidding how you think the bills get paid); that he had an affair (Ummm . . . the wife quits or shuts down sex to nothing, becomes unattractive, and non-supportive and then is shocked when he steps out) what did she think was going to happen . . . Food and Frickin go a long way to helping a man overlook a lot of BS."

December 30th, 2009: "Let me explain women to the young high schoolers visiting us. From my years in the courtroom: 1. All women have an agenda. 2. Women look at two bulges on a man. A. The front and/or B. the back (wallet). 3. As long as either one is big enough they can make do without the other."

January 26th, 2010, with the subject "Guys, would you make out with another guy for a million?" the judge wrote: "You make a hole in one . . . Doesn't make you a golfer. But make out with another guy . . . You a homo. You know I make a hole-in-one and it doesn't make me a good golfer BUT you su[c]k on pecker or take in pooper . . . You are a homo/gay."

July 13th, 2011, with the subject "story of an upset Free Mason, the judge stated: "What about Mexican masons??? I mean that all I ever see laying bricks."

August 16th, with the subject being "worst tattoo ever," the judge wrote: "I have never understood why African Americans just don't use white ink in their tattoos."

October 18th, in a discussion on whether racial profiling is good or bad, the judge wrote: "It depends on if you are the profiler or the profilee."

October 24th, with the subject, "Should you be able to legally beat up a friend caught sleeping with your wife?" Judge Maggio using his forum name geauxjudge wrote: "His defense attorney can argue defense of wife/chattel. He thought it was rape in progress."

November 16th, with the subject "Before you over-marry," the judge wrote: "I have found the slender ones to go nuts at 40 right after the boob job."

January 17th, 2012, on subject of "Bengals Cheerleader accused of sex with minor," the judge wrote: "Please, please, please let me get this case . . . The discovery process would be outstanding."

January 29th, under the forum subject, "Ever been to the Grand Canyon?" the judge wrote: "Let's see you taking lady friends to Vegas and you want to see Grand Canyon??? OT ballers just gamble like Arabs, drink like Indians, and do the humpty-hump like rabbits. But, hey you want to go and see the Grand Canyon. Go ahead."

September 26th, in a discussion on "what's the best advice," the judge wrote: "F rule: if it flies, floats or F—ks . . . rent it."

October 12th: "Yeah. I am looking for a 69 GTO Judge. I want to put Guilty on the license plate."

Commission records state that the judge posted "many comments on how [he] wishes to be assigned cases involving attractive women, sexual subject matter and nude or explicit pictures."

December 23rd, in "offering" what appears to be legal advice on how to beat a drunken driving case, under the subject of "To Blow or Not to Blow," the judge wrote: "You have the right to remain silent . . . so don't say a word. Don't open your mouth 'smell of intoxicants' that is the probable cause for FST [field sobriety test]. Just hand the LEO [law enforcement officer] your license, insurance and registration. Everything they need to write you the ticket (reason for the stop) is on those papers . . . Never say a ward. If ordered out of car. Get out and lean against car. Don't move. Yes, very possible you will be cuffed and stuffed. But at that time all they have is the violation for the stop . . . Refuse the BAC test. Yes another ticket but better than the alternative. In the end the less evidence the best . . . That being said 99 percent of folks on the side of the road all think, Hey, I can talk my way out. Of course, the single best advice is don't drink and drive ever. LEO don't play."

December 27th, the judge posted a comment which showed he did a little "independent investigation" on an upcoming case, which is unethical. "OK, I have a case this afternoon involving backpage.com. . . . Seems this may be an issue in a divorce [and] custody case. I never had any idea about this [web] site. So I just asked a LEO cyber investigator . . . Well, this could be interesting. Especially since a lot of subpoenas have been issued. Hey, here I thought it was going to be a slow week."

February 20th, 2013, with subject "Vegas woman arrested for sex with pit bull," the judge wrote: "How old was the dog? Hey look if you can have TGGLBS [apparently stands for Transgender Gay Lesbian Bi-sexual] sex then it is just a small step to this. I wish I could say, I never. But I once had a case where the couple argued over a German Shepard . . . for this reason."

December 24th, under the subject of "baby names: where's the line between creative and obnoxious?" Judge Maggio wrote: "I do agree about names may not be predictors of future success, but in reality. How many Doctors do you hear named Dr. Taneesha or HaHa? How many bankers do hear named Brylee?" In another post the judge used this phrase: ". . . Cause he da cutest baby I has."

January 15th, 2014, with the subject "has anyone here dated an Indian chick?" Judge Maggio wrote, tersely, "Teepee or hotel?"

There was sweet irony in this case, which could be easily overlooked. In a post in November 2011, Judge Maggio warned others on the LSU web site about how easily it was for people to find out your identity from posts. "I cannot tell you the amount of information on FB, Twitter, etc. that opposing parties look up. Not only is your direct info being looked at so are your 'friends' info. The Photos that people are in on their friends sites, they are tagged and date stamped. It just amazes me some of the things posted."

Yes, but was he amazed when journalists and investigators for the commission quickly learned the true identity of geauxjudge?

Stated the judicial discipline commission, not showing what must have been group bemusement: "Your statements online were not anonymous. It took little time once the posts were sorted to find numerous facts in the posts that proved your actual identity. Examples include: a sitting circuit court judge; someone who lives in Arkansas; attended the University of Mississippi law school for two years; attended a Catholic high school growing up in Mississippi; attended Millsaps College in [Jackson] Mississippi for an undergraduate degree; . . . was appointed to his position by a governor and subsequently won election to his current position; the screen name geauxjudge was also used on the Arkansas sports site, Hogville.net and in those posts geauxjudge also talks about information that reveals your identity as Circuit Judge Michael Maggio . . . There were dozens, if not hundreds, of other posts identifying you as the poster through context and comments. Additionally, you made no secret that you were in fact a sitting judge and continually commented on your job and your role as a judge. Even your screen name indicated your official position . . . What you actually did was use a pseudonym and identify yourself through context while broadcasting to the public the comments that would ultimately bring you to discipline" and, the commission should have added, removal from office.

◊

The case of Minnesota Senior Judge Edward W. Bearse is another example of a jurist getting in hot legal water because of his internet ramblings.

A judge since 1983, he retired in 2006 and was then appointed a senior judge to assist with case backlogs in his state.

Here is a fact that doesn't excuse the old guy's misconduct, but it does help to explain it. He thought his posts on his Facebook page were being read by only 80 friends, family and members of his church. Hardly. His posts were public and could be read by Facebook's more than one billion users. He should have consulted with a 10-year-old for advice on the finer workings of the web.

In his three-decades-long judicial career Judge Bearse had never been disciplined by the Minnesota Board on Judicial Standards until his Facebook posts about cases he handled in 2015. Normally judges know they cannot discuss their cases, although some talk about cases which have concluded, like after sentencing of a defendant. But even then, with appeals underway, it can be ethically dicey for a judge.

Here is a post the judge wrote during a felony trial he was presiding over of a woman charged with "intentionally engaging in the sex trafficking of an individual." After the first day of testimony, the judge posted this on Facebook: "Some things I guess will never change. I just love doing the stress of jury trials. In a felony trial now [the] state [is] prosecuting a pimp. Cases are always difficult because the women (as in this case also) will not cooperate. We will see what the 12 citizens in the jury box do." After the woman was convicted by the jury, the county prosecutor learned about the judge's post, and as required, alerted the woman's attorney. Before she was sentenced her lawyer sought a new trial, and the request was assigned to another judge to consider. After reviewing Judge Bearse's post, the other judge granted the woman a new trial, stating: "The posting at 7:57 p.m. in the evening which followed jury selection and opening statements . . . imply the premise [that] the defendant is guilty of the charge and the corollary that the woman involved is a prostitute. They imply a pre-judgment of the case before any evidence is heard . . . The court will vacate the verdict and order a new trial." One post – 52 words – caused the trial to be done over again at public expense. That's not mentioning the three days the poor wretches on the jury suffered, trying to stay awake in the jury box.

In another post the judge mentioned a petition filed by a medical school graduate, asking that her conviction for disorderly conduct be wiped from the courthouse record. In other words, no record, no crime. She said she couldn't get a medical license with the crime on her record. Judge Bearse posted, "Listen to this and conclude that lawyers have more fun than people." He went on to say why, by giving details of the crime, stating that the medical graduate assaulted her boyfriend when she discovered him having sex with her best friend. In the post the judge said he granted her request to clean her record, and said he doubted prosecutors would appeal it, but if they did, "I think I will be reversed."

A Facebook reader of the post, commented: "I am always heartened by the application of common sense. An excellent decision, in my opinion." Another commented: "You're back in the saddle again, Judge."

In other posts the judge mentioned defendants who repeatedly turn up in court after being arrested on warrants issued by judges: "We deal with a lot of geniuses!" Noting a person was charged with possessing a shotgun, the judge posted: "Just awful his son turned out to be such a Klunk." He called the Hennepin County, Minnesota District Court "a zoo!" because it was busy.

He also commented on Facebook on two serious cases he had been involved in. "My day yesterday in the Hennepin County

District Court in Minneapolis: . . . Criminal Vehicular Homicide where defendant stoned on Xanax supplemented it with a lot of booze and then drove wrong way down a freeway colliding with an innocent citizen driving the right way down the same freeway killing him . . . and most interesting – three kidnappings . . . where the three were physically tortured to try and find the drugs."

His last post on courthouse business came in August 2015, telling of a non-jury trial he presided over. During the trial the defense attorney had a "panic attack" and was taken to the hospital by ambulance. The judge put the following message on Facebook: "Now we are in chaos because defendant has to hire a new lawyer who will most likely want to start over and a very vulnerable woman will have to spend another day on the witness stand . . . I was so angry that on the way home I stopped to see our District Administrator and told him, 'Michael, you are going to have to just listen to me bitch for a while.' . . . We know the new lawyer (probably quite justifiably) will be asking for another continuance. Terrible day!!!"

As is often the case, another judge snitched Judge Bearse off over the post, and told the court's chief judge about it, saying "Sounds like it is likely to be raised as a legal issue soon." The chief judge sent the other judge's e-mail about the post to Judge Bearse, and recommended he delete his post from Facebook, which he did. Judge Bearse also removed himself from hearing the trial he mentioned in his post, and stopped putting things about his cases on the web.

The Minnesota Board on Judicial Standards posted its own message for Judge Bearse, publicly reprimanding him for violating ethics rules prohibiting a "judge from making a public statement that might reasonably be expected to affect the outcome or impair the fairness of a matter pending . . . in any court," among other code misconduct.

◊

When Judge Gerald Webb of Chattanooga took to the web he hadn't gotten the message from Tennessee's high court about the internet being "live ammunition." His posts exploded in his face and he was reprimanded for them by the state's Board of Judicial Conduct.

In a Facebook post called "Legal Tip of the Day" on June 18th, 2021, the judge wrote: "When stealing stealth is key. You want to blend in with your surroundings." He continued, giving this example: "You and your 5-foot-10 sister walk in [Walmart] with green hair and green toenails and green flipflops that smack the back of your feet with every step you make and you don't blend in and you are caught with three steaks shoved into your pants. You forgot to be stealth." In another post on August 5th, the judge wrote: "It is downright damn humiliating when police are pulling crack from your crack. Find some other place to hide your stash."

To almost anyone, the judge's posts were sacksful of sarcasm, ions of irascible irony, tongue-full-in-cheek stuff – you know, "Hey criminals, how stupid can you get?" But not to the humorless crowd at the state's judicial conduct board, whom, one must assume took his words as the "Illegal Tip of the Day."

Even the judge in responding to the complaint filed against him said he wrote the posts to "get a laugh, and to make people think about life choices." The judicial board countered that maybe the judge should have thought about his own choices. Like when he posted: "The goal of criminal and bad behavior is to get away with it."

The board stated his posts did not show "caution and reflection" especially for a judge like Mr. Webb who handled criminal cases. Perhaps realizing that his humor was best saved for the Improv, the judge took responsibility for his posts and cooperated with the board's inquiry.

◊

The case of Limestone County, Texas Judge Daniel Burkeen is of particular interest because of its political mutterings. In 2017 on his public Facebook page which identified him as a county judge, Judge Burkeen posted a photo of U.S. Marine Corps General James "Mad Dog" Mattis who had been appointed as secretary of defense by then-President Donald J. Trump. On the photo were the words: "Fired by Obama to please the Muslims, hired by Trump to exterminate them." The post ignited a firestorm of people claiming the judge supported "genocide." He quickly deleted it but the horse was out of the barn. The Texas Commission on Judicial Conduct sent him a complaint letter, to which he later responded. He explained that the photo "showed an interesting contrast" between Presidents Barack Obama and Trump and their "attitudes" towards Mad Dog Mattis. However, he said, he "never would have shared this post if I thought it would be taken as an endorsement of genocide. I realized afterwards that I should not have posted it, because it's not just about how I interpreted it, but how others might."

In another post, a supporter of President Donald Trump, Judge Burkeen wrote this after the 2016 election: "The best part of Trump's election has been that it has revealed once again how hateful, intolerant, arrogant and divisive liberals are, not to mention the fact that they have taken the word hypocrisy to new extremes . . . Hope apparently is defined by liberals as hatred and intolerance, persecution of Christians, embracing criminals, murdering police officers, racial violence, and of course, a welfare state financed by borrowed money . . . A good example of the shallowness of liberal thinking is the fact liberals have convinced themselves that the norm is the lunacy we have gone through in the last eight years, and that anything else is not survivable. In the last eight years, police officers and firefighters became the bad guys, criminal conduct was justified if not glorified, the Bible became 'hate speech,' Christians became targets of private and public discrimination, and the government began telling us where to go to bathroom, and who our children have to go to bathroom with."

A month later the judge put up this on his Facebook page: "Do the morons claiming Trump is another Hitler not know who Hitler was? I realize liberals have not been much blessed with brains, but surely they can figure out that Hitler was a socialist. It was the National Socialist Party. He was one of you! His goals were your goals."

Called out by the commission for his political messages, Judge Burkeen explained that he "was railing or venting about the intolerance displayed by those who claimed to be open-minded and loving. The intolerance was incredibly obvious when they lost the election. The intolerance breeds hatred and violence, which we continue to see." He also assured the commission that his Facebook missives "never impacted his judicial duties, and did not cast discredit upon the judiciary." He said "everyone here knows I'm a conservative Christian," and his "liberal friends" have "never expressed anything but confidence in my role as a jurist."

In rethinking his actions the judge later told the commission that "wording" in his posts was "tacky and insulting."

The commission ruled that his posts violated his judicial ethics.

In another case involving politics but 1,250 miles north of Texas in Minnesota, Judge Matthew M. Quinn was publicly reprimanded in 2021 by the Board of Judicial Standards for posting support of political candidates, piloting a boat September

5th, 2020 on the Mississippi River "which displayed at least two Trump flags," and for calling Democratic presidential candidate Joe Biden a "dipshit" online and saying he would "never support Biden."

No, not all members of the board were Democrats.

◊

In the famous 1964 obscenity case of *Jacobellis vs. Ohio*, U.S. Supreme Court Justice Potter Stewart wrote one of the most memorable lines ever to describe pornography. "I have reached the conclusion . . . that under the First and Fourteenth Amendments criminal laws in this area are constitutionally limited to hard-core pornography. I shall not today attempt further to define the kinds of material I understand to be embraced within that shorthand description; and perhaps I could never succeed in intelligibly doing so. But I know it when I see it." In 2021 the Kansas Commission on Judicial Conduct knew it when it saw it, and recommended removal of Russell, Kansas Magistrate Judge Marty K. Clark for posting X-rated photos of himself on a swingers' website called "Club Foreplay." Ironically, the judge had been named "Outstanding Magistrate Judge of 2020" by a Kansas justice reform group which he had served as its president.

The case is memorable for more than X-rated photos, including one, according to press reports, showing Mr. Clark standing in water with his penis exposed. For the first time a member of the Kansas Supreme Court, Justice Caleb Stegall, said that while he concurred with sanctioning the judge it was a slippery slope to attempt to regulate a judge's "lawful, private, consensual practices."

The Commission on Judicial Conduct recommended the judge's removal from the bench but the state Supreme Court decided to censure him instead. A non-lawyer judge, Mr. Clark resigned, making it possible but improbable that he would seek re-election.

Kansas Commission on Judicial Conduct records showed that the magistrate judge had an anonymous account at the website for swinger couples for a couple of years. At the Lake of the Ozarks in 2019, the judge and his wife met and talked with another couple, and afterwards, the other man's wife e-mailed the judge and they "discussed their attraction to each other and the prospect of sexual activities with each other."

An official of the Commission on Judicial Conduct, Todd Thompson, was more explicit in describing one of their messages, telling a Kansas newspaper: "Their rather salacious texts included messages wherein Judge Clark and his paramour actually discussed the details of a wished-for sexual encounter in the judge's chambers."

The commission pointed out that they never had sex in the judge's office, however.

Photos of the judge and the wife of the other man, who had filed the complaint against Judge Clark, became crucial evidence in the case, even though the other man let the judge see "sexually revealing" photos of both himself and his wife. After that, the man's wife and the judge traded explicit photos with each other, commission records showed.

Judge Clark testified before the discipline commission and said the commission was attempting to regulate the morality of a judge when it had nothing to do with his judicial responsibilities. He said his actions should be left to "the ballot box" where the public would decide if he deserved removal from office.

In his concurrent opinion of censuring the magistrate judge, Kansas Supreme Court Justice Caleb Stegall somewhat agreed. "While Judge Marty K. Clark's behavior was embarrassing, foolish and grossly immoral, it was not a violation of any of our rules governing judicial conduct," the justice wrote. "The behavior we are talking about consists entirely of the lawful, private, consensual sexual practices of Judge Clark." Added Justice Stegall, a conservative, "Judge Clark's actions did not have any real, factual connection to his role as a judge . . . So, what is really going on? In short, Judge Clark has embarrassed us – the examiner, the commission, this court, the judiciary and the wider legal community. And, this may be the unforgivable sin of our day . . . The complex and ubiquitous shaming and shunning rituals our society has concocted and enacted in recent decades may best be understood as an elaborate response to collective embarrassment. Scapegoating and 'cancelling' the most embarrassing among us becomes a quasi-religious way of purging collective shame and guilt . . . I may be an unexpected defender of 'consensually non-monogamous' judges – and I have no difficulty condemning adultery as morally destructive – but above all else, the rule of law condemns the arbitrary and unaccountable power of the state to pick winners and losers, reward friends and punish enemies, and protect its own interests above the public's. Such abuses and the hypocrisy they reveal are the real threat to the legitimacy and integrity of the judiciary."

That said, the justice went along with the censure.

◊

Obviously Kansas Judge Clark wasn't the first nor would he be the last jurist to send nude photos of himself to a woman online or on his cellphone. It is no surprise that Smith County Texas Judge Joel Patrick Baker resigned from the bench after the discipline commission claimed he had "exchanged sexually graphic . . . photos and videos with a woman" in 2016. But in one of the most hilarious ironies in American jurisprudence, at the time Judge Baker was serving as commission vice chair of the Texas Commission on Judicial Conduct, the very body that punished him. In an additional dash of spicy derision, the judge was in the Texas capital attending a commission meeting when he ran afoul of his judicial ethics by allegedly sharing the sex photos. A good fiction writer couldn't have made this stuff believable in a novel.

Judge Baker added to his woes by allegedly "deleting" the information from his cellphone and donating the sanitized phone to charity after commission investigators sought it for evidence. In other words he had refused to cooperate with the watchdog commission he had vice chaired, the very same commission which expects other judges to cooperate when they are under investigation.

Holy moly. Talk about a public black eye for this commission. You quickly get the idea that all it wants to do it get this stupid judge as far away from the commission as is possible, and that's what it did.

In what might be called a "plea bargain," Judge Baker agreed to resign from the bench without admitting any guilt in the sex-photo scandal. For its part, the commission agreed to drop its investigation into the incident.

One of those sweet deals the public gets cynical over.

◊

"My life is an open book," Alabama Probate Judge Leon Archer told a newspaper after it all hung out. There's plenty of people in Tallapoosa County who must have wished that his life wasn't so open.

In 2016 the Alabama Judicial Inquiry Commission launched an investigation, finding that the 70-year-old judge sent a nude photo of himself to a 37-year-old Facebook friend who had appeared in his courtroom a couple of years before to get married. The commission found, and the judge admitted, that he had sent the woman "sexually explicit dialogue, including sexual propositions and invitations" online and on his cell phone "during office hours and from the office of the probate court." The commission suspended the judge for six months, and he retired for medical reasons. He was a one-time court commissioner who was elected judge in 2012.

How did the commission learn of the judge's sexting? The woman said the judge made her feel cheap when he wrote her this: "What you got going today . . . I got some money I need to spend." It made her feel like a "prostitute," she complained. She ratted him out to a newspaper which published the texts. The woman and judge never had sex, the investigation found.

The commission report stated that photos exchanged between the woman and judge included female breasts and male and female "genitalia." The woman claimed she sent nude female photos she found on the internet, and not photos of herself.

Oddly, while some of the sexting took place on Facebook's private messaging, it was linked to the judge's Facebook page titled "Judge Leon Archer" and included a photo of him wearing his robe. The woman said she was well aware of who she was messaging.

◊

The sin of Arkansas Judge John Throesch was continuing to chat online after a woman informed him she was a defendant in his court 2018. While he stepped down from the case, in what the courts call a "recusal," he continued online and telephone communications with the woman while her case was handled by another judge. As the chatting continued it turned from "friendly to flirty" and then to "sexual in nature," and the woman sent the judge some sexually revealing pictures. Afterwards, according to the investigation, the judge asked for more such photos.

While the judge is said to have never met the woman for sex, nor had he sent her explicit photos of himself, the Arkansas Judicial Discipline and Disability Commission ruled that he had violated judicial ethics and was "unworthy of the robe." In a plea bargain with the commission, the judge agreed to resign, and with it, the commission warned him against making any "inaccurate comments" to the press about the case.

◊

Talk about lying to the media.

California Superior Court Judge Vincent J. McGraw, who quit the bench in 2002, was barred from ever serving as a judge in California again for lying to a television news reporter in Fresno.

In 2002, during the judge's re-election campaign a male TV reporter asked the judge if he had ever used the government-owned computer in his office to surf the web for pornography. "No, that is not true," he said in a taped interview at the TV station. "I categorically deny that." As politicians often do when faced with uncomfortable questions, he attempted to dissimulate, claiming that his "campaign" had "spent almost all day today trying to uncover some substantiation for this story and we have not been able to substantiate the story. The story is not true."

Well, not really not true.

Judge McGraw, likely seeing his re-election being flushed down the toilet by the revelation, knew that he had already been privately admonished by the Commission on Judicial Performance for accessing porn sites on his office computer during working hours and on weekends. He knew it because he had declined to fight the allegation, tacitly admitting that in 1998 he had used his computer ten hours a month to see sexually explicit material on the internet, access provided by the county which had rules against such misuse. His accessing of porn was known by his presiding judge because in a meeting with the top judge in 1999, "Judge McGraw admitted that he was the person accessing the [sexually explicit] sites reflected in county internet records."

In a follow-up, when the TV reporter asked Judge McGraw if he had ever been disciplined by the state judicial commission for improper use of his office computer, the judge responded, "I have not been disciplined for these things that you are talking about."

In vehemently denying the TV reporter's allegation, the judge tried another tact. "I'm concerned if these allegations are on your newscast that my reputation, my career, twelve years on the bench, a sitting judge, is going to be damaged," Judge McGraw told the reporter. "I've heard of no evidence so far to substantiate the allegations. And it sounds to me like this is reckless." He went on to say, "It troubles me that if this is the subject of media coverage, that my reputation will be injured. And I'm seriously considering whether or not I shouldn't be seeking counsel and considering a lawsuit."

What he should have been considering is how to bow out of running for re-election, gracefully.

Days later the television station aired a newscast about the judge and included his false statements about his misuse of the county computer to access porn. In what was certainly a death blow to his campaign the station also included a "live" statement by the judge essentially retracting his earlier denials, saying he should have stated "no comment" to the allegations. He apologized for his misstatements.

Before the November election the judge resigned and moved from the area. In barring him from ever being a judge in California, the commission said all that needed to be said in this statement: "Honesty is a minimum qualification expected of every judge."

Chapter Two

In the early 1970s when this author first covered and wrote about the courts as a rookie newspaper reporter, it shocked me – all of the "humor" going on in courtrooms. Four decades later, hearing judges and lawyers cracking funny even during death penalty trials became almost routine, and was usually welcomed to lessen courtroom tension. Today a newcomer at the courthouse that opens a courtroom door in a capital murder trial and is jarred by a sudden blast of laughter from the judge, attorneys and jurors inside, and maybe even the defendant himself, is going to have conflicted emotions. "Is this a comedy club or a courtroom?"

Be that as it may, occasional humor and banter in courtrooms is essential. Courtrooms are tense places during trials, especially criminal cases involving crimes such as murder. Humor can diffuse courtroom tension. It is absolutely a welcome tonic for everybody involved, especially judges and jurors who decide facts, apply the laws and render decisions of life and death. As the otherwise humorless judicial discipline commissions, like California's, acknowledge: "A sense of humor is essential to judicial demeanor, and the modest injection of humor at the appropriate time can reduce tension, and can be a tool for restoring control in court." The working phrase here is "modest injection of humor at the appropriate time." If joking in court is not "modest" and "appropriate" then you can bet that a judicial discipline commission will pounce on a sitting judge as if his wit was learned in kindergarten rather than law school.

The official handbook for California judges addresses what it calls "the problem" of judges making jokes in open court. "The problem . . . is that much of what seems funny in court relates to the conduct or demeanor of those standing before the [judge], creating the temptation to get a laugh at their expense. The temptation is especially great given how easy it is for a judge to get a laugh from the adoring audience of those seeking the favor of the judge. In addition, one must always remember there may be people in the courtroom under very serious or grave circumstances who may not appreciate jocular and humorous exchanges between the judge and [attorney]. A judge needs to always keep in mind that breaks to joke around and have a few laughs may not be in the service of the goals and objectives of the judicial proceeding." Therein lies the rub. Humor, and judging what is funny is in the minds of the speaker and the hearer.

This chapter covers examples of things judges have said in courtrooms in efforts to crack funny, but, which have instead backfired because even though people laughed at the time, the judge's remarks offended someone who later complained to a state's judicial discipline investigative body. Because you are reading it here, the following remarks were not considered "funny" by commission members, but "inappropriate."

◊

If there was ever a comedian serving as a judge it was Gary G. Kreep of the San Diego County Superior Court. No doubt that at a private party his quips could send a roomful of boozed-up party-goers into uproarious laughter. The problem was he had to reckon with the much-too-sober judicial disciplinary commission of California, and courtrooms aren't parties. In the annuals of the state's discipline board, no judge ever got into so much hot water over his jokes, nicknames, and other ill-chosen words sometimes in Spanish than Judge Kreep, even as good-natured as they might have been. What follows is an arm's-length list of examples of the kinds of things the judge, who practiced law for 37 years before becoming a judge, said on the record (tape-recorded or typed by a stenographer) in his courtroom. During an eviction case the defendant was testifying in a voice with, what she called a "Texas" accent. The woman had just testified about what had happened after her landlord "filed" the eviction notice on her.

Judge Kreep: "Ever since she *what* on you?"
Defendant: "Ever since she, um, gave me . . ."
Judge: "Filed on you?"
Defendant: "Yes, filed."
Judge: "I thought you said fouled on me. I'm sorry, filed on me."
Defendant: "Oh, sorry. We talk with, I got Texas; my parents are from Texas."
Judge: "Don't worry about it."
Defendant: "We might say, Y'all or something like that."
Judge: "Doesn't bother me a bit. I just misunderstood what you said."

At this time the landlord's attorney joined in and volunteered: "My husband asks for a *pin* all the time, but it's a *pen*."

Judge Kreep: "That's okay I, I talk about doing the *warsh*, so. Anyway, people look at me like, are you crazy? Anyway. And I had a Filipino teacher who always used to ask for a *shit* of paper."

His "shit of paper" joke ended up for commission review. In censuring the judge in a case over this comment and other more serious allegations, the humorless commission members failed to say whether the courtroom erupted in laughter at the judge's "shit-of-paper" remark, but it's a good bet it did.

The judge explained he made the remark in response to the defendant's joke about her own accent and the attorney's joke about her husband. He was trying, he said, to bring "some levity and relaxation into the proceeding," but admitted it was wrong.

After weighing many charges against Judge Kreep, some of which have not been listed here, the commission voted to impose a "severe public censure, the highest level of discipline short of removal" on the judge, stating that "Judge Kreep is hard working and has helped reduce the backlog on default matters at the superior court."

The city attorney's office in the San Diego handles a heavy load of prostitution cases, and many turned up in 2013 in the courtroom of Judge Kreep. Many of these sex cases were prosecuted by a female deputy city attorney, and we'll call her Miss Wagner. Judge Kreep was on the bench and his court staff and other attorneys were all present when 'Miss Wagner' walked into the courtroom. "Speaking of prostitution," the judge said, "here's Miss Wagner." Now you can almost hear the snickers in the courtroom still today, and the deputy city attorney said she knew the judge was trying to be funny, but, she told the discipline commission that the remark was "ridiculous."

Judge Kreep told the commission he didn't remember making the remark but conceded he may have used that language in referring to her and the prostitution cases her office handles. Unconvincingly the judge's attorney tried to wiggle out of this client's legal pickle by arguing that the judge "may have actually said 'prosecution' rather than 'prostitution'" and that the female attorney had "misheard" what was said. The commission considered the argument groundless. Stated the commission: "Although Judge Kreep's comment was made in jest, it was disrespectful and undignified for a judge to suggest or imply that an attorney appearing before the court was a prostitute." It said his remark was misconduct.

In a separate case, Judge Kreep asked a female charged with prostitution: "Ma'am, anything I can do to get you out of the life?" Then he said, "Is it, you like the money? Or you just like the action?" When the defendant attempted to respond and discuss her plans for the future, Judge Kreep cut her off and asked, "Are you going to try to get a job at the Bunny Ranch in Nevada?" He then told her, "I don't think it's a good lifestyle choice, but it's your lifestyle choice and it's your decision."

Answering a commission complaint, Judge Kreep told the panel that he was trying to show support for the woman, but may also have been trying to shame her into changing her lifestyle. He said he was not trying to embarrass or demean her. He explained that his comment about the "Bunny Ranch" prostitution business in Nevada was a reference to the woman having said that she wanted to go somewhere prostitution is legal.

In another case involving a conference at the bench between Judge Kreep and attorneys in a prostitution prosecution, including a San Diego Deputy City Attorney with a Korean surname, the judge used the words "Chinese prostitutes." After he was given an "angry look" by the deputy city attorney, the judge added, "No offense to Chinese people." The attorney said she was offended by the judge's remarks because "Judge Kreep constantly mentioned her ethnicity," commission records stated. She recalled that when a group of Koreans visited his courtroom he told them that she was "from China and spoke Mandarin." She was not from China, and even though the judge denied saying she was from China, a tape of the session showed he did mention her "Chinese heritage" to the Korean visitors.

The state judicial discipline commission cited the judge for "improper action" and stated that "Gratuitously singling a person out based on ethnicity or national origin can be offensive to that person and can also be perceived as indicating bias." In a separate complaint involving the same attorney, Judge Kreep told a defense attorney that if she were late for a hearing, "I'll kick her in the butt." She was there when he made the remark, which the commission found inappropriate. On another case of his words running afoul of his ethics, the commission found that Judge Kreep told someone in his courtroom that he took care of a friend with whom he traveled because the friend had seizures. Judge Kreep shared that he showered and slept with the friend, but "there was no sex involved. We were just friends. It was purely platonic." Here the commission accused the judge of TMI. It stated in its report: "While it is not necessarily improper for a judge to share personal anecdotes in the courtroom, Judge Kreep's disclosure was an example of sharing too much information." The commission ruled his anecdote "gratuitous" and was misconduct. Another time during a hearing in which a law student intern appeared in Judge Kreep's courtroom, the judge picked up a box of animal crackers and told the intern that "If you're good during your argument, I'll give you some cookies, little boy." The student said the remark was demeaning and the commission ruled that it was "undignified" for a judge.

When a San Diego County Deputy Public Defender of Mexican heritage walked into Judge Kreep's court to change the plea of her client, she wasn't expecting this exchange.

"I love her accent," said Judge Kreep.

"I'm Mexican," said the deputy public defender.

Kreep: "Are you a citizen of the country of Mexico?"

Defender: "No."

Judge: "Okay. Okay. There is an attorney in town that I know that is actually a citizen of Mexico who does immigration work here in California."

Defender: "Oh no, your honor. I am a U.S. citizen and proud of it."

Kreep: "I wasn't planning on having you deported."

The exchange was reported by a local newspaper. While the deputy public defender said she was not offended by Judge Kreep's comments, she reported them to a supervisor, who complained. In this one the judge told the commission that he "did not intend to belittle" her "by commenting on her accent. He intended his comment as a compliment." He said his "deportation" comment was "inappropriate" and he apologized to her. He contended he was "trying to get a laugh" and "put people at ease." The commission stated that "drawing attention to a person's ethnicity and questioning a person's citizenship when these are not issues in the matter before the judge, can reasonably be perceived as offensive and reflecting bias."

It is imagined if you work in an office or a factory there are nicknames for colleagues and bosses floating around, and they are sometimes good for a laugh. Often nicknames are terms of endearment, but sometimes they are used to ridicule. If you work in a courtroom, calling people by a nickname can get you into trouble, as Judge Kreep learned. His problem was he had this habit of referring to attorneys who appeared in his courtroom by nicknames that he arbitrarily assigned to them. A 6-foot-7 male attorney-intern was called "Shorty," an African-American woman who worked in the city attorney's office was "Star Parker" which was not her real name, and another woman intern-lawyer became "Bun Head" in his courtroom, while he labeled another female attorney "Miss Dimples." The woman he called "Star Parker" said the name made her "uncomfortable" in his courtroom. Once Judge Kreep was called out on this annoying nickname, he explained that the female attorney "resembled 'Star Parker,' who was a beautiful African-American woman" who looked like the female attorney.

The judicial commission found that his use of nicknames violated his duty to keep decorum in his courtroom, and in particular his calling the African-American attorney "Star Parker" because she looked like a black woman he was friends with "could have reasonably been perceived as improper attention based on her gender, race and physical appearance." The commission ruled that the judge's "unilateral creation and use of nicknames for attorneys . . . appearing in his courtroom was discourteous and did not convey proper respect for them. Furthermore, his use of nicknames created an atmosphere in the courtroom that was too informal and lacked appropriate decorum. The nicknames used by the judge could suggest a lack of impartiality or a sense of inappropriate familiarity, which could undermine public confidence in and respect for the judiciary."

In another case, after Judge Kreep apparently either did not hear the man's name or forgot his name, he called the representative of an insurance company, "Mr. Insurance Man," which on its face seems harmless, but the commission ruled that he should have asked for the man's name again rather than invent a nickname for him. The judge said he did not remember the name stating his name for the record in the small claims case and anyways, the judge reasoned, small claims court is "informal" and the nickname went along with that informality. The stuffy members of the commission decided that all sessions of court are formal and it was "improper" for the judge to call him "Mr. Insurance Man."

The commission didn't end there with Judge Kreep, and one begins to wonder whether it had something other than his judicial conduct driving it. Kreep had publicly opposed President Barack Obama's 2012 re-election, a fact known to the commission members, and in California which is controlled by Democrats that was a capital offense, speaking politically. The commission listed as inappropriate a bucket full of other comments Judge Kreep made in his courtroom, mostly remarks about the attractiveness of females. Said a woman who testified about the attorneys in his courtroom: "We've got all sorts of very attractive, young public defenders around here, so."

On July 12, 2013, "Judge Kreep said to someone in the courtroom, 'She's a pretty girl, you know you could smile.'" The commission acknowledged his comments did not rise to the level of sexual harassment.

Deputy Public Defender Leticia Hernandez testified that Judge Kreep commented on the physical appearance of female attorneys who appeared before him. She said he once said to a defendant, "The lovely attorney next to you went over the form, correct?" Other female witnesses said Judge Kreep referred to a deputy public defender as "the pretty brown one." Judge Kreep conceded he may have said to a defendant, "The lovely woman next to you is your public defender." The judge defended himself by saying he "believed the comment was descriptive, not demeaning." The judge admitted that during an appearance by a female defendant charged with prostitution who was represented by a male deputy public defender, he made a comment about how attractive the male deputy public defender was to a defendant. Judge Kreep said he "was going for a laugh" but now agrees his comment was wrong and he has not made such a comment since then.

An attorney's pregnancy also was part of a complaint against the judge. San Diego Deputy City Attorney Danielle Stroud appeared before Judge Kreep in 2013 when she was pregnant. During one appearance, Judge Kreep said to a defense attorney: "Let's get on with this case" and then added something like, "we don't want Ms. Stroud to have her baby in the courtroom." On other occasions Judge Kreep made comments to Ms. Stroud about her pregnancy such as "it's getting closer, Ms. Stroud" and "she wants to go home and have her baby. I'll pick on her today." The judge made these comments in open court, sometimes on the record. Judge Kreep testified before the commission and said he asked Ms. Stroud how she was doing and when she was due, but that was the extent of his comments about her pregnancy. However, Ms. Stroud's testimony, which the commission stated "we find more credible," contradicts this, and is "corroborated by the testimony of bailiff, Deputy Sheriff Piper Paulk." Deputy Paulk said Judge Kreep told Ms. Stroud, "Ooh, I hope you don't have this baby in here." Judge Kreep explained his conduct by stating that he regularly overheard conversations between Ms. Stroud and other attorneys regarding her pregnancy. But Ms. Stroud denied that her pregnancy was a matter of regular discussion in the courtroom. Deputy Paulk likewise did not recall Ms. Stroud talking to anyone about her pregnancy when she was in court. The commission ruled that the judge should not have made comments about the attorney's pregnancy. The judge's handbook states: "Unprofessional remarks made in the courtroom concerning an attorney's personal appearance, pregnancy, or sexuality, can have an impact on the credibility of women in court; and when addressed to a woman lawyer, such remarks make it difficult for her to effectively represent her clients."

Judge Kreep might have wanted to dress up like Santa Claus for Christmas, who knows, but when it came to running his courtroom on sentencing day he was famous for his "gifts." "When sentencing criminal defendants," the commission noted in its findings, "Judge Kreep on multiple occasions mentioned giving a defendant or defense counsel a 'gift of the day,' 'gift for the day,' or 'gift for today' at sentencing. In other words, his decision to not fine or jail a defendant was his "gift" from the bench. In one case Judge Kreep said, "Here's your gift for your new child" before he vacated a fine. On another day he said, "I already gave the gift of the day." In another case, after indicating he would stay the payment of a fine pending the defendant's successful completion of probation, he said to the defendant, "That's a gift, ma'am . . . don't take it for granted, all right. If you come back before me on another case, you'll have to pay that fine plus whatever you got to do on the other one." In another case he said he was giving a "second gift of the day since we're going so long."

Sentencings are serious emotional affairs and no place for brainless levity.

In his defense Judge Kreep said he used the term "gift of the day" to convey that he was giving the defendant "a break" and the defendant needed to "live the straight and narrow," but conceded it was a mistake. The commission analyzed the situation perfectly. "Judge Kreep's characterization of discretionary rulings as a gift suggested unequal treatment and bias and may have improperly suggested to court participants that Judge Kreep was ordering something that was not deserved under the law, that he was dispensing favored treatment to certain defendants or defense counsel and withholding that special treatment from others, and that such special treatment was only available once a day to a lucky recipient." It called his remarks of giving "gifts" misconduct.

In another case, after a defense attorney requested reinstatement of probation for a client, Judge Kreep said: "Yeah, your client's no virgin . . . as far as these cases are going." On another day the judge was counseling a defendant whose case was dismissed upon successful completion of diversion to stay off drugs. When the defendant's mother identified herself, Judge Kreep said, "His mother, okay. Slap him upside the head a few times, make sure he stays off the drugs." The judge told the commission he did not intend for the mother to beat her son, but wanted her to take an active role in making sure he stayed off drugs. He testified he no longer uses such language in court. In another case a defense attorney informed Judge Kreep that the defendant was in an abusive relationship. Judge Kreep said to the defendant: "Just so you know, ma'am, I grew up in a relationship where I used to get the crap beat out of me on a regular basis by a stepfather . . . So I have some understanding of what you're going through, okay? From a child's perspective." Judge Kreep testified he wanted to convey that a person does not turn to a life of crime just because they are being abused. Stated the commission about the judge's language: "Judge Kreep used language that was crude and undignified. Swearing is unbecoming, injudicious and unsuited to the proper decorum of a courtroom." And the commission stated, "The words 'butt' and 'crap' may be relatively tame examples of crude language, particularly when compared to the vulgar language rampant in culture, social media, and entertainment. But a higher standard of conduct is required in our courtrooms, and for good reason."

In another complaint, after the court's presiding judge learned that Judge Kreep was speaking Spanish to Spanish-speaking defendants, the presiding judge told him to stop the practice. In fact, the chief judge told him not to speak Spanish on three occasions. Nonetheless, Kreep continued to speak Spanish in his courtroom. He addressed defendants as "señor or señora" and greeted some defendants Spanish interpreters with 'buenos *dias*' [or] '*vaya con Dios*.'" The judge said he merely used Spanish in greetings or to wish defendants well. But, the commission found, "his characterization is incorrect." He asked one defendant with the last name Ontiveros, "Habla Ingles?" When Mr. Ontiveros indicated he did not speak English, Judge Kreep said, "*Señor*, we'll explain it to you all in *Español. Un momento por favor.*" Judge

Kreep then asked Mr. Ontiveros's attorney, "Would you explain to his mama, *por favor*?" In telling a defendant with the last name Sanchez that she should retain certain paperwork, Judge Kreep said, "Keep your paperwork, okay? *Muy importante*." The commission said there was no indication that Sanchez spoke Spanish and had greeted the judge in English. In a different case, Judge Kreep spoke to a defendant in Spanish even though a court interpreter was present. He asked the defendant, "*Culpable o no culpable*?" He addressed another defendant in Spanish even though a court interpreter was present. The judge told him, "*No cerveza. No tequila. No alcohol. Nada.*" A witness told the commission that "Judge Kreep used Spanish when the defendant was Hispanic-appearing and the judge was not always correct that the defendant spoke Spanish." The witness said she heard defendants tell him in response to his Spanish: "I actually speak English." When told this, the judge stopped speaking Spanish. In one court proceeding, Judge Kreep greeted a defendant with the last name Torres in Spanish even after the defendant said she understood the terms and conditions of her probation in English. In a case involving a defendant whose last name was Silva, Judge Kreep spoke in Spanish to the defendant's mother and girlfriend, who were in the courtroom. He asked them in Spanish whether they spoke English. When they said they did, he spoke to them in English. Two public defenders testified that "Kreep's use of Spanish did not upset their clients or make the clients feel uncomfortable." Although, another attorney said his use of Spanish in the courtroom "could be naive and insensitive towards Hispanics." The discipline commission reminded the judge that state law required "judicial proceedings must be conducted in English only." It stated: "While Judge Kreep may have thought he was simply being welcoming to litigants, he failed to recognize that speaking Spanish to people based on his perception that they were Hispanic could be perceived as offensive or suggest differential treatment."

What's astounding is Judge Kreep would later tell the commission that one reason he had gone afoul of the rules for judges is his lack of training for the job. Members of the judicial discipline commission found the assertion ridiculous given the fact that Judge Kreep had practiced law for nearly four decades before becoming a judge.

◇

Stupid nicknames also got a Tennessee judge reprimanded in 2009. Judge John W. Walton called two clerks in the courthouse by nicknames that weren't flattering. "You made these statements in a demeaning and disrespectful manner," stated the discipline board. "One such comment was made concerning Leslie C. Sharpe. Ms. Sharpe's maiden name was Leslie C. Hill. On one occasion in open court during a proceeding, you called Ms. Hill "Liar Hill" and demeaned her professional capabilities as an employee of the General Sessions Court Clerk's office, saying that she was incompetent." Judge Walton also called another female clerk, "Dora Dumb."

◊

Over a span of months in 2013, you could count on Superior Court Judge Timothy D. Dooley of Nome, Alaska to say something that brought either a chuckle or a moan when he opened his mouth on the bench.

In a courtroom lecture on drinking, the judge said during sentencing of a defendant: "Has anything good ever come out of drinking other than sex with a pretty girl?" A few months later, during a criminal sentencing in a sexual assault case, he told a defendant: "What you've done with this young girl, it's a strange thing, routinely done in Afghanistan where they marry 6-year-old girls. In our society, and in the society of the local tribal communities, supposed to be totally forbidden." A little more than a month later in a case involving the sexual abuse of a 14-year-old girl the judge said, "This was not someone who was, and I hate to use the phrase, 'asking for it.' There are girls out there that seem to be temptresses. And this does not seem to be anything like that."

The following year he invoked "medieval" Christian values in discussing the charge of lying under oath in court to a group of litigants without attorneys. "I'm gonna enforce these oaths and they're enforceable with a two-year sentence for perjury. And I'd be the sentencing judge. I also have a medieval Christianity that says if you violate an oath, you're going to hell. You all may not share that, but I'm planning to populate hell."

During a trial a victim testified in a soft voice and the judge asked jurors if they could hear, by saying, "I'm sorry folks, but I can't slap her around to make her talk louder." He made the remark despite the fact that it was a domestic violence case. Ouch!

The Alaska Judicial Conduct Commission voted that the judge's remarks were insensitive and that he be censured by the state's Supreme Court, and assigned a "mentor" to train him "in the areas of gender sensitivity, cultural awareness, domestic violence and interaction with . . . litigants." The Supreme Court agreed with the punishment, saying "Judge Dooley was negligent in making the statements. We accept the commission's findings that it is reasonable to assume Judge Dooley's statements adversely affected the witnesses, victims, and others who directly or indirectly heard the statements and that [his] conduct caused actual injury to the public perception of the judiciary's integrity."

Before the final ruling, the judge gave up his $226,000 a year position by not seeking re-election to the Nome bench. The judge had been appointed to the bench a year before he made the first of his offending remarks, having filled the position of the former Nome Superior Court judge who retired in 2012. Curiously, at a hearing on the allegations, the judge's attorney used the judge's inexperience in his defense, arguing that his troubles were also the fault of the Alaskan judicial system itself because "Judge Dooley was in a one-judge town and did not receive sufficient assistance or training." In effect, he blamed the administrative arm of the Supreme Court, which had the judge's fate in its hands.

◇

This happened during jury selection in the courtroom of Los Angeles Superior Court Judge Edmund W. Clarke, Jr. in a murder trial involving defendants who were gang members. An actress wrote on her jury form that she could not serve as a juror because she had a role in a movie called, "The Big Balloon." The judge granted her request to be excused, and told her he would not disclose the name of the film in court. After she left the courtroom, Judge Clarke said: "It sounds like a nice PG project, by the way, for those of you letting your minds run a little bit." The woman said she heard laughter in the room after she walked out.

Called before the commission, Judge Clarke testified that after he told the juror in open court that he would not disclose the name of the film, he became "concerned that the attorneys and other jurors could be speculating that it was a gang-related movie." The judge told the commission he wanted them to know that it was a "wholesome film" title. One of the defense attorneys in the case told the commission that the female juror was "attractive and that there was whispering among the defense attorneys about whether it was a pornographic film." Judge Clarke testified that he did not hear this conversation.

The commission agreed with investigators that the judge's explanation that he was attempting to curb speculation that the movie was about gangs (rather than a sexually explicit film) was "implausible." It said: "The judge's assertion that he thought the jurors might be speculating that the movie was about gangs or violence makes no sense." The commission ruled, however, that the judge did not violate his ethics in making the "PG" remark.

But, ethical concerns for the judge didn't end there. Another female juror in the same murder trial wrote that she only had $25 in her checking account and requested to be excused from jury duty because of financial hardship.

Judge Clarke: "Hello."

Juror: "Hello."

Judge: "You actually told me how much you have in your checking account."

Juror: "I can show you, too."

Judge: "No. No. It's an impressive and convincing figure."

Juror: "Thank you for not sharing it."

Judge Clarke: "Well, every one of these lawyers spent more than that on lunch today."

Juror: "Great."

Judge: "Probably. But, yes, I know some wait staff make a lot of money. Sounds like you're not in that category yet, so I'm going to excuse you. Thank you."

Juror: "Thank you."

The juror left the courtroom and the judge blabbed what she had thanked him for not blabbing.

"That's [juror] 7132," said Judge Clarke. "She has $25 in her checking account. I know you all eat for less than $25. Sometimes we don't. That's cutting it close."

Before the judicial performance commission the woman complained that the judge's comparison of the amount in her checkbook to the amount the lawyers spent on lunch was "embarrassing and condescending."

Judge Clarke denied any intent to demean or embarrass the woman and testified that he intended his "exchange with the juror as light-hearted banter meant humorously." He said, "The juror acted like she was doing comedy and was kidding and joking." Additionally, "he stated he disclosed the amount in her account because he realized that it was impolite to make a joke comparing the amount in her account with how much money the attorneys spent on lunch when the attorneys did not know the figure," the commission reported. "Yet another explanation offered by the judge was that he revealed the specific amount in the juror's checking account to provide the attorneys with a factual basis for the hardship excuse."

The commission ruled that "Judge Clarke . . . engaged in conduct prejudicial to the administration of justice that brings the judicial office into disrepute. Even if [he] thought he was engaging in humorous banter, joking about a juror's limited financial resources and revealing personal financial information in open court, particularly when the juror expressed that she did not want that information to be disclosed, is manifestly discourteous and undignified."

Under the heading of you can't teach an old judge new tricks, Judge Clarke also disclosed the amount of money, $33, in another juror's checkbook in the same case. Said the judge to the juror: "[You have a] little bit more than the other gal. [Thirty-three] bucks," and "You are putting her in the shade with that big account." He then excused the juror by saying, "Good luck on getting paid and being able to bring that number up a little bit better." The juror told the commission he was not offended by the judge's remark in court, and Judge Clarke testified he was making a light-hearted joke.

◊

This antic by Judge John D. Harris of Los Angeles Superior Court could have been a scene right out of "Saturday Night Live." In October of 2003 at the courthouse, Judge Harris arrived at work and approached two female security officers at the weapons screening area near the door. He put his hands against the wall and asked the women if they were going to search him. He did this as 30 people waited in line to be checked for guns and knives, which could not be brought into the courthouse.

You can imagine how surprised the two officers were as they watched the judge spread-eagle against the wall. "Judge Harris then asked if he could choose who would search him, and said he wanted to be searched in [his] chambers," the commission stated. Calling his antics "unsuitable for a judicial officer in a public setting," the commission stated, "it was inappropriate for Judge Harris to make fun of an event that the public is expected to take seriously." Commissioners also stated that his silly act delayed the weapons screening.

The same judge also got heat for "joking" during jury selection. In a case of a male flasher charged with several counts of exposing himself to two women, the state prosecutor asked female jurors if a man had ever "made a pass" at them which made them feel uncomfortable? She then asked prospective male jurors if a female had ever made a pass at them which made them angry. To that, Judge Harris couldn't resist. "Did some woman make a pass at you and get you angry?" he said, repeating the prosecutor's question. "I've been waiting for that to happen to myself."

Well, guess what? His apparent joke was subject of a complaint, and the commission, although stating, "His comment . . . reflects a troubling pattern of insensitivity to women" and was "poor judgment," the remark wasn't improper. The commission dismissed it from the overall complaint.

◊

No doubt about it, judges have keen senses of humor. But in the case of New Jersey Municipal Court Judge Hector I. Rodriguez, it was not knowing when to use it.

In December 2017, a female defendant in his courtroom pleaded not guilty to criminal charges, and then the question of her bail was brought up by the prosecutor, also a female. The defendant's public defender responded that his client was eligible for a no-bail release, and Judge Rodriguez agreed, stating, "Your bail is ROR – you're released on your own recognizance."

However, the female defendant seemed confused by the judge's words, probably the use of "ROR," and because of that, the judge then asked her, "Do you understand? You seem a little . . ."

Still confused whether she had to pay something, the woman asked the judge: "Do I owe you anything?"

To which the quick-witted Judge Rodriguez responded: "Not that you can do in front of all these people, no."

It must have brought a few chuckles in court because, hey, come on, it was a funny retort. Yet, the humorless New Jersey Supreme Court's Advisory Committee on Judicial Conduct didn't see the humor, and even if it did, it decided the judge's remark was inappropriate and reprimanded him in 2018.

Rather than simply say that, okay, he was trying to crack a little joke, the judge "denied that his remark could be interpreted as sexual innuendo." In his defense he gave the board of judicial inquiry this word salad:

"You can't take it out of context. You take a statement and flip it around, throw it in the air, put spice on it and put it back into that – it's going to be the same when you – in the context of what I said. It was all about the monetary bail. And I – and she [defendant] seemed confused. I said, well, you seem – I didn't say confused. And she goes, do I owe you anything and I was like not that you would give me in front of all these people, referring to money, a monetary bail."

To which the discipline board responded: "By his conduct" the judge "demonstrated an inability to conform his conduct to the high standards required of judges and impugned the integrity of the judiciary."

◊

Sometime jokes that seem funny in words are humiliating when carried out in deeds. Here's an example from the courtroom of Riverside, California Judge Arthur S. Block in 2000. When a Spanish interpreter was late for court a joke on her was hatched in a conversation between the judge, courtroom staff and attorneys. They decided the interpreter would be held in contempt of court for being late. When she arrived in the public hallway outside the courtroom, a deputy sheriff in on the joke handcuffed her. The interpreter protested and resisted as courthouse visitors looked on. Inside the courtroom, the judge told the interpreter to listen to what the deputy district attorney had to say.

Interpreter: ". . . This better be a joke. Take them off."

Judge to the D.A.: "What were you going to say?"

D.A.: "I was going to say perhaps this is the appropriate time for the order to show cause re contempt."

Judge: "All right. I understand bail is not available; is that correct?"

D.A.: "There is no bail for that."

Judge to the interpreter: "I'm sorry but your vacation plans are somewhat awry."

At that point the judge disclosed it was all a yuck-yuck joke, and the cop unlocked the cuffs.

The interpreter wasn't laughing. She told the commission the episode made her feel "humiliated."

◊

Judge Gary T. Friedman of Kern County, California Superior Court called to order the sentencing of a criminal defendant who was acting as his own attorney in 1987. "The defendant told the judge he had been unable to read the probation report in part because he had observed and smelled a snake outside his cell in jail," the judicial commission stated, recounting the sentencing. "He told the judge that [his] fear of snakes outside his prison cell had kept him awake at night." As a result, the sentencing was rescheduled. Later, when the defendant was brought back to the courthouse for sentencing, he was placed in a holding cell outside the courtroom, and "a rattlesnake enclosed in a plastic ball" was "displayed to the defendant when he was locked in a holding cell." The judge who had played the "joke" on the defendant might have gotten a laugh, but the defendant had an "emotional outburst," according to commission files.

Several years later the judge learned that a criminal defendant had a "thing" for an unidentified television personality, and the judge acquired a photo of the star and "pressured" a court staffer to write a "personal inscription" from the star to the defendant on the photo. Judge Friedman then had the photo given to the defendant "to play on the defendant's bizarre obsession."

The commission "reproved" the judge for playing jokes on "vulnerable" prisoners. "Humor and levity can oftentimes reduce tension in the courtroom. When appropriate, humor can assist in humanizing the otherwise intimidating atmosphere of our courts, and may even assist in improving communications between the judges, attorneys and litigants," the commission stated. "However, humor at the expense of another, or humor intended or likely to demean or belittle another is unacceptable. This is particularly true when the object of the joke is someone who has been deprived of his liberty and who is submitting to the jurisdiction of the court."

◇

You know the Politically Correct Police are swarming when a judge is called "unprofessional and demeaning" and is disciplined for calling women at the courthouse "sweetheart," "honey," "sweetie" and "dear," but that's what happened to Municipal Court Judge David M. Kennick in California. The state's commission said while it "lacked evidentiary support" to say the judge used such terms in his courtroom, "it could be fairly inferred that the judge used the expressions in and about the courthouse during business hours to people he knew principally or solely in connection with his judicial duties." Folks, a judge who refers to women as "sweetie" and "dear" isn't trying to score more than a friendly hello. That's something even the discipline commission itself hinted at by stating, "The fact that the judge proceeded properly and courteously on many, or most, occasions, did not excuse the instances of misconduct . . . ." Be that as it may, Judge Kennick was also investigated for being "intemperate" in open court by "screaming" at a female attorney who made a motion. He wasn't punished for that, but, when another snitched Judge Kennick off and testified that he "became loud, impatient, and abusive toward witnesses who hesitated in answering questions" in his courtroom, that waxed it. He was punished with a slap on the wrist by the commission.

Chapter Three

When a judge, especially one who has been on the bench for many years is arrested for a serious crime, the public reaction is predictable. Take the case of a city judge in Tennessee, Woodrow Adams, 70, who was indicted for child rape in 2019, and later suspended from his job as a municipal court judge by the state's judicial watchdog commission. "It's just a shock and disbelief for our city," Mayor of Tennessee Ridge, Stony Odom, told a newspaper at the time. "Woody is well known, well liked . . . We're still in shock from hearing of him being arrested, accused of that. Anything but that." This chapter details cases in which judges were arrested for major crimes and how judicial watchdogs ruled on the misconduct.

In modern times no case involving a judge was more shocking than the revenge murders of three people by North Texas ex-Justice of the Peace Eric Lyle Williams in 2013. For full understanding, it is a story in which its background must be brought forward.

Attorney and former prosecutor Rick Harrison ran for district attorney of Kaufman County in 2006 and was elected over rival, Michael McLelland who narrowly lost in a runoff. An issue in the 2006 campaign was a drunken driving conviction of Mr. Harrison in 1994. During the campaign something happened, which at the time caused only a tiny spark of controversy but its true significance would remain unrealized for five more years. In 2006 Kaufman County private attorney Eric Lyle Williams wrote a letter endorsing Harrison and opposing McLelland and it was used as advertising material for Harrison's campaign, according to court records.

Four years later in 2010 District Attorney Rick Harrison again faced rival Mike McLelland, both Republicans, for the top prosecutor's office in Kaufman, a town of 6,000 near Dallas-Fort Worth. Adding to the 2010 election excitement, in another pollical race attorney Eric Williams who had been in the community since the early 1990s and was a good-standing member of the Chamber of Commerce, ran against a long-time Justice of the Peace.

The key issue in the 2010 D.A. race was a fresh drunken driving charge against incumbent Harrison. "It's the only issue in the race," Harrison said of his DWI case in June of 2009, for which the local Republican Party chair called for his resignation. Mr. McLelland, 60, won the district attorney job in April 2010, with 59 percent of the vote. According to court records, the new D.A. didn't forget those who had opposed him. "[Mr.] McLelland, even after he became the elected D.A. [in 2010], continued to harbor a grudge against [Rick] Harrison and his supporters, including [Eric] Williams" whose "letter during Harrison's first campaign was absolutely not forgotten." Meanwhile in the Justice of the Peace election on November 2nd, 2010, the five-foot-10, 200-pound, blue-eyed Eric Lyle Williams, 43, a Republican, won with 60 percent of the vote, defeating Johnny Perry for Justice of the Peace in Precinct 1 of Kaufman County, according to election records. Two months later, Justice of the Peace Williams had settled in to handle typical cases in justice court such as misdemeanors "punishable by fine only" and small claims. His duties included issuing search and arrest warrants, conducting preliminary hearings, performing marriages and serving as a coroner.

So from the get-go, the new D.A. and the new local judge were political enemies.

Justice of the Peace Williams also had an impatient side. "Eric had a reputation for ordering whatever he wanted instead of going through the [county] bureaucratic processes," wrote a newspaper. His impatience would send his life into a spiral, and stir within him hatred and revenge for District Attorney Mike McLelland that by comparison would render any grudge Mr. McLelland had against Mr. Williams over the campaign letter little more than schoolground rivalry. In the months after being sworn in, Eric Williams was caught several times on surveillance cameras removing computer equipment including three monitors from a county warehouse. On May 24th, 2011, police came to his office, and in an act of heavy-handedness, they handcuffed him and hauled him off to jail on D.A. felony charges of burglary and theft. The computer equipment was valued at $1,500. Under Texas law governing attorneys and judges a conviction would have led to loss of his license to practice law, and end his judgeship. Mr. Williams would say later in court records that the "prosecution was done in such a way that [he] would lose his law license upon any conviction for a crime of moral turpitude" and the charges were vindictive. In November of 2011 additional charges were piled on, stemming from supplies Judge Williams had billed to a local law library he managed.

    A highly skilled and experienced Kaufman County prosecutor who had tried organized crime cases in Dallas was assigned to prosecute Judge Williams. At the time, unmarried prosecutor Mark Hasse was also involved in an investigation of the white prison gang Aryan Brotherhood of Texas, a fact that would become relevant later. Before trial, plea bargain negotiations broke down. Mr. Hasse, who did not share his boss McLelland's dislike of Williams, offered a plea deal that would have saved Williams's law license but would mean he'd have to relinquish his $70,000-a-year job as Justice of the Peace. Williams would plead guilty to a charge of abuse of power in the plea bargain, and offer he rejected. Williams suggested he pay restitution for the computers and have criminal counts dropped. D.A. McLelland rejected it, and Judge Williams was tried in March 2012. Judge Williams contended that he had taken the computer equipment for office use. He said he was "setting up a video conferencing system" so he could conduct magistrate duties from his office. However, prosecutor Hasse introduced evidence that showed investigators found a computer monitor from the warehouse in Judge Williams's truck. In addition, jurors saw the damning security video showing him stealing the stuff. After four hours of deliberations he was convicted of theft, and sentenced to two years on probation. Afterward, Mr. Williams said it meant losing his law license. "I will have to seek another career . . . My life has taken a drastic turn." For a man who had earned his law degree at the relative late in life age of 33, it was a crushing blow. Mr. Williams resigned from his judgeship and lost his county health insurance for his wife, Kim, a sickly woman who suffered from rheumatoid arthritis and chronic fatigue syndrome, and was addicted to pain-killers. Williams also claimed "that he had been falsely convicted and accused D.A. McLelland of pursuing a political grudge," according to local press reports. It was well-known that Eric Williams had high-power guns at home. After the trial, prosecutor Hasse who had never owned fire arms bought a handgun for self-protection. A newspaper reported that "both prosecutors feared he [Williams] might seek revenge." In months that followed his anger festered, and Williams confided to a friend he had money problems and was "at the end of his rope."

Around 8:40 in the morning on January 31st, 2013, senior prosecutor Mark Hasse had parked his vehicle and walked on a sidewalk a block from the courthouse when a person in dark clothing and wearing a mask, jumped from a car and overpowered him. A witness who worked at a nearby auto repair shop heard Mr. Hasse, 57, say, "I'm sorry." The next thing the witness saw was the masked person shoot Mr. Hasse. "The deceased falls down," the witness stated. "He comes up to him and fires again while he's on the ground." The witness said the shooter fired two pistols at him. The witness said he retreated because he feared the gunman would kill him. Another witness, attorney Linda Bush said she arrived at the Kaufman County Courthouse when she saw two people scuffling. "There was another shoving, and at that point in time, the shooter put the gun to Mark's neck and shot him," she said. A onetime police officer, Bush said she saw the gunman jump into a "silver colored sedan" driven by a second person, and she tried to follow it in her vehicle, until she saw the car had no license plates. She said she turned around in an effort to aid the victim. She started CPR on Mr. Hasse. "I wanted him to know help was coming." At that point Kaufman Police Officer Jason Stastny, who had been investigating a nearby theft and heard five gunshots arrived. The officer parked his patrol car so its video camera recorded the scene. The film showed Officer Stastny administering CPR, Mr. Hasse struggling for breath and screams of onlookers. Mr. Hasse was rushed to Kaufman Presbyterian Hospital where he died from wounds to the chest and head. In the emergency room a nurse saw a gun Mr. Hasse wore on a belt beneath his coat, which he never used.

A $70,000 reward for information leading to the shooter was offered, and as police searched for two "masked shooters," reports surfaced that Mr. Hasse had been "fearful for his life" and took different routes from the office. Asked about the stories, Mr. McLelland called them "total B.S." He told *The Dallas Morning News*, "He [Hasse] and I, three-quarters of the time, we went out of the building together [and] went out the same door. He was never cowering in any corners . . . He was not afraid of anybody or anything."

At Mr. Hasse's funeral the outgoing 20-year Army veteran Mr. McLelland vowed to arrest his killer.

The prosecutor's murder immediately sent shockwaves through the county and sparked suspicions by investigators and public officials that the Aryan Brotherhood of Texas had ordered a "hit" on Mr. Hasse because he had prosecuted gang cases. Statewide, prosecutors and officials became so fearful that police heightened security for them. Locally, D.A. Mike McLelland told a newspaper that he "carried a gun everywhere, even to walk his dog around town." Said the district attorney: "The people in my line of work are going to have to get better at it [dealing with danger] because they're going to need it more in the future."

His words were prophetic.

Just short of two months after Mr. Hasse's murder, the mother of Dallas Police Officer C.J. Tomlinson called her son. It was Easter weekend, Saturday, March 30th, 2013. His mother told him she had tried to call Mike McLelland and his wife, Cynthia, to arrange delivering vegetables that Mrs. McLelland, a nurse, was preparing for Easter dinner. The officer's family was friends of the McLellands who, between them, they shared five children in a second marriage. Officer Tomlinson and his step-father, Skeet Phillips, drove to the McLelland home near Forney, 20 miles east of Dallas, to check on them. Arriving, Tomlinson found the front door of the ranch-style bungalow unlocked, which he knew was unusual given heightened security after Mr. Hasse's murder. He said he "noticed shell casings on the entryway floor as he carefully opened the door." Inside he found McLelland, 63, and his 65-year-old wife dead from several gunshots, including one shot directly into the top of Cynthia McLelland's head. Here is the description of the horrific McLelland murders at 6:40 in the morning, which appeared in records of the Texas Supreme Court: "McLellands went to bed in their home on Friday night. On Saturday morning, they were awakened by their murderer. The perpetrator was in their home for less than two minutes. The severity and number of the McLellands' injuries left no room for doubt concerning the perpetrator's intent to kill the couple. Using high-velocity ammunition, the perpetrator shot Cynthia between five and eight times, including several shots to her chest and abdomen. After Cynthia had fallen to the floor, the perpetrator fired a shot that entered the top of her head and exited under her chin. Additionally, the perpetrator shot Michael at least ten times, including several shots to his neck, chest, and abdomen. Some of these shots were fired after Michael was lying on the floor."

On Easter Day, March 31st, a day after the McLelland murders, the killer made a fatal error. He sent an email to law enforcement officials in Kaufman County that stated "unless law enforcement responded to the demands of the writer, another attack would occur." It would take computer investigators a week before they could find "unique identifiers" to determine where the email had been sent from. Also in a chilling message following the McLelland murders someone called a "Crime Stoppers" tip line and said: "Do we have your full attention now? Only a response from Judge Bruce Woods will be answered. You have 48 hours." A law enforcement officer responded: "You have our attention. How can the county judge contact you?" The voice responded: "The message through this secure format only. Your act of faith will result in no other attacks this week. Judge Wood must offer a resignation of one of the four main judges in Kaufman, district or county court, list stress or family concerns or whatever else sounds deniable." The voice went on: "The media will understand. My superiors will see this is a first step, ending our action. Do not report any details of this arrangement. You have until Friday at 4 p.m. We are not unreasonable, but we will not be stopped."

The email and chilling message with its mention of "my superiors" remained secret, but as obviously intended, it fueled hysteria among officials that the Aryan Brotherhood was behind the slayings.

Days after the McLelland murders, mourners gathered at a memorial service attended by many in law enforcement and Governor Rick Perry. When family friend Chris Heisler stood and spoke about the slain couple, he got applause after he declared of the killers: "Chase 'em down. Go get 'em. Bring 'em to justice . . . Take them out of the hole they come from."

Reward for the killer's capture rose to $200,000.

The couple's murder renewed fears that the Aryan Brotherhood of Texas was behind the slayings. D.A. McLelland had played a key role in the prosecution of a senior member of the prison gang who had gotten life in prison following a shootout. Fear of the gang rose to such a fever pitch that a federal prosecutor in a major case against the Aryan Brotherhood in Houston quit the case over concerns for his personal safety. Other possible suspects remained, however under more subdued suspicion, including the one person that D.A. McLelland himself believed had murdered his friend, prosecutor Hasse – Justice of the Peace Eric Lyle Williams.

Shannon Herbert was one of a dozen prosecutors in the Kaufman office who got increased security. She said that after Hasse's murder, McLelland told her that he was convinced Eric Williams was involved. Herbert later told a newspaper that

McLelland "went to the police. He went to the FBI." She said while ex-Justice of the Peace Williams remained on the suspect list, his attorney refused to let him talk to investigators. Although Williams had volunteered to have a ballistic expert test his hands for gun powder residue. Yet, the overriding theory was still that the three murders were work of the notorious Aryan Brotherhood of Texas. The wicked irony of what could have been prevented had investigators taken Mr. McLelland's suspicions more seriously, cannot be understated.

It took ten days for computer experts to determine that the threatening email sent to law enforcement on March 31st had been sent from a computer with certain kinds of "identifiers" owned by Eric Williams. He was immediately arrested for making a "terrorist threat" and jailed. "A search warrant was executed on April 12th, 2013 at the residence of defendant, Eric Lyle Williams at 1600 Overlook Drive, Kaufman, Kaufman County, Texas. During the search of the residence, it was learned that the defendant had utilized these unique identifiers to send the threat via the electronic communication from his personal computer," an affidavit stated. Further investigation would show that Williams also used his computer to search for information about his victims, and he had made the threatening phone call to the "Crime Stoppers" line. His arrest for making a "terrorist threat" was so police could keep him in custody as they gathered evidence against him. The search of Williams's house found computer messages that "confessed to the killings and threatened more acts of violence against county officials." Night-vision goggles, tactical boots, a balaclava-type ski mask and cellphones were also found. A significant break came when a friend of Williams called police and said he had rented a storage unit in Seagoville, 15 miles from Kaufman, in his name at the request of Eric Williams. In the unit investigators discovered weapons and tactical gear, a crossbow and homemade containers of napalm that Williams had planned to use to kill another judge. More importantly, they found the getaway car, an old "retired" white police Crown Victoria that fled the scene of Mr. Hasse's and the McLelland murders. Williams bought the car using a phony name.

On April 17th, when confronted with the mountain of circumstantial evidence, Kim Irene Williams admitted she'd driven the getaway car and told investigators her husband shot Mr. Hasse and the McLellands. She said Eric told her of his plans. She had waited in the driveway of the McLelland home and heard the gunshots. In crucial evidence, divers recovered the gun used in the Hasse murder from a nearby lake, where his wife said Eric had thrown it, and where he had target-practiced. "I was so drugged up and I so believed in Eric and everything he said," she would state later. "His anger was my anger."

The former justice of the peace was charged with first-degree murder.

Kim Williams was also held in the homicides but her case was left in abeyance because she agreed to testify against her husband.

Charges in his trial for murdering Cynthia McLelland, with a possible finding of double murder in the death of Mike McLelland, made Williams eligible for the death penalty under Texas law. He pleaded not guilty, and maintained his innocence, arguing that evidence against him was largely circumstantial, and that another, possibly his wife or the friend who had rented the storage unit because they knew the weapons and getaway car were stored there. While prosecutors did not have to show "motive" to prove murder, Williams certainly had one, and the state's Supreme Court would later spell it out in one word: revenge. Court papers filed after the trial also pointed out that "both the state and the defense presented evidence that the instant offenses [murders] were motivated by a desire for revenge against a few politicians who ruined his life, and not by [an] impulse toward violence against society." Court records told how Mr. Williams described his life prior to his theft conviction and losing his job, saying he was "living a good, normal, law-abiding life of practicing law, taking court appointments, and helping people in the court system."

At his trial in 2014 for murdering Mrs. McLelland, the jury found him guilty, and after a second penalty trial in December, sentenced him to death. Kim Williams provided bone-chilling details of the murders in the penalty phase of her husband's trial, which obviously aided jurors in recommending his state execution. While she later divorced her husband, she took the witness stand and admitted guilt to murder. She said she hoped to save her own life by testifying. She said there was "excitement in the air" the day she and her husband killed Mr. Hasse. She said that because the prosecutor had convicted her husband of stealing county computers they had decided he should die. She said they waited in the car near the courthouse and when Eric saw Hasse he got out of the car. She said Mr. Hasse said, "No, please, no" as her husband shot him multiple times. She described the ride home as "happy, satisfied and quiet." She said they also planned to kill other officials, including a judge with a crossbow. She also told jurors what happened the morning the McLellands were murdered. She had driven the getaway car, and was "happy" when she heard the shots coming from inside the house. "When Eric returned to the car, he told [me] that he'd had to shoot Cynthia McLelland one more time because she was still moaning." (This *coup de grâce* bullet essentially assured his death sentence.) Evening of the murders, in celebration, Eric Williams grilled them steaks for dinner.

At the close of testimony, Williams's attorneys pleaded for his life. Prosecutors argued that the former North Texas justice of the peace was a "serial psychopathic killer who planned to kill even more of his enemies." Before a judge accepted the jury's death sentence, family members of his victims had their say in court. "You are going to die and our family will be there to watch it happen," Hasse's mother said in a written statement to the court. "And long after your corpse has been disposed of, and your name forgotten, this county and state will remember the good people – Mark Hasse, Mike McLelland, Cynthia McLelland – who gave their lives putting scum like you in prison."

Accepting the jury's sentence, Judge Mike Snipes told Williams he was like other serial killers. "You made yourself out to be some sort of Charles Bronson-death-wish-vigilante . . . At the end of the day, you murdered a little old lady," he judge declared. "That puts you right there with Charles Manson, Jeffrey Dahmer and Richard Speck." The judge also addressed the fear in Kaufman County. "I know you've been scared for the last couple of years. Nobody's gonna be scared anymore."

After Eric Williams's case concluded, Kim Williams, 48, pleaded guilty in the murder of Mark Hasse and was sentenced to 40 years in prison, sparing her own life.

Finally, in one of the most superfluous actions in the annals of crime, on February 3rd, 2014 the State Bar of Texas revoked ex-Justice of the Peace Williams's license to practice law for stealing the county computers.

◊

An Ohio judge was sent to prison in 2004 for what the media called an "arson for hire" scheme, and right out of the chute, it had trappings of a made-for-TV drama, including use of a code-worded escape plan, threatening witnesses with death, and accomplices wearing "wires" to get the goods on the judge. Its chilling detail is unlike any felony case Judge Don S. McAuliffe ever heard in his

Fairfield County courtroom, which handled small claims, speeding tickets and barking dog complaints.

After earning a law degree in 1972, Don McAuliffe had been prosecuting attorney for the City of Pickerington, Ohio, a town of 19,000, before being elected to the municipal court in 1997. Until a fateful night in March of 2002, when a halogen light sparked a blaze and destroyed his lakeside house in Millersport, Ohio, by all accounts the 58-year-old judge lived a cushy, although not without controversy. In 1999 his former wife claimed he had "choked" her in an argument, according to a report in *The Columbus Dispatch* newspaper. The judge denied the allegation, and an investigation concluded the case was too old to do anything about. That same year taxpayer-money paid for a former state Supreme Court justice to investigate an affair between the judge and his court's probation officer, a woman who became his on-again, off-again girlfriend and who would testify against him, backing up accusations of chief prosecution witness, Darrell "D.J." Faller.

The judge's former business partner, Faller had actually ignited the blaze in the early morning of March 8th, 2002 by tilting a hot halogen lamp against an interior wall of the house on Northbank Road at Buckeye Lake in Millersport. After the fire, and well before federal agents began investigating it as arson, a sharp-eyed insurance investigator looking into the fire's origin suspected wrongdoing. She noticed fire damage on the lower floor of the house, but even "more extensive fire damage on the upper level of the home," which, in her mind, made the fire's cause "suspicious." Consequently the home's insurer Grange Insurance sent an electrical engineer to the burned house to take photos and collect debris. "He observed the burn patterns near the [halogen] lamp, but also noticed a second set of burn patterns at the base of the stairs to the upper level." In the final report the electrical engineer gave the opinion that the "cause of this fire loss was an intentional human action." At this point, the insurer sent the judge a letter stating the fire at his home was "deliberately set." Therefore, the insurance company mailed the judge a form, essentially making him swear the fire wasn't arson. In signing the notarized form the judge agreed that "the loss did not occur because of any act or design on [his] part" and that "nothing has been done to conceal or misrepresent any material facts concerning this claim, nor to deceive the company." He also responded that the "cause and origin" of the blaze was "unknown" to him.

It would be these forms that laid the groundwork for multiple counts of federal mail fraud against the judge.

The insurer ended up paying the judge a total of $235,000 for damages to the house and contents. Of course at his trial it didn't help his defense when it was disclosed that days before the fire the judge had increased insurance coverage on the house. (Curiously at his trial the judge testified that "I had absolutely no idea" the insurance amount on the home had increased.) And ironically, and probably something the judge wholly regretted, the federal investigation was launched only after he filed a civil lawsuit against business partner Faller over "differences regarding their joint demolition and excavating venture." (Name of the company was cleverly, "Judge-R-Work." The judge was the money man for the business venture and Faller was to do the actual work of demolition.) As a result of the judge suing him, Faller called a lawyer, who in turn, contacted the federal Bureau of Alcohol, Tobacco and Firearms, which initiated an investigation. In exchange for his spilling the beans about the arson plot, and describing to "authorities his role and [the judge's] involvement in the planning and execution of the fire for the purpose of obtaining insurance proceeds," Fallers was given immunity from prosecution.

A year after the fire and following a five-month investigation by federal authorities, on April 23, 2003 Judge McAuliffe was indicted by a federal grand jury in the Southern District of Ohio on several charges stemming from the arson – six counts all together of "using fire to commit mail fraud," "conspiring to use fire to commit mail fraud" and "money-laundering." It included demands to return the insurance funds, $143,000 of which was used to pay off the mortgage on the burned house, $67,000 for purchase of another house in Millersport, and to buy a 1997 Jeep Wrangler.

The charges carried a maximum 20 years in prison.

As timing would have it, the judge's arrest and jailing came in the midst of his re-election campaign in 2003. As the chairman of county Republican Party acknowledged, the indictment virtually handed the judge's seat to his opponent, a former city administer who was a Republican who changed party allegiances after the election. "For all intents and purposes, the election is over," the GOP chair was quoted by the newspapers. But, he expressed a belief in Judge McAuliffe's innocence. "I believe that Judge McAuliffe has been an excellent judge, and I believe he's innocent." Arrested, Judge McAuliffe refused to resign and continued to collect his hundred thousand annual salary, languishing in jail. Although state rules barred him from taking the bench after the indictment, there was little chance of that, especially in light of a required bail hearing days after his arrest, in which chilling evidence was revealed.

The following account is based on state and federal court records and media reports at the time.

At the hearing a federal magistrate denied bail for Judge McAuliffe after prosecutors presented secretly recorded conversations between the judge and accomplices, business partner Faller and Beth Westminster, the former probation officer and the judge's girlfriend. Unknown to him, they had been wired by federal agents and wore eavesdropping devices to snare the judge. His attorney, arguing that the judge should be freed on bail, said he was non-violent, a "respected jurist" and wouldn't flee if released. In contrast, evidence tended to show a dark side of the handcuffed man's personality. Dressed in familiar garb like he saw criminals wear over the years – a drab shirt, drawstring pants and flip-flops – the judge listened stoically as a federal agent testified and played damning recordings.

In testimony the agent said the judge had threatened the other plotters if they turned on him. "If I'm able to verify anyone is cooperating," the judge was quoted, "I'll have them killed." In another conversation the judge, possessing a handgun owned by Faller, said, "It would be a shame if I had to shoot you with your own gun." The .38-caliber turned up in a search of his home. A conversation between the judge and girlfriend Westminster, taped when he knew he was under investigation, had the judge saying, "Look into my eyes . . . If you (expletive) ever leave me, I'll kill you . . . I'll go to jail for you. I'm going to jail anyway." Threats of death continued in other recordings, including one in which the judge and Faller expressed mutual distrust of each other. "How do I trust you?" said Faller. "You got me scared, Don." The judge responded, "You need not worry about me . . . But, if you're asking me if I could kill somebody, hell, yes." The federal agent also testified that a former wife of the judge told investigators that her ex had talked about having witnesses against him killed.

Death threats aside, as much as any other evidence, what probably sank him at the bail hearing was testimony that he had an escape plan worked out with his girlfriend, if agents were ready to arrest him. She was to retrieve their passports and meet him at an undisclosed location in either Ohio or Iowa. The escape plan would be launched by uttering code – either the word "none" or numbers "6663."

Even before his arrest, the judge had been asked about the fire at his house and denied wrongdoing, telling a reporter for *The Columbus Dispatch*: "If arson was committed on the property, I certainly want to find out who committed it."

At his federal trial in 2004, a jury would say he did.

The plot was fairly pedestrian, as told by unindicted co-conspirators D.J. Faller and Beth Westminster in court testimony. The two-story house would be torched to collect insurance money. The cash would be used to build a new house on the valuable lot at Buckeye Lake, east of Columbus, where today homes sell for as much as $750,000. Having cooperated with authorities, Faller and Westminster were placed under federal protection and granted immunity from prosecution for testifying against the judge at his federal trial in 2004. Trial evidence showed that the judge, as arranged, was on vacation in the Virgin Islands when the house fire was set by Faller, after Westminster removed photos, antiques and other valuables from the house. Prosecution evidence at the jury trial was straight forward. Faller claimed that it took two tries to burn the house. He said a first attempt by the judge and himself to ignite the fire by rupturing a gas line in the basement failed, and the second attempt of using the hot halogen light did the trick. He essentially portrayed the judge as the heavy, and said they "conspired to burn down [the] house so that [the judge] could obtain insurance proceeds and use the [money] to demolish the house and rebuild it." Girlfriend Westminster added credibility to Faller's testimony, and of course all the documents the judge had filed with the insurance company, stating he had nothing to do with starting the fire, came back to bite him.

There are two kinds of defenses in criminal cases. The first is the SODDI defense, which stands for Some Other Dude Did It. The second becomes obvious when more than one person is involved in the same crime. The other guy did it. That was essentially the judge's defense. The judge testified in his defense on February 10th, 2004, and quotes from the testimony come from solid coverage at the trial by *Columbus Dispatch* reporter Mary Beth Lane and by Kristin Gordon of the *Lancaster, Ohio Eagle Gazette*. Dressed nattily for the jury in a dark blue suit, the judge spoke in a confident but calm voice and denied that he had anything to do with an arson-for-profit plot. He testified that it was Faller who had "suggested" burning the house down for the insurance. "He offered to burn down the house," Judge McAuliffe testified. "Well, I took a deep breath. I was flabbergasted. I said, 'D.J., let me think about it?'" He said he made that statement because he was "so caught off guard . . . Here was someone who was my partner offering to commit a felony." The judge said he did tell Faller no, after discussing his offer with girlfriend, Westminster. The judge told the jury he used "extraordinarily bad judgment" in not forcefully rejecting the idea immediately. After he told Faller not to torch the house, the judge testified that Faller said, "I wouldn't be surprised if it caught on fire while you're on vacation." While he was in the Virgin Islands on vacation, a neighbor called the judge and told him about the fire, he testified. Returning home, he said, "I asked D.J. whether he had any involvement in this." The judge said Faller explained that the fire started when Westminster's son had knocked over a lamp in the basement. Westminster had testified that she removed items from the house but that her children were not with her. Judge McAuliffe said he gave her permission to remove a grandfather clock, chest, bookshelves and rugs from the house, and that the items were to be put in another house. The judge tried to explain two untidy but significant facts: insurance on the house was increased by more than $200,000 before the fire; and Westminster removing valuables from the house prior to the blaze. In testimony he called these events "unique coincidences." He accused the insurance agent of upping the insurance coverage on his own initiative. He denied instructing Westminster, as she had testified, to remove family photographs, his boyhood toy chest and other heirlooms from the house before the fire.

    Two additional points, and there were likely others, which probably made his version of events unbelievable for the jury, stood out as well. First he didn't call authorities right after the fire to report Faller for offering to burn it down. Jurors aren't stupid, and one might have insisted in the deliberation room: "But he's a judge, sworn to uphold the law, why didn't he report it?" The judge tried to smooth this rough edge by acknowledging that he handled the situation improperly by not calling police. Secondly, why didn't he just tell the insurance adjustor he was told the fire started when his girlfriend's son knocked over a lamp? After all, he had testified that's what Faller had told him. (Sounds like an accidental fire which insurance would have covered.) He insisted, telling jurors, "I had no intent to injure or defraud the insurer." He believed he had no legal obligation to inform the insurer about Faller's offer to destroy the house, and told the jury, "I would answer what they asked truthfully but not volunteer anything." He likened his silence to President Bill Clinton's policy on gays in the military, don't ask, don't tell. A basic flaw in the testimony of guilty people is their overall stories invariably contain both truth and lies, and oftentimes a lie here and a lie there taints the whole thing in the minds of jurors.

The jury convicted the former judge of six federal charges of mail fraud, using fire to commit mail fraud, conspiracy to use fire to commit mail fraud and money laundering, and was sentenced. The trial judge sentenced him to a total of 17 years in prison but because of changes in sentencing laws, the term was shortened to 13 years. McAuliffe appealed his conviction and it was upheld. Of course the Ohio judicial discipline agency, the Board of Professional Conduct, filed a case against the former judge. There was little the board could do. He had left the bench, been tried and convicted and sent to prison, after all. But the board moved to lift his license to practice law in Ohio. The factors "in aggravation" were overwhelming, including his "acting with a dishonest and selfish motive; multiple offenses; refusal to acknowledge the wrongfulness of his conduct; and making restitution only when ordered to do so." The state's high court bought the board's argument that the judge had "brought disrepute to the judicial system and breached the public trust." In the discipline case the ex-judge "stipulated that he had been convicted of the crimes charged in the federal indictment, but maintained his innocence in those charges. He declined to present any mitigating evidence at the hearing, on the ground that presenting such evidence would be inconsistent with his protestations of innocence." In his favor, the discipline body found that Judge McAuliffe had "paid a $150,000 fine and $235,000 restitution to the insurance company." He also offered well-reasoned defenses to the judicial board's legal findings, with even justices of the Ohio Supreme Court who ruled in his discipline case admitted, in rejecting them, that some of his arguments were unique. However, as expected in such a serious case of criminal wrongdoing, the top Ohio court ruled against the imprisoned ex-judge, and disbarred him.

In a last and highly unusual legal maneuver in a state judicial discipline case, the ex-judge petitioned the United States Supreme Court to hear his disbarment, seeking what is called in law a *writ of certiorari*, which is a request for the highest court in the nation to instruct a lower court to send the case file up for the Supreme

Court's review. Few cases are accepted by the Supreme Court each year – about 100 of 7,000 – and usually only when a case has national significance. The former judge's request was denied, which essentially ended his various appeals.

◊

Circuit Court Judge Ronald R. Duebbert gave the judicial discipline board of Illinois no choice than to fire him for lying to police in a murder in which his friend was a suspect. The state's Judicial Inquiry Board removed the judge from office in January 2020.

The board said that in 2013 Judge Duebbert became "close friends" with David Fields who was charged two years later with assaulting a pregnant woman, and remained friends with Mr. Fields while he served a prison sentence. After Mr. Fields's release he moved into Mr. Duebbert's home, and a few days later Mr. Duebbert was elected judge.

Beginning in 2014 Mr. Duebbert provided a cell phone for Mr. Fields to use. At some point Mr. Fields returned the phone to the judge, but on December 29th, 2016, Mr. Fields asked for the phone back, along with other items he had left at the judge's house. The two men met in a gasoline station parking lot where the phone and other items were given to Mr. Fields. Hours later on December 30th, at around five in the morning, a man named Carl Silas was shot to death. It didn't take long for homicide investigators to name Mr. Fields as a prime suspect.

Sometime that same morning the judge got a call from a woman who knew Fields and reported that "she had heard" Fields was a suspect in a homicide. Shortly afterward, Mr. Fields telephoned Judge Duebbert and, according to the judicial inquiry board, the call lasted "just over three minutes." The official record showed that during the call, the judge advised Mr. Fields to "turn himself in to police." (Mr. Fields turned himself in to police later.) Around 4 o'clock that same afternoon two detectives talked to with the judge and recorded their interview. They said they wanted to make sure that any gun the judge might have was not removed from his home by Mr. Fields. During the police interview, the board alleged, the judge "made statements he knew to be false and deceptive" and "omitted facts he knew were relevant" to the murder investigation. For instance, he did not tell police that he had "been in contact" with Mr. Fields and had told his friend to turn himself in. Police admitted later they had not specifically asked the judge if he had talked with Mr. Fields after the murder.

Police said they asked about the judge's cell phone which was periodically used by Mr. Fields, and based on the responses they got from the judge, they believed the phone was still in his possession.

At a discipline board hearing later, Judge Duebbert testified that, yes, the cell phone was among items he returned to Mr. Fields at the gas station after Christmas, and just hours before the homicide. This contradicted statements police said he told them at his house on December 30th, 2016. The judge explained that he had answered the questions from the officers "very literally . . . whether or not followed up on." For example, when an investigator asked, "Do you have that phone?" he said he answered, "I do." What he meant by his response was that it was his phone and he was paying for it. They did not ask me if I possessed that phone," he explained. "I think I literally answered their question," he testified. "I believed that during the interview, I was in possession of the phone number, but not in possession of the phone, of the actual phone, because I wasn't." The judge admitted his responses to police could have caused "misperception" and he was "ghast about that."

Curiously the cell phone was later found in the judge's garage, and Judge Duebbert said he "had no idea" how it got there. Like you dear reader, the Illinois judicial discipline board had had about enough of this and ordered Judge Duebbert fired. The Courts Commission said the testimony of police was "credible, believable and without bias." On the other hand, the board stated that the "implications" of what it called the judge's "false and misleading" statements "were significant because his answers effectively misdirected the police investigation of a homicide." Folks, when it comes to reasons for removing a judge it doesn't get much worse than that.

As a footnote to the discipline case, in December 2018 Mr. Fields, who was charged in the shooting death of Mr. Silas at an apartment, was found not guilty by a jury in Illinois.

◊

In a second case in Illinois involving a judge who lied to police, the courts commission removed Circuit Judge Patrick O'Shea from the bench in 2019. The case involved a complaint by the judge's neighbor who found a hole in the wall of his apartment in 2017, and later found a bullet. When police questioned the judge he said he had made the hole with a "screwdriver" and a "nail gun." When police said a bullet was found inside the neighbor's next door apartment, the judge said his "son" must have accidentally fired the shot. Finally, the judge told police that he had fired the handgun. He had shot a revolver in his bedroom and it smashed through a mirror and the apartment wall. Judge O'Shea contended he had told police he had shot the hole in the wall when they initially asked, a statement the judicial misconduct board found "untruthful" and made under oath. Imagine, a judge lying under oath.

◊

All this judge did was lie to the FBI.

It was a perfect, sunny and cloudless September day in suburban Cleveland, with temperatures touching a pleasant 79 degrees, when Cuyahoga County Judge Bridget Marie McCafferty was pulling her empty garbage cans up her driveway in 2008. Suddenly a vehicle with two smartly dressed G-men pulled unannounced into her drive, and boy, did they have some trash to talk over with the Court of Common Pleas judge, who had had an unblemished record on the bench since 1999. She invited them into her kitchen, little knowing, her life's weather was about to turn gloomy and nasty.

FBI agents had tapped her phone and others and had listened to 44,000 conversations in a probe of one of Ohio's biggest county government corruption scandals, which involved bribes and racketeering. "These calls included conversations between [Judge] McCafferty, [Cuyahoga County Auditor] Frank Russo and others in which she revealed that she had used or intended to use her influence in cases in her courtroom to advance the interests of Russo and [Cuyahoga County Commissioner James] Dimora and to get more favorable settlement terms for local businessman, Steven Pumper," according to court records. Russo and Dimora were heavies in the scandal, and both would get long federal prison terms later, 21 years and 28 years, respectively. Construction company executive Pumper, who cooperated in the probe, got eight years.

Sitting at her kitchen table, the agents wasted no time. "The agents asked [Judge] McCafferty numerous questions about Dimora, Russo, and Pumper," stated court records. "McCafferty denied that Dimora had ever attempted to influence or intervene in any cases before her court. She also denied that Dimora had any involvement in any cases before her court. When questioned about Russo, McCafferty told the federal agents that she had never spoken to Russo about any of her cases. And when asked about

Steve Pumper, McCafferty denied ever attempting to sway settlement negotiations for Pumper. And she denied ever telling Pumper that she had tried to settle his case for less money."

With her denials, the FBI men stopped the interview and told McCafferty that they "knew she was being dishonest." They warned her that "lying" to them was a federal crime. "They even told her about the wiretapped conversations and offered, multiple times, to play the tapes for her," according to the official records.

Judge McCafferty repeatedly refused to listen to the recordings.

Though an itty-bitty figure in the scandal, she was indicted for making "false statements" to federal authorities. In 2011, a federal jury convicted the judge, then 49, of lying, all a result of the kitchen table conversation with the FBI agents, who had gone to her home to see if she'd assist them in the probe, which had begun in 2007.

She was suspended from the bench for the felony conviction.

Court evidence included a wiretapped one-minute conversation between Judge McCafferty and the politically connected businessman, Pumper, in May 2008. In the conversation the two talked about a lawsuit against Pumper's company over work at the stadium where the NFL Cleveland Browns play. The suit was settled for $190,000, although the judge says she tried to settle for less.

"I know it's more than you wanted to pay, but I hope you can live with it," the judge tells Pumper. Later she says, "I was trying to get it out at 175 but just couldn't get it done," meaning $175,000.

Pumper replies: "Nah, you know what I mean, it's you know, we're gonna spend another twenty, $30,000 getting this thing done."

Showing deference to the politically connected businessman, the judge ends the conversation by saying she had told Pumper's attorney that, "I don't want Steve throwing a beer on me when I see him."

Pumper then asks when he will see her again.

"Oh, who knows," she says, laughing. "I'm sure I'll see you soon."

Pumper: "Next fundraiser."

McCafferty: "Yeah."

A big problem for Judge McCafferty was that the contractor later pleaded guilty to having enlisted County Commissioner Dimora to intervene in the lawsuit on his behalf. Whether Dimora ever asked her to help Pumper in a case was one of the questions she denied at her kitchen table with the agents.

Specifically the agents had reportedly gone to her house to see if she would assist them in their probe of Mr. Russo, the county auditor, and Commissioner Dimora.

Judge McCafferty had a reputation of handing down stiff sentences to criminals in her courtroom, and a federal judge gave her the maximum sentence of 14 months in prison, ordered her to perform 150 hours of community service and pay a $400 fine. In what must have stung her severely, at her sentencing a federal prosecutor said she had lied to the federal agents to "protect her political godfathers." Dimora was one-time chairman of the local Democratic Party, which endorsed McCafferty's election.

She declined to make a statement at her sentencing.

In prison the judge was a model inmate, and helped women incarcerated with her to get their high school equivalency certificates. She also "displayed a cooperative attitude during the disciplinary proceedings, she submitted many letters attesting to her good character and reputation, she had a record of extensive community service, and she had suffered prior penalties for this misconduct, such as the loss of her judgeship, incarceration, a fine, court-ordered community service, and supervised release," the records of the discipline board stated. In one of her good character references a lifelong girlfriend wrote that the judge had "a fantastic sense of humor and has always had a gift for putting people at ease and making them laugh." The woman also said Judge McCafferty was "polite and outgoing," "intelligent," "truthful" and "serious about her studies" when they attended Miami University of Ohio together, and she shared an anecdote about an incident in high school. "Our physics instructor once accused Bridget of cheating on a test. He couldn't believe that she could have gotten an A without help. She was new to our school and he assumed she wasn't a serious student. He made her take the test over. She scored the same and she was angry and humiliated to have been unfairly accused and was upset that anyone thought that she wasn't intelligent enough to get an A without help. I don't think she ever got over that. She always worked incredibly hard at her studies as if she had something to prove."

A year before her troubles with the FBI, however, a Cleveland magazine surveyed 300 attorneys in 2007 about judges, and Judge McCafferty didn't fare well, although she won what was called the "most improved" award. The magazine noted 16 of her rulings were overturned during two years by higher courts, including a case in which "a black couple sued their landlord for racial harassment and won $80,000." On appeal the appellate "judges discovered [Judge] McCafferty had allowed the defense to show the jury re-enacted pictures of the landlord's friend showing up on the couple's porch wearing a Ku Klux Klan hood. The jury had been hopelessly tainted, the appellate court ruled," the magazine stated.

◊

It isn't often that a judge comes along who is every bit as sleazy as the criminals who appear before him, but it happens, and Orange County, California Superior Court Judge Ronald C. Kline was one of them. Appointed by Republican Governor Pete Wilson in 1995, Judge Kline was elected to his first term a year later when he won a six-year term, which expired in 2002. He was running unopposed for re-election but dropped out when raids by law enforcement in November 2001 discovered child pornography on his home and office computers, and he quit the race. You can bet Governor Wilson wished he could have taken that appointment back. It took a few years but Kline pleaded guilty to federal charges of possessing child pornography in December 2005. At his sentencing in federal court, the then 66-year-old ex-judge collapsed after learning he was being sentenced to prison for 27 months. His federal sentencing judge also ordered Kline to serve three years of probation and to not possess any way to access the internet, including having a cellphone. In addition he was barred from loitering near schools and parks where children gather. Kline's own attorneys told the federal judge that Kline suffered a sex addiction and was being treated for it. In addressing the judge at his sentencing, the former Orange County judge said he owed society an apology. "The problem is, I can't think of a way to say it to make any of it right," he said. "It would be a lifetime of apologies for what I did."

For its almost irrelevant role in the case, the California Commission on Judicial Performance put a hold on discipline until after the judge pleaded guilty. The state constitution required that judges convicted of such felonies be removed from office, but because the judge was then off the bench, the commission barred him from ever serving as a judge again in the state. By entering into a stipulated settlement with the commission, the dirty details of the judge's crime were not included in the commission's public report.

Chapter Four

Her court was in Southern California where you'd expect a little glitter from Hollywood to wear off. Still it was bizarre when in 2009 Judge DeAnn M. Salcido turned her courtroom into what amounted to her own audition for a "Judge Judy"-like TV reality show. As a production crew's camera recorded every rude word, she pelted litigants with snarky one-liners. If you've ever been in a modern American courtroom you know such wild things just don't happen. Judge Salcido seemed to confuse her courtroom with a comedy club.

During one court session she defined how she viewed humor in her courtroom, which helps explain why she got into so much trouble with the state judicial discipline agency. Demonstrating her talent of warming up her courtroom crowd, kind of like a yesteryear Ed McMahon warming up Johnny Carson's audience for the *Tonight Show*, Judge Salcido told spectators before calling her morning calendar of cases: "You guys have no sense of humor. Did we steal it when you came through the electronic metal detectors or something? Yeah. Get back your sense of humor. You're allowed to have one in court, even though they try to suck the life out of you here in the courthouse . . . God, you guys are dead, you guys are like, dead." When a man in the room raised his hand, she said, "Yes, sir . . . You're volunteering? All right . . . We're getting the fun back in the courthouse. Fun, courthouse, they don't have to be separate."

The state's Commission on Judicial Performance didn't agree, nor laugh. While it stated that some humor in courtrooms helps relieve tension, Judge Salcido's antics crossed the line into judicial misconduct. In November 2010 San Diego County Superior Court Judge Salcido resigned after the commission censured her. In settling the matter, she admitted nearly 40 improper remarks, including getting a crowd of courtroom spectators to chant "woo-woo-woo" at a bewildered defendant. Stated the commission in disciplining her: "Judge Salcido failed to appreciate that a courtroom is not the Improv and the presider's role model is not Judge Judy."

Records showed her comical antics were stuff of legend and gossip around the city of El Cajon, near San Diego, and it makes one wonder whether she came up with the idea of becoming another TV Judge Judy, or if others suggested it. Whatever, oftentimes in court she acted like she was acting in a comedy skit rather than administering justice. When a defendant accidently called her "sir," Judge Salcido wheeled her chair away from the bench and while still sitting down, said, "Do these look like the clothes of sir?" She dramatically raised her leg "above the bench" and held it by the ankle. "Do these look like the boots of sir?"

On the bench since 2002 and blessed with the good-looks of a TV personality, if Judge Salcido had visions of success like Judge Judy – Judy Sheindlin – it's understandable. Sheindlin made $47 million in 2013, becoming the highest paid TV star, and reportedly bought a condominium in Beverly Hills for $11 million.

It's how Judge Salcido outlandishly went about obtaining dreams of stardom that were so objectionable.

In January 2009 the judge laid the ground work for her TV-star-in-the-making audition by having someone videotape her for an hour on the bench as she presided over regular court business. She then gave the tape to an entertainment attorney who showed it to a producer of reality TV shows, featuring judges. Apparently impressed by her courtroom persona, the producer indicated he'd like to film the judge, administering justice. Through e-mails between the judge and an entertainment lawyer it was decided that the filming would be done on May 1st in her courtroom. She told the lawyer in an e-mail: "I will line up my most interesting cases for the afternoon."

The commission would claim it appeared she loaded her calendar with "more interesting" cases to "promote herself" for a TV show. In other words, manipulating her docket for "non-judicial" purposes.

As a newspaper court reporter for many years I had to file requests with judges to bring cameras into court. This is a requirement under California's court rules. No permission was sought either for the one-hour videotaping of the judge previously or for the May 1st filming by the reality show producer. The state commission opined: ". . . Nor would an order granting [cameras] . . . have been properly issued as the filming was for the judge's personal purposes."

Despite this, filming commenced, and in snappy sit-com-like banter the judge kept the courtroom gallery entertained. For instance when a defense attorney was tardy getting to court, the judge quipped to an employee, likely her courtroom bailiff, a female deputy sheriff: "Do you want to Taser him?"

The most injudicious insults of this Judge Judy wannabe, however, were saved for unsuspecting defendants who had arrived for what they thought was their day in court. Instead they got a near non-stop barrage of judicial putdowns and mockery.

At 10:43 a.m. in a case involving a man who wanted to change his plea in a marijuana case, the judge asked him if he was born in 1980. When the defendant said yes, Judge Salcido remarked: "You look older than me. That's what smoking will do to you."

At 10:53 a.m. a defendant pled guilty to urinating in public and exposing himself. After the judge noted how long he had already spent in jail, she joked, "Wow, 72 days in custody, giving new meaning to the term zip it." Then she ordered him to stay away from the area where he had urinated, and added, "Because, think they'll recognize you in more ways than one."

At 11:07 a.m. she placed a defendant on probation and said, "What that means is don't come before the court on another case . . . 'cause you will definitely be screwed and we don't offer Vaseline for that."

She would go on to use the word "screwed" to other defendants as the day progressed, such as a defendant who had previously not appeared in court as ordered. "You basically screwed yourself by not coming in."

At 11:13 a.m., Judge Salcido learned that a county deputy public defender wanted to talk with her in her office, she told him to come to the "sidebar" – close to the bench instead. She then laughed and said to a staff member, "Did roll my eyes at the camera." One way to interpret it is nobody was gonna get her off the bench and remove her mug from the hungry camera that might make her a reality television star.

At 11:24 a.m. a defendant appeared before her and asked to be taken off probation so he could join the military. He told the judge that he had moved to North Carolina with his mother after she had lost her home. In her best impersonation of the acerbic Judge Judy, Judge Salcido made denigrating remarks about the defendant being "tied to the hip" of his mother. She also mocked his desire to enter military service: "I'm supposed to put my national defense in your hands, but you can't come up here without your stepdad . . . ."

At 2:34 p.m. she handled a child custody case, modifying parental visitation. She told the child's parents who were in the courtroom: "I don't mean any disrespect to either one of you, but thankfully don't live with either one of you. So don't know where the daughter has been."

Ten minutes later, the "show" went on.

At 2:44 p.m. a defendant, admitting having violated his probation, asked that a domestic violence program be reinstated rather than being jailed. Reminding him that she could sentence him to 60 days in jail, the defendant said he would rather be allowed back into the anti-violence program. At that point the judge "warned him twice that if he returned with another excuse she would slam him like tidal wave," records stated. She told him that if he violated probation again he would "do double or nothing," meaning that he could serve 60 days now or 120 days later, and she asked him whether he were a gambling man. When he said no, she said, "Well, you're gambling, you're gambling right now." To that remark the defendant said that he was "trying to show that [I] can do what I'm supposed to." With that said, Judge Salcido invited the courtroom "audience," which in normal courtrooms sits and listens in complete silence, to verbally recite a slogan made famous by Master Yoda in *Star Wars*, which was posted in the courtroom, "Do or do not, there is no try."

At 3:21 p.m. a defendant who was in jail custody appeared in court with his attorney and admitted to a violation of probation. Judge Salcido gave him the option of getting a 60-day sentence or re-enrolling in a program, which if he didn't complete would mean an even longer jail stay as punishment. The man said he'd re-enroll in the program, and his attorney asked the judge for a moment to talk it over privately with his client. As the defendant and his attorney talked privately, the judge spoke into the open courtroom at people in the "audience," and gave this long-winded, TV game show host speech, reminiscent of a cross between *Who Wants to Be a Millionaire?* and *The Price Is Right*: "You guys know he doesn't want to do that, don't you? Yeah. Does he need to call the lifeline? Try to tell him. Let's make deal. Think he needs to call the lifeline. Yeah. Want to poll the audience? What should he do? Take the deal, take the deal, take the deal. The audience says, of course, the audience isn't going into custody. Really easy for you to tell him to take the deal because you're going to go home tonight and sleep on your pillows." The judge and courtroom spectators "repeatedly laughed" at her stream-of-consciousness comments. At that point the man's attorney told the judge that his client did not want to be jailed "because he was the only person available to take care of his 75-year-old mother, who was in poor health."

To that the judge quipped, "Then God help her."

At 3:29 p.m. the judge was informed that a defendant who had appeared before her earlier in the morning had "tested positive for" pot. Said the judge to the audience, "He's not too clean." To which the courtroom of spectators, all greased up and ready to join in the fun, said loudly in unison: "Woo!" The judge then said, "THC" – meaning the stuff in pot that makes people high. To that the audience gave her another loud, "Woo!" That prompted this response from Judge Salcido: "Can get woo, woo, woo?" Of course the audience gave her what she wanted, loudly, at which the judge and others in the courtroom laughed. "See why my sons are screwed? Can just look at someone and can tell." Later she said, "If had dollar for everybody who told me they were clean wouldn't need to work anymore."

At 3:37, the judge told a defendant who had failed to appear in court the day before, "Do you want tissue now or later because you're going into custody right now." Prior to the man being hauled off to the pokey, Judge Salcido remarked, "Did you think by coming in the next day, they wouldn't let you see me? You thought by coming in the next day, oh, won't see Judge Salcido, they'll send me next door. How do you like me now? Things don't work that way."

At 3:45 p.m. a defendant admitted she had an alcohol and drug abuse problem. The judge asked her "what type of alcohol" and the woman said, "vodka." The judge then asked, "Any type of vodka?" The woman answered yes, "any type" and the judge said, "Blame it on the a-a-a-a-alcohol." Her comic voice brought laughter from the courtroom gallery.

At 3:51 p.m., a defendant came into court who had mental health problems. After the defendant said he had been "hearing voices" – a classic symptom of schizoaffective disorder – the judge asked, attempting a joke, "Okay. And we talked, right? You're going to tell me if they say 'hurt the judge, hurt the judge.'"

At 4:06 p.m. after the judge added a term of probation to a defendant that stated that he not consumed booze and that he would be subjected to random testing for alcohol, she couldn't resist: "So that means if you come here and you test . . . and they find that you had some Budweisers, not only will put you in jail because it was Budweiser instead of Heineken, you will be in jail because it's a violation of your probation."

At 4:10 p.m. after the judge caught a male defendant "smiling," she classlessly remarked, "They might like your smile in jail." The audience responded loudly, "Oooo!" The ethics commission was particularly disturbed by this and her earlier remark about the defendant being "screwed" without "Vaseline." It stated: "We have previously condemned joking or making casual comment about the possibility of an inmate having to endure same-gender rape while incarcerated, which may be perceived as not only an indifference to and acceptance of tragic reality in our criminal justice system, but as perhaps unintended admission of its inevitability under present conditions."

At 4:27 p.m., a defendant on probation appeared without necessary paperwork to show he had done court-required volunteer work. He blamed his mother for not following through. Judge Salcido asked if his mother was in court, and he said she was at work. The judge responded, "I'm surprised, she hasn't cut the cord obviously. Cut the cord, Mom. Cut the cord." After the defendant was placed in custody, the judge remarked, "I suggest you don't call your mama."

At 4:29 p.m. when a defendant responded to a question the judge had asked earlier in the day about how he was able to control his anger, the judge reacted with mocked appreciation, saying, "Hallelujah, amen, praise the Lord, thank you very much." The audience applauded. She then asked for a "woo-woo-woo" and the audience tossed one back.

A short time later the game show, I mean court, adjourned.

Following Judge Salcido's May 1st, 2009 courtroom impersonation of Judge Judy, she continued her shtick, perhaps gearing up for her own TV show, given how her enthusiastic "audience" in the courtroom gallery had reacted. A month later in questioning the actions of another judge in a criminal case, Judge Salcido called the other judge "a.k.a. assistant public defender," in an apparent suggestion of the other judge's soft leanings on crime. Later the same day she turned to a court staff member and criticized the other judge again, this time in a low voice. "Is that ridiculous that [the other judge] did that. Mean it's a sex offender case. Yeah, whatever, you know . . . Statute says it's mandatory but, you know, we're the judge, we can do what we want. Quote. Justice be damned."

In another case on the same day, Judge Salcido listened to a defense attorney cite legal precedents and explain their significance in a domestic violence matter, stating that "there was a dating relationship for purposes of the domestic violence statutes." In response the judge summarized the cases by saying the precedents "tell me that booty calls are exempt from domestic violence statutes." She continued to use the words "booty call." In the same case she remarked: "Yeah well, he got a taste of it though right? That's what I'm saying. If he's stalking her, he got taste of it. They don't stalk unless they've got something."

At the end of June, an attorney told the judge that his client was on the East Coast and felt unable to travel because she was pregnant. He gave the judge a letter from a medical doctor that mentioned the woman's due date for her baby, and asked the judge to postpone the case. The judge remarked that pregnant women travelled all the time and said that the doctor's letter didn't say the woman "was at high risk or subject to bed rest." When the prosecutor agreed to the postponement, the judge granted it but not because the woman was pregnant. She then ripped the doctor's letter to pieces.

In July after a defendant walked into her courtroom wearing a jersey with the Oakland Raiders football team on it, the judge asked him which door he wanted to use to leave. "That's the [San Diego] Chargers' door," she said, referring to the public exit. "That's the Raiders' door," she added, referring to a courtroom door that led to jail. Then she repeated: "Chargers' door? Raiders' door? Chargers' door? Raiders' door?" She said that "365 days of the year I'm a Chargers' fan. Hello, we don't take break." Following this she turned to a woman who was connected to the man's case. "Would you say he's smart, coming here in a Raiders' shirt? No? What does that say about you, [woman's name] and the kind of men you pick?"

Also in July a female defendant was asked why she had not brought proof of having attended anti-alcohol meetings. Judge Salcido remarked, "I really feel like need some popcorn to listen to this."

When a female defendant was considering whether she wanted the advice of an attorney before she entered a plea she looked around at her father who was sitting in the gallery. To this Judge Salcido said, "Proud moment there, Dad, huh?" (Under state court rules she could not enter a plea of guilty without consulting a lawyer.)

In October 2009 the judge mocked a litigant who claimed the court wasn't "allowing him to complete his program," likely having to do with probation. "East County Court is being immature," said the judge, to laughter in the courtroom. "Being sore losers."

In another case after a defendant had difficulty explaining whether he had talked his case over with his lawyer, the judge ridiculed him. "I need some aromatherapy spray right now," she said, and sprayed something from a bottle. "This is my stress relief spray." She then "sighed heavily and laughed." Later when the same defendant stated that he had not talked to anyone about his case, the judge mocked him again, saying of his lawyer: "What do you think, she was your secretary?"

Sometimes the judge's courtroom fluctuated between a comedy club and a house of horrors. In January 2010 a defendant arrived in court to change her plea to guilty, and the judge called the case using the woman's name.

Judge: "Oh, [woman's name]."

Woman's attorney: "Good morning, your honor." He added that he was representing the woman who was not in jail and was there to plead guilty to a misdemeanor."

Judge: ". . . All right. And it's going to be an added what count five?"

Attorney: "Think that's correct, your honor."

Judge: ". . . So, [woman's name] is that how to pronounce your last name?"

Defendant: "Yes."

Judge: "Why don't you have her speak next to the microphone? [Woman's name] have you had chance to talk about the facts of this case with your court-appointed attorney?"

Defendant: "Yes."

Judge: "Did you get all of your legal questions answered?"

Defendant: "Yes."

Judge: "Can't hear you. You need to speak up or use the microphone."

Defendant: "Yes."

Judge: "Thank you. Were the consequences of pleading guilty explained to you?"

Defendant: "Yes."

Judge: "Oh, no, no, no, no. Counsel?"

Attorney: "Yes."

Judge: "You know how [I] am with the defendants who don't show the proper respect to the judge. Don't deal well with eye-rolling attitudes. And am about to sentence her. So maybe you want to take her outside and let her know whose courtroom this is."

Attorney: "Sure. We've discussed the case, your honor, just need to . . . ."

Judge: "Just directed you to take her outside."

Attorney: "Sure."

Judge: "And let her know whose house she's in."

Attorney: "Thank you."

Judge: "Mm-hmm. I'm about to sentence her."

Defendant: "For what?" [The woman might have said "so what" because the record isn't clear.]

Judge: "Excuse me, go grab her. Yeah, go grab her for direct contempt of court."

Bailiff: "Come back in."

Judge: "Don't play in here. Don't know who you think you're playing with."

Bailiff: "Come back in, take seat."

Judge: "Put her in, in the tank."

Bailiff: "Okay. Come on over here actually."

Judge: "She's in direct contempt of court."

Bailiff: "Come on over here."

Judge: "For saying 'so what' when [I] said [I] was about to sentence her."

Defendant: "Didn't say it, said, do what."

Judge: "Be quiet. Anybody else feel like they're lucky today?" Laughter followed this remark. Then the judge said, "Guarantee you we're not in Las Vegas people."

Sometime later the woman's attorney asked if the judge would recall the woman's case and the judge said, "I'm not ready to deal with her yet." Later the judge told the attorney to go handle other cases because she was going to give his client "time to reflect" on her actions.

Sometime later the judge announced she was removing herself from the woman's case and the defendant was taken to another court, changed her plea and was released. A contempt hearing was never held.

The state commission said the judge had become "embroiled" in the woman's case and had abused her authority of finding her in contempt and holding her.

The judge had the same distain for the staff at the courthouse as she did litigants. She called staffers "cucumbers," and said, "they aren't even potatoes because potatoes have eyes." Other times when she called court employees "potatoes" she told her courtroom "audience" that "they aren't corn because corn has ears."

She also seemed to like to focus her stupidness on sports stars. One time she essentially slandered a professional football player, accusing him of using drugs. Another time in open court she told spectators that golfer Tiger Woods was probably a nice guy. "I'm sure he's nice," she said. "Ask all the hookers in the nation, he's very nice to them."

When a woman defendant appeared in court, the judge criticized her shoes, calling them "hoochie" shoes and repeated it several times. After the woman said she was trying to get a job as a waitress the judge joked, "And this is restaurant to be waitress where you actually get to wear clothes?" [The record isn't clear whether the case was for prostitution.] After the judge made corrections to the woman's resume in front of courtroom spectators she told the woman that she could "take" or "leave" her suggested changes but "You can see where my effort has gotten me."

We do.

Off the bench.

No hiding it, she made a mockery of the court.

Having seen the judicial commission writing on the courtroom wall, and by retiring, the judge was eligible to collect a public pension of up to $53,000 a year at age 70.

In its discipline records the commission wrote that "Judge Salcido concedes that her conduct" ranged from being "prejudicial to the administration of justice that brings the judicial office into disrepute" to simple "prejudicial misconduct." The commission blasted her for her antics. "Judge Salcido's misconduct made mockery of the judicial system," the Commission on Judicial Performance stated. "She used her court proceedings as an audition for her own television entertainment program, giving the unseemly appearance of playing to the cameras and the audience. While the cameras were rolling, the proceedings took on the atmosphere of [a] game show."

Unseemly?

Game show?

Woo-woo-woo.

It continued: "Even when not auditioning for her own television show, Judge Salcido engaged in conduct that was seriously at odds with her duty under the canons to be patient, dignified and courteous to litigants, attorneys, and those with whom she deals in an official capacity and to maintain decorum in the proceedings . . . Judges are expected to administer justice and resolve serious issues, not to provide entertainment," the commission said.

Courtroom entertainment?

Yikes.

"Judge Salcido's misconduct cheapens the dignity of the court and undermines public confidence in and respect for the judicial system."

Cheapens? Until then, the author had never read the word in a judge's discipline case.

◊

Gotta admit they were colorful characters, even if the first was booted off the bench for his "gesture," and the second was publicly scolded.

Back in 1975 Alameda County, California Municipal Court Judge William D. Spruance had only been on the bench four years when he tangled with the judicial ethics commission. He had practiced law for two decades so he knew his way around the courthouse. During a criminal trial in 1972 at the Fremont courthouse the judge became upset at a public defender for refusing a proposed plea deal, which forced the case to trial. At the trial, the defendant took the stand to testify in his own behalf. The judge listened for a while in disbelief until he had had enough. Then he did the only thing a judge would naturally do.

Read him the perjury statute? No.

He gave him a "raspberry."

That same year a defendant arrived late to the judge's courtroom, which was a telltale sign in the judge's mind that the dude didn't respect the court. Judge Spruance reprimanded him for his tardiness, Nelson Rockefeller style. That is he gave him the middle finger.

(Footnote: German tribesmen gave the middle finger to Roman soldiers, the symbol is that old. But it was New York Governor Nelson Rockefeller, a Republican, who made it famous in popular culture when in 1976 he flipped off protesters in Binghamton, N.Y., and his photo was taken and broadcast worldwide.)

◊

But for sheer colorful judicial antics, few can best the rip-roaring actions of Los Angeles Superior Court Judge Alexander H. Williams, III, a generation later in 1995.

Talks had broken down in a settlement conference involving the Los Angeles County Chicano Employees Association. After Judge Williams took a courtroom break, he walked into the hallway and spotted the association's attorney and 20 group members. Angrily and in a loud voice the judge said, "Your demand for money is bullshit . . . If you keep making this demand, you can stick it right here." Saying it, he thrust papers rolled into a stick towards his own butt, as if showing where they could stuff their demand. When another attorney in the case walked up the judge also told him the demand was "bullshit." The judge walked back into the courtroom, and as people sat in the gallery, he turned to one of the attorneys who had followed him back into the room. Again in an angry voice, Judge Williams said: "If you think you are going to get money out of this case, you've got shit for brains. If you want war, you'll get war. And if you still think you're going to get money, I've got a Brooklyn Bridge I can sell you."

At that point the judge went into his office. Having perhaps thought better of it, he returned to the courtroom and "apologized to the attorneys for his language." However, he wasn't done making his point. "No jury I know of is going to give you money for this case. I'll set it for 1999 [four years later] and make sure it goes nowhere. You did not want to settle, so now you are my enemy." He then told the attorneys that he would "sanction" the lawyer if he lost the case in a trial, and that he "had no respect for him."

The following day the attorneys appeared in his court and filed papers to disqualify the judge from the case. Judge Williams suggested the motions be withdrawn and the attorney said no. The judge then removed himself from the case, saying: "Well, now I don't have anything to do with your case, and you can leave. I just told the truth. This case is worth nothing and now you'll get a judge who's been disqualified three times from other cases and I hope you enjoy that environment. You will not find another judge who will show the patience and give you the time that I did." When one of the attorneys tried to say something, the judge cut him off. "This is my courtroom and you have nothing to say here. Get out." At that point the attorney managed to say, making a record, "You said this case is not about money and you've got shit for brains. We weren't asking for money." Judge Williams shot back: "Well, I was half right."

The commission found that the judge's conduct "involved vulgar, abusive and demeaning language toward attorneys and constituted an improper display of personal hostility and embroilment."

Yeah, but it was entertaining.

◊

An associate judge of Cook County, Illinois Circuit Court, Lambros J. Kutrubis, a judge since 1989 who retired in 2004 and collected a $159,000 pension, allegedly "forged the signature of a former friend on 20 federal and state income tax returns for himself and entities in which he and (or) his wife had a beneficial interest," according to a complaint filed in 1999. Gambling also played a role in the complaint. The Illinois Courts Commission claimed he failed to remove himself from hearing a gambling case against a person with whom had a "personal relationship."

That 1990 case involved a woman who later became his stepdaughter. The judge was living with her mother who owned a tavern that was raided by Chicago police in 1989. The cops seized a video-poker machine and prosecutors charged the stepdaughter with illegal gambling because she was a waitress there. The state commission claimed the video-poker machine was placed in the tavern by the judge's wife. The stepdaughter was later convicted of a misdemeanor by another judge, but Judge Kutrubis improperly heard arguments on return of the video-poker machine.

Commission files included a statement from the judge's lawyer, which puts part of the blame on his bad marriage at the time. "Some of his difficulties arose during his calamitous marriage to a lady of very strong personality who operates taverns," the attorney wrote. In continuing the dominant wife theme, he added, "Judge Kutrubis recognizes that his wife is not a judge, and is not expected to know what it is that a judge must do and not do." Yeah, can't you just hear her?

Henpecked or not, the commission suspended the judge for six months without pay in 2002.

◊

Whenever former Napa County, California Superior Court Judge Michael S. Williams was invited to a house party, the hostess watched the whereabouts of her silverware. That's because the California Commission on Judicial Performance charged the judge with "taking without permission" (notice they didn't say steal) two business cardholders from the City Club of San Francisco during a dinner he attended hosted by the American

Academy of Matrimonial Lawyers. Tragically the cardholders, worth $80, led to his voluntary resignation from his $190,000-a-year judgeship. This after serving on the bench for nearly 20 years, five as a judge and a dozen years as a court commissioner filling in for regular judges.

The jig was up for the judge after he was identified on surveillance cameras, and later returned the cardholders to the City Club, blaming the incident on drinking "wine." Once he agreed to report the theft of the cardholders to the state discipline commission, it ruled to censure him and to accept his resignation. Judge Williams said of taking the club's property: "I have no excuse but that I had a couple of glasses of wine and was not thinking of what I was doing." He admitted having had an "unexplainable impulse" to take them. The art deco cardholders held business cards of the City Club's managers and sat on a table on the tenth floor of the building. He "pocketed" one holder and walked away. He then returned and took the second before getting on the elevator. Sounds like a pretty long impulse. He told the commission he took the cardholders to display "joke business cards that he and a friend had printed 40 years ago, and that he recently found." The former judge expressed "deep remorse, embarrassment and regret" for his actions.

◊

Decades ago California newspapers used a Department of Motor Vehicles service to find names and home addresses of people by knowing their license plate number. Jot down a plate number and you'd find anyone in the state. According to barroom talk among reporters, there was a guy at the paper who, when he saw a pretty woman driving alone on the freeway, he'd write down her plate number. He'd use the DMV to find her address and send her an invitation for a dinner-date. If true, pretty slick Casanova.

In 1990 a California judge, D. Ronald Hyde of the Alameda County Municipal Court was in a bind. A class reunion fast approached and organizers needed an updated list of class members. The judge had a solution. He asked courthouse employees to access DMV records and create a list of fresh addresses for class members. He then instructed an employee to send the list to a reunion organizer who had no affiliation with law enforcement.

A year later, when word must have leaked out, the courthouse administrator sent employees a memo, asking them to acknowledge the tight restrictions on use of DMV records.

Believing he was not a "court employee" the judge declined to sign the acknowledgement.

Over the next four years the judge asked court workers to access DMV records to obtain "information regarding motorists that was not related to court business." During this span of years, as well, his use of court workers to perform personal tasks for him got out of hand. He used them to type personal letters, to prepare course work for a paralegal class he taught, type dozens of pages of material for a service club the judge belonged to, babysit his school-aged child at the courthouse and even pick the kid up at the dentist's office because the judge couldn't leave the bench. He even had a court employee type up his application for a federal judgeship, which was driven to the federal court in San Francisco by a court "attendant" in a county vehicle.

The judicial conduct commission stated in its findings that "none of the acts . . . concern the manner in which Judge Hyde conducted his courtroom proceedings or deported himself while on the bench." In other words when it came to dispensing the law he was good at it. Nevertheless the judge was censured.

In his defense, Judge Hyde told the commission that it was his "impression that utilizing the work time of court personnel did not result in the impairment or nonproduction of necessary court business." That was open to argument, of course.

In the past the judge had "received three advisory letters and a private admonishment" from the commission. As is all too common in these discipline cases, Judge Hyde was booted off the bench several years later, in 2003, for new misconduct, which included telling a "story concerning a former court employee engaging in oral sex in the courthouse parking lot to the new court executive officer and a member of the clerk's office, in a manner that could be overheard by other court employees."

Chapter Five

Of all the cases in which the California discipline commission kicked a judge out of office, none tugged at the heartstrings like the firing of Judge Richard W. Stanford, Jr., in 2012, then the longest serving judge in Orange County, California. Here was a Superior Court judge who also worked 300 hours a year at a homeless shelter, cared for an old woman who had been blinded by acid, was a deacon in his church and, by accounts of fellow judges, was one of the hardest-working and most compassionate jurists they'd ever met. He was booted off the bench for fixing traffic tickets for family members and friends, including his pastor. In total, the nine cases of handling these tickets cost the county about $2,000 in lost traffic fines.

But, as the Commission on Judicial Performance stated in its findings, it had to consider the damage the incident involving nine traffic tickets between 2003 and 2010 caused to the integrity of the courts. "Members of the public know instinctively that a judge should not handle traffic tickets of family and friends," stated the commission. "Common experience and common sense indicate that ticket fixing is a quintessential bad act of a judge. It is an abuse of power that citizens unquestionably understand and are suspicious about . . . The vice in a two-track system of justice does not turn on whether there was a classic ticket fix in the sense of a dismissal of a ticket, but rather, in the damage to the reputation of the judiciary from the double standard."

Ironically, the first traffic ticket improperly handled by Judge Stanford was for a juror in a criminal trial being presided over by the judge in 2003. The juror was late for court because he had been stopped for speeding and issued a citation. It probably wouldn't be too outrageous to say that anybody who has been forced into the last form of legal slavery, which is mandatory jury service, would have agreed with the way the judge handled the juror's ticket.

"I felt bad for the guy and here I am chewing on him (for being late)," the judge who had been on the bench since 1985 told the commission. "And in his mind, I'm the reason he got his traffic ticket to begin with, which is not really fair . . . . He's doing his civic duty" by serving on the jury. In open court, Judge Stanford offered to either suspend the fines or order traffic school with payment of only the county fee, about $50. The juror choose suspension of the fines, agreeing to attend traffic school.

Two years later an elderly friend of the judge's wife, whose son had been in the same college fraternity as the judge's son, got a ticket for "impeding" traffic. The judge heard about the ticket. The commission's examiners stated that ". . . Judge Stanford handled the ticket based on hearsay information from his wife." The judge told the commission later that he felt sorry for her because she was 82 years old and appeared "frail and in ill health" when he saw her at church on Sundays. The judge "conceded that he also was motivated to help her because she was upset about the ticket." Like the ticket for the juror, the woman's ticket ". . . was transferred to Judge Stanford's department (and) at the judge's direction, his clerk entered a disposition of guilty with all fees and fines suspended." Judge Stanford also fixed two ticket for his friend and church pastor, in 2003 and 2006. The first ticket was for failing to stop at a red light and the second was for speeding, going 10 miles per hour over the limit. The judge explained that he "offered his assistance" because the pastor was "living on a pastor's salary with four children and probably could use the money . . . I just felt sympathy for him." The judge made it so his pastor got out of paying $326 for the first ticket and almost $500 for the speeding violation. All the pastor had to do was plead guilty and pay a traffic school fee of $50, which under county rules could not be waived. What's interesting is that in 2005, the pastor also got a speeding ticket but never told the judge about it, and instead, paid a $179 fine. If it was because he had second-thoughts about the handling of the 2003 ticket isn't known. But, it isn't hard to imagine that faced with the huge bill of nearly $500 for the 2006 speeding ticket, the pastor felt he needed help. The judge and the pastor knew each other well because they volunteered at a homeless shelter run by their church, and the pastor played tennis at the judge's home.

The ticket fixing continued in 2006 when Judge Stanford's longtime clerk was cited by police for failing to stop at a stop sign. His clerk was a friend of his family and attended his church. Because of a prior traffic ticket, the clerk was required to pay a fine if she pleaded guilty, and she was upset about the ticket because she felt she had properly stopped at the sign. "When she discussed the matter with Judge Stanford, he offered to suspend her fine if she was willing to plead guilty," the commission stated. The judge testified that he "made the offer because he thought it would be awkward for (her) to go downstairs to traffic court; that she might need time off to go down there; and that 'it would be easier for me to do it for her.'" The judge therefore suspended her fine of $141, and another clerk entered the case in the court's record. Another time a friend of the judge's wife got a speeding ticket while driving on the street his house is on. She had been on her way to visit the judge's wife, and the judge said he wanted to help her because "the speed limit on his street had recently changed, and he felt bad for her." He ended up handling her ticket even though he wasn't assigned to traffic court by ordering a guilty plea for her and suspending fees of $249.

These last two incidents of professional misconduct against the judge showed that he should have been more mindful of who he helped. The first was an aerospace engineer friend who also volunteered at the church homeless shelter and attended barbecues at the judge's home. In 2009 the engineer was cited for going 16 miles over the speed limit and faced a fine of $332. As the two men worked one day at the shelter the engineer mentioned his traffic ticket to the judge, and expressed surprise at the hefty fine involved. After other volunteers left the shelter, commission records showed, the judge told his friend that "he would take care of the ticket" so that he "did not have to court and could pay a lower fine." As with the other tickets, the engineer's ticket was fixed and he paid a $51 traffic school fee.

Problem was, without the judge's knowledge, his friend blabbed to his wife and other friends – including a police officer – about the judge fixing the ticket. Because the identities of those who file misconduct complaints against judges generally remain secret, it isn't know whether the "police officer" had complained. Be that as it may, the wheels fell off the judicial wagon when the judge fixed another traffic ticket, this one for his own son-in-law. In March 2010 his son-in-law got a ticket for running a red light, and like many of us in similar circumstances, the son-in-law thought the light was yellow when he crossed the intersection. The judge and his son-in-law talked about the ticket and the judge told him "he would process the ticket, but he would not be able to help him with future tickets." The son-in-law ended up saving $456 in fines and fees. When the judge gave his clerk his written directions to put the case into the court's computer system, the clerk recognized the son-in-law's name. She told the judge she was ethically barred from putting the cases of people she knew into the system. The judge agreed she should take the paperwork to her supervisor for entering into the system. At this point the clerk's supervisor alerted others at the courthouse and, ultimately, it was reported the court's presiding judge.

"You can't handle cases for family members," his presiding judge, Kim Dunning, told Judge Stanford of the traffic tickets. Judge Stanford explained that suspending fines and fees was little different than the way traffic citations were handled years ago when he was a lower court judge. The presiding judge responded that "traffic tickets are not as simple as they used to be, and that fiscal issues in 2010 have impacted the collection of fines and fees," the commission stated. What the commission doesn't say, but what the presiding judge probably was hinting at, is that by eliminating traffic ticket money the judge also reduced revenues to government, a big no-no in fiscally rough times like 2010 in Orange County.

After meeting with the presiding judge, Judge Stanford wrote a personal check for $456 to cover all fines and fees for his son-in-law's ticket. "The judge testified that when he was adjudicating the tickets of friends and family, it did not occur to him that his actions were improper."

The judicial discipline commission ruled that the judge could not have "failed to recognize the impropriety of using the power of his judicial office to help his friends and family." The commission even pointed out that his own clerk knew of the ethical problems of handling his son-in-law's ticket, so the judge should have as well.

Judge Stanford admitted his ethical lapses, and accepted all responsibility for his inappropriate actions and articulated remorse for them.

In a flutter of support unseen at the time by the commission, 62 people wrote good-character letters on behave of Judge Stanford, including many judges, justices and lawyers. They said the judge would "not intentionally do something he believed was wrong."

For example, California appellate court Justice Kathleen O'Leary called the judge's actions "gross stupidity" but not the result of a "lack of integrity."

All of the letters in support mentioned Judge Stanford's "fairness" and "honor."

Despite the outpouring of support, which also was highly praiseworthy of the judge's work in the community in helping poor people such as the homeless, the commission removed him from his judgeship in 2012. It issued this statement: "This pattern of misconduct between 2005 and 2010 created both the appearance and the reality of a two-track system of justice – one for his friends and family and another for all others. Removal is necessary to restore public confidence in the integrity and impartiality of the judiciary and honor the commission's mandate to ensure the evenhanded administration of justice."

Regrettably, the state Supreme Court shamefully failed to take up the appeal of his dismissal.

Frankly, at the time, of all cases in which the commission booted judges from the bench, this one probably caused commission members more lost sleep than others. It should have and should continue to. Over the years killers have gotten bigger breaks than did Judge Stanford, who should have been publicly censured instead of being canned. Exhibit A: Ethan Couch, the drunk-driving kid known as the "affluenza teen," was shamefully given probation after killing four people in Texas. He later served a sentence of two years for violating probation. He was called the "affluenza teen" because he came from a rich family and his defense included that his wealthy, dysfunctional upbringing made him not know the difference between right and wrong.

And he never helped the homeless.

◊

Loose lips sink ships is what they warned on the home front in the Second World War. It sinks judges, too. There's plenty of lessons to go around in this case. The first is a judge probably shouldn't fix a traffic ticket, even to help a person out of a jam. Second is, if a judge fixes your ticket to get you out of a jam, shut up about it.

When Judge James B. Scales, III, took the bench in Municipal Court in Bridge City, Texas in 2015, he never knew his good deed would get him into a kettle of stinking fish. A woman pleaded "not guilty" to a ticket she received for not stopping for a school bus. Judge Scales set the date for her trial. The woman protested, saying she had already paid for a cruise for that date. The clerk told the judge and he asked the woman to come into his office, where, with no prosecutor in the room, she watched him use "a pen to change the charging instrument" from failure to stop for a school bus to "Expired Motor Vehicle Inspection." The judge asked her if she wanted to pay the $275 fine for having an expired inspection sticker and she paid it in full. In a stroke of the pen the judge saved her boat cruise vacation. Then, she began to blab. She told friends what the judge had done, and one of them mentioned it to the Bridge City police chief, who, of course, called the judge about it.

You can imagine how Judge Scales felt. He had helped this woman and now – bang! He telephoned her and left the following voice message: "Yeah, this is Judge Jimmy Scales, city of Bridge City . . . I need you to call me back. It seems like you're running your mouth on something that you shouldn't be. And, uh, maybe we need to have a little discussion on it. Be sure and call me back now. I don't want to have to send somebody after [you]." Afterwards, the woman got a letter from Judge Scales, telling her that he had ordered a new trial on the original failure to stop for a bus citation. Her $275 was refunded. From then on the case was assigned to another judge.

It wasn't long that the Texas judicial commission took action against the judge in the ticket controversy. The woman told the Commission on Judicial Conduct that she though the telephone message was "threatening, intimidating and harassing."

In his defense the judge said the woman "embellished" her story but he confirmed the basics of the case against him. He blamed the problem for his inexperience as presiding judge of the court and said he had been "buried" by work at his construction company at the time. He had been a judge since 1996 and was named presiding judge in 2015.

"Judge Scales believed at the time that he had the authority to take such action, but he now understood that he did not," the commission stated in its public statement. In its reprimand of the judge, the commission stated, "The commission has taken this action in a continuing effort to protect the public confidence in the judicial system and to assist the state's judiciary in its efforts to embody the principles and values set forth in the Texas Constitution and the Texas Code of Judicial Conduct."

◊

Every judicial commission in the nation has loads of case where judges have been punished for fixing speeding tickets for buddies and relatives. Sometimes the cases are particularly egregious. Take the case of Municipal Court Judge William C. Romo in Hidalgo, Texas. He was disciplined after leaving his judgeship because a local newspaper put together a story in 2012 that reported as many as 839 traffic tickets had been dismissed over a 15-month span "at the request of local politicians and city officials," or as favors to friends and court staff. At the center of the controversy was Judge Romo, and he wasn't about to go down without taking City Hall with him. It was claimed that city school district officials "hand-delivered stacks of tickets to the courthouse . . . for dismissal." In testimony before the Texas Commission on Judicial Conduct, the judge said that "a culture of intimidation" existed in city government which "led him to believe that if he did not dismiss cases when requested, he would be fired." He said he felt "pressured" to "dismiss the citations without a prosecutor's motion because city officials had expressed a desire not to pay a prosecutor to prepare and present dismissal motions." As if to prove his point, when Judge Romo's term of office expired following the ticket brouhaha, the Hidalgo City Council failed to renew his contract. Perhaps the judge should have applied for "whistleblower" status. In any event, given the severity of the case the Texas commission reprimanded the judge after he had left office, and in its ruling it left little doubt that it believed the judge's allegations against the city. "Judge Romo's description of the political landscape and culture in his community highlights a fundamental flaw in the system of justice that has been administered in the Hidalgo Municipal Court for some time," the commission stated. "Given that the foundation of the justice system in a modern democratic society rests on the guarantee of an independent and impartial judiciary, a judge who disposes of cases out of fear that those in power will terminate him, or to satisfy the political or financial interests of an entirely separate branch of government, cannot be – nor can he be seen to be – independent. By definition, a judge who is not independent cannot be impartial. Based on his own testimony, Judge Romo was neither independent nor impartial when he dismissed cases without a prosecutor's motion; however, to the extent that the practice appears to have stopped with Judge Romo and if Judge Romo's successor refuses to succumb to pressures from local politicians, city officials, friends and court staff, it is possible that public confidence in the judiciary in the City of Hidalgo may eventually be restored."

No action against city officials was mentioned.

◊

For a blatant case of cronyism involving traffic tickets look no farther than the courtroom of Municipal Court Judge Bruce A.

Clark of Ventura County, California in the late 1980s. When the daughter of a state assemblywoman got two speeding tickets, Assembly member Cathie Wright, a Republican from Simi Valley in Ventura County, went to the home of Judge Clark to talk about it. The cases were pending in his courtroom.

The assemblywoman, who once described herself as "irascible" and a "fighter," certainly fought for her daughter. "Based" on his conversation in his home with the state lawmaker, the judge handled both speeding tickets in his private office rather than in open court. In neither instance was a prosecutor present to protest the judge's actions, nor was the press or public able to view them, which they would have done if handled in open court. The judge first "struck the requirement that the defendant appear in court on the tickets," and then "permitted [the assemblywoman's daughter] to attend traffic school in connection with both tickets," according to commission records. The judge then "ordered that both speeding counts be dismissed upon receipt of a traffic school certificate." While the commission acknowledged that the judge handled the tickets "lawfully," his actions were "unusually lenient."

In "reproving" him the commission stated the judge failed to "comply with" rules stating a judge "should conduct themselves at all times in a manner that promotes public confidence in the integrity and impartiality of the judiciary." Additionally, the commission stated the judge was in violation of the judicial ethics code which states "judges should not allow their families, social, or other relationships to influence their judicial conduct or judgment." Without mentioning cronyism, the commission summed up: "Judges should not convey" the "impression" that others "are in a special position to influence them."

◊

By all accounts Merced County, California Superior Court Judge Robert D. Quail was a devout Christian with a warm heart, proven by years of leading volunteers on medical relief missions to Kenya and Tanzania to treat African children for malaria. These poor kids would be given clothing and eyeglasses and Bibles.

Saving the lives of children wasn't a sin in the eyes of the California Commission on Judicial Performance, and who knows, maybe they didn't even mind the Bibles. But, to do-good, do-gooders need green. And it was how Judge Quail raised this money that crossed the icy perimeter of his ethics. Nothing hardcore criminal, mind you. He just did a little arm-twisting. To pay for these missions the judge organized charity "auctions" in which business leaders and others donated items like bales of hay for horses and cases of wine to be sold to the highest bidder at an annual auction attended by 400 people, including law enforcement and courthouse workers.

Shucks, angel-tongued Judge Quail was even the auctioneer.

In the stuffy world of judicial ethics it was all right to solicit charitable donations from fellow judges because they were unlikely to appear in his courtroom behind the defendant's table. But, the ethics code barred him from hitting other people up for charitable donations. He sought donations from county officials, attorneys that appeared in his courtroom, courthouse employees and many others in his community. His pitch to an attorney who possessed season tickets to San Francisco Giants baseball games was typical. For five years he had asked her to donate a pair of tickets, and she did once. "One request occurred in the courtroom while [the attorney] was asking for a continuance," stated records in the discipline case. "The judge called her up to the bench, alone, and asked her whether she was going to donate Giants tickets." Afterward the attorney complained about being pressured this way, and the court's presiding judge told him to knock it off – not to ask attorneys for auction donations. Later, Judge Quail asked the attorney to come to his office, and told her that "somebody had snitched me off about the auction." He asked her if she had done it. To his question she asked another – (how lawyerly). Did he think she would do such a thing? Well, a good Presbyterian and too gullible, the judge suggested and named another attorney who had probably squealed on him. Still in his office and undeterred, the judge "again solicited" the attorney for her Giants tickets, saying, "Are you still going to get me those tickets?" It isn't hard to believe that the judge knew full-well that his conduct trampled on his judicial ethics, but, of course, his was involved in a higher cause.

After the state judicial commission got wind of his conduct, it hit him with a public admonishment. But to be charitable to the commission, it wasn't all about soliciting donations. Judge Quail also had used a courthouse secretary to type letters for the African trips, even after being warned about it by the presiding judge.

Some might argue Judge Quail put his religious good work before his judicial duties. He retired in 2007 after 28 years as a judge. By then he was probably more concerned about his immortal soul than about the workaday happenings of a mere earthly courthouse.

◊

Here we go again, another do-gooder judge slapped aside the head. This time Douglas County, Nebraska District Court Judge Michael Coffey was reprimanded in 2006 for helping the local National Multiple Sclerosis Society. He had volunteered to serve as "honorary" co-chair of a fundraising dinner for the charity. Sounds worthwhile for the judge who had been on the bench since 1998, and had graduated from Creighton University School of Law in 1974.

The judge got involved when the MS society asked him to approach a friend of his about the friend possibly being honored at the dinner, and the judge did so. The friend said he wanted the judge to introduce him during the dinner.

"By the time Judge Coffey approached his friend, he had become aware that the honoree would be required to make a financial contribution to the MS society," the Nebraska Commission on Judicial Qualifications stated in its reprimand order. "The commission notes approaching anyone to participate in an event that raises funds or solicits membership is prohibited by the Nebraska Code of Judicial Conduct, which makes no exception for friendship."

Or for worthwhile charities, apparently.

To add to the judge's sins in the divine eyes of the commission, it noted that letters seeking donations to the MS society were sent out that mentioned the fundraising dinner and the judge's honorary role in it as co-chair. The commission acknowledged that the judge didn't know about the letters before they were mailed and "he took no steps to advise the MS society that he was unable to participate in any fundraising or solicitation efforts, or that neither his name nor his judicial position could be used." Of course the commission also scolded him for attending the dinner as promised and introducing his friend as the group's honoree.

The rule-sticklers at the commission said they knew the judge didn't intend misconduct – (how could he, money was actually raised for a very good cause, Multiple Sclerosis). Nonetheless, rules are rules, and he had "participated personally in the solicitation of funds" and "permitted the prestige of [his] judicial office to be used for . . . membership solicitation." Therefore, he violated Nebraska's judicial ethics code.

Oh, and the clincher?

"The commission is aware that Judge Coffey's own family is affected by multiple sclerosis," it stated, in publicly punishing him. After all, a violation is a violation is a violation. Attempting to portray themselves as human beings, the commissioners added, he deserved a reprimand "regardless" of "how worthy the cause, or sympathetic the circumstances."

◊

Courts nationwide are clogged with cases of domestic violence, usually husbands beating up their wives. It comes as no surprise then that judges have also been charged with beating their spouses, such as the case involving Judge Ralph L. Perkins of Pend Oreille County District Court in Newport, Washington in 1993.

What makes the case somewhat unusual is that the judge allegedly assaulted his then wife twice in two months, on February 27th and on March 27th. In both attacks, according to records of Washington's Commission on Judicial Conduct, "with or without provocation [he] intentionally" struck and caused "bodily harm" to his spouse at their home, and sheriff's deputies were called.

Six months after the last attack the judge pleaded guilty in Pend Oreille County Superior Court to charges of "assault in the fourth degree." In Washington fourth degree assault amounts to simple assault and is a gross misdemeanor, punishable by a year in jail and a $5,000 fine.

The commission censured the judge, and in December 1993, the judge resigned from office.

Unfortunately for ex-Judge Ralph L. Perkins, who later got a job as a prosecutor in Okanogan County, Washington, his legal troubles didn't end with his quitting the bench. Ten years later, after deputies were called to his home, his wife accused him of rape, according to press reports. In a search of the house deputies found child pornography on a computer. While the former judge wasn't charged with rape, he was charged with possessing child porn, a federal offense.

Ironically his job in the county prosecutor's office was handling child porn cases. The former judge "admitted in court documents that he got hooked on child porn while researching the topic as part of his job prosecuting people for the crime," stated a newspaper report in 2003. "His initial research turned into sexual gratification, and less than half of the pornography on his computers was work related court documents said," it was reported. "An examination of Perkins's computers turned up more than 10 images of children younger than 12 involved in sexually explicit conduct," the news report said.

Avoiding a trial in 2004, at age 55 the former judge was sentenced to 27 months in federal prison after agreeing to plead guilty to possessing child pornography. At the sentencing he told a federal judge that as a former judge he had "heard every self-serving excuse" from criminals, and he was ready for punishment. "I did this crime, and I'm guilty," he said in court in Spokane. "It cost me everything."

◊

As a newspaper reporter the author once covered a case in which a man shot and killed a baby in the arms of its mother – on Mother's Day, no less.

On the first day of the killer's trial 20 people who were friends and family of the baby's mother showed up wearing badges with a photo of the baby on it. After a bailiff told the judge about the badges, the judge told the people if they didn't remove the badges pronto they'd have to leave the courtroom. I say this to demonstrate how benign the spectator's gallery is supposed to be in a courtroom, and to draw a marked distinction with the discipline case of Minnesota Judge Richard G. Spicer of Dakota County in 2008.

After calling a defendant some "disparaging" names, the judge "asked the courtroom gallery to weigh in on his own conduct and that of the defendant, creating the appearance that he was either delegating his decision- making authority to the gallery of spectators or asking the gallery for its opinion on how he should decide an issue placed before the court," official records stated.

Lesson? Turning to the mob for directions in court or out is never a good idea. The Minnesota Board on Judicial Standards reprimanded him for his lack of "dignity."

◊

The following cases are head-scratchers because they make you ask, how did the judge even do that?

The 1976 removal from office of William D. Vanderwater, associate judge of the Circuit Court in Kane County, Illinois came after the judge issued "speedy" justice. To quote the complete description of the case, here's what he allegedly did. "He detained a former tenant with the aid of a hand gun, had him arrested and charged with theft, procured a guilty plea and jury waiver, conducted a midnight proceeding in the police station and sentenced the tenant to eight months in jail."

Montgomery County, Illinois Circuit Court Judge William A. Ginos was censured in 1974 for "pressuring" jail inmates into becoming "his informants," and when an inmate refused, the judge raised his bail amount as punishment.

In presiding over a hearing, St. Clair County, Illinois judge, James M. Radcliffe, allegedly forced a state liquor control agent to "reveal publicly that the FBI was investigating" a litigant who was participating in the hearing, even after the state agent, who had learned of the hearing 15 minutes before it began, asked for time to get a lawyer to represent his interests, and thereby was denied any opportunity to defend himself from being forced to disclose the secret FBI probe. In 2001 the judge agreed to a three-month suspension without pay.

◊

Michigan's Judicial Tenure Commission recommended and the state's high court accepted a one-month suspension without pay for a Jackson District Court judge who took his romantic interest in a woman he had sentenced and invited her on a date in 2014.

The woman was arrested for domestic violence and the case was assigned to Judge R. Darryl Mazur. The woman ended up pleading guilty and the judge sentenced her to a year's probation, with the prosecutor's approval. A few months later the woman sent him a Christmas card and thanked him for being an "extremely firm yet fair judge." Rather than doing nothing because the woman was still on probation, the judge decided to write back to her on courthouse stationary. And rather than simply thanking her for the card, he wrote, "You continue to sound well. No need to thank me. Well, maybe you can. I am not sure of your marital status. But if you are not, would you be interested in seeing me? Being on probation is a complication. I am interested if you are."

Commission documents don't show whether any kind relationship ever developed but stated the judge and the probationer "continued to e-mail each other through the month of January 2015." The commission noted that the judge's actions amounted to judicial misconduct and said that he willingly cooperated in the commission investigation, and agreed to a speedy settlement.

Chapter Six

Art Linkletter hosted a very popular radio and television show for 25 years called "House Party" and one of the segments was "Kids Say the Darndest Things," (1952-1969), in which the host interviewed youngsters, often about their own families, causing much embarrassment for unsuspecting moms and dads.

Yolo County, California Judge James L. Stevens, Jr., as far as is known never appeared on Linkletter's show. But, he could have. After a juvenile defendant became upset and rushed towards Judge Stevens, the youth was tackled by a bailiff, and restrained in the courthouse. Later the judge said the juvenile "did not have a Chinaman's chance of reaching" him. Well, the expression from the 1800s refers to Chinese immigrants who worked for peanuts and faced racism in America, and is considered a racist and derogatory epithet. Once the judicial misconduct commission called him out for using it, the judge said, he "is now aware that 'Chinaman's chance' may be considered offensive" and agreed not to use it again. The judge was also "reproved" for other comments. He referred to two female juveniles as "bitches." In a case in which he apparently didn't like the looks of a male defendant he turned to female clerks in the courtroom and said, "Ladies, how would you like to wake up with that naked in your bed?" In a case involving parental rights of a sperm donor, the judge made a legal point by using a hypothetical example, saying, "She said to him, sweetheart make me a baby." Later in the case Judge Stevens said, "As I look at it, I frankly get the very distinct impression that this child is conceived as a sort of a toy for the mother and her friend, something to fill their lives up and to hell with the needs of the child, and to hell with the rights of the father." He once said goodbye to a court stenographer who had worked in his courtroom for years and gave her a "partially rotten zucchini," which according to commission records, "some observers [thought it] conveyed a sexual connotation."

The commission stated that "the judge has acknowledged that he has offended people and has apologized and he has agreed to refrain from further conduct as exemplified herein and to attend appropriate communication and sensitivity classes."

◊

One thing that never plagued the Art Linkletter show was profanity. We've all seen and heard it. The coarsening of America. Whether it's a group of teenagers flipping each other off on the sidewalk or a fan at a football game shouting that the referee needs "fucking" glasses. So, it was just a matter of time before it landed on the bench. Unfortunately foul-mouthers have always occupied the benches of jurisprudence.

Take the classic case, which judges and lawyers still talk about, of Los Angeles Municipal Court Judge J. Noel Cannon. She had a rough way of expressing herself, and it helped get her booted off the court in 1975.

In November 1972, a police officer spoke to the judge at the intersection of Spring and Arcadia streets in Los Angeles about her "excessive use" of her car's horn.

Here's their conversation, according to the cop.

"She rolled down her window when I pulled up alongside her, at which time I said, 'Ma'am, there is no reason to honk your horn.' The gentleman was just waiting for a pedestrian, like he should have."

"At which time she told me she would honk her horn any time she damn well pleased.

"At that time I said, 'Ma'am, there is a Vehicle Code Section that covers excessive use of the horn.'"

"At which time she told me, 'You go to hell, officer.'"

Arriving at the courthouse, Judge Cannon said to her bailiff, "Find the son of a bitch; I want him found and brought in right away. Give me a gun: I am going to shoot his balls off and give him a .38 [caliber] vasectomy." She then told another bailiff: "God damn. Get that son of a bitch here; find that bastard; I'm not going to start court until that son of a bitch is here: when I find him, I'm going to cut off his balls and have them hang over my bench: I'm going to castrate him; I'm going to give him a vasectomy with a .38." Afterwards, the judge and a bailiff went to the "police officer's waiting room" at the courthouse, and Judge Cannon spoke to a police sergeant there.

"God damn it, find him," she told the sergeant. "Find that son of a bitch for me. I am not going to take the bench until you find that male chauvinist pig."

About this time several police officers began arriving at the courthouse, and went to the judge's office, including a lieutenant and a captain. With the officers there, the judge "appeared to be hysterical" and her "voice was harsh and loud." She told her two bailiffs: "God damn it. No one is to leave; if anyone tries to leave, shoot the bastard." Then, with the officers listening, Judge Cannon declared that she could sound her "God damn horn any place in the city and no male chauvinistic officer" is going to tell her otherwise. Then she said, "I'd like to slap that mustache off that officer's face for what he did. We have too many of these motor officers out there laying their pecker on the line for their pay checks."

Later, the patrol officer who had talked to her at the corner about excessive use of her car's horn arrived. He said he could hear the judge yelling at the police sergeant, and after ten minutes walked into her office.

The judicial misconduct commission asked the officer what happened then.

Officer: "Yes . . . I walked into the chambers and I stood behind my chair, and Judge Cannon said, 'Good morning,' and I said, 'Good morning.' She said, 'Have a seat' and I said, 'Thank you,' and I sat down. . . There was a momentary silence for about thirty seconds. We just looked at each other, because I did not know what to say or do. Her opening statement was. 'You've been a very naughty boy.' And I stated, 'Well, if you say so, your honor.' She said, 'What do you mean, if I say so?' I said, 'Well, you are the Judge.' At this time we just talked about things in general, such as public defenders and court cases and how the public defenders ask some ridiculous questions like, 'Officer, did you have your gun out when you did this? Did you have your gun out when you did this?' she said. 'There is nothing but a revolving door here,' she said, 'All of these people are going to be back, they just come in and out.' Then it was – she just changed. The conversation changed back and forth. Then she started talking about some religious seminar that she attended over some holiday, just a couple of weeks prior to this, I presume. And she started going through some religious pamphlets that she had. And told me that she wanted me to have a copy of it. And she looked for a copy of it and she could not find one. She gave me her own personal copy of a couple of these pamphlets and told me to look at the dog-eared pages of the pamphlets in my spare time. She also stated the guillotine had been used in France again: she wished it would be brought back in the United States."

Commission: "Did she ever ask you to apologize during this conversation?"

Officer: "No, sir."

Commission: "Did you leave with how many pieces of religious brochures?"

Officer: "Three or four."

Commission: "And later on did you receive a letter of commendation from Judge Cannon?"

Officer: "Yes, sir. I did."

Commission: "How many weeks after this incident was this?"

Officer: "Two weeks.

Commission: "And could you relate in essence the substance of this letter of commendation?"

Officer: "Yes, sir. It was just addressed to Chief [Ed] Davis . . . and it said the Los Angeles Police Department is the finest in the world, and the T.E.D. motor squad was the finest of L.A., and [I] was the finest of the fine. It was signed Noel Cannon."

Interesting how this she-lion of judge turned into an emasculated lamb, spouting religion once her prey sat cross from her, looking her in the eye. She probably realized her outburst of expletives just might land her in judicial hot water. Alone they didn't but, they didn't help her case. The commission ruled that the judge had engaged in willful misconduct by "not only using profane, abusive and inexcusable language, but she also misused the authority of her office by ordering [police] to appear in her court where no matters were pending requiring their attendance and by directing her bailiffs to use force if they attempted to leave."

She was fired from the bench for other problems.

◊

In a contest of the most disgusting things ever uttered in open court by a judge, the "joke" told by Orange County, California Superior Court Judge James Randal Ross ranked skyscrapers above all others. It's the number one worst, and not only because of its content. The context in which it was said, in a civil trial in a child molestation case, made it shocking as well.

The case involved a woman whose attorney told the jury what had happened to her as a child. "The allegations involved my client from the time she was 12 years old, for several years being sexually abused by the defendant, including sodomy, use of alcohol, use of vodka enemas, use of pins penetrating her nipples and other foreign objects, involved the use of rubber clothing. To summarize, disgusting conduct over at least six years of time . . ."

During the trial a medical professional took the witness stand to talk about what the child had gone through, and with the victim and the defendant in the courtroom along with about 30 other people, Judge Ross told the following joke after telling the jury to wait in the hallway. "Did you hear about the psychologist that had this man in for testing for the Rorschach test," the judge began. "He said what's this one, and the man looks at him and says that's a man and a woman having intercourse. So, he showed him the next one. He says that's two women making love. He turned over the third one. What's this? Oh, that's a gang intercourse. And turned over another one. Oh, they are having sodomy, a man and a woman. About that time the doctor said, man, I think you're a pervert. The man looked at him and said, don't talk about me, doctor, they are your pictures."

The woman who had been molested told the state commission on judicial misconduct she was "stunned" the judge told the joke. The commission called it an "inappropriate, undignified and offensive joke."

Because the judge retired in 1995 before being possibly being removed from the bench, the commission made sure he was never allowed to take the bench in California again.

Complaints against him also included losing his temper in court and fabricating testimony before the commission during its investigation.

For instance there was an insurance liability case involving State Farm. In his office the judge met with two representatives from the insurer and the company's attorney, and according to the judge, when he asked the company's adjusters "How much money do we have today?" – meaning how much money could the adjusters approve to settle the case, the attorney, "Out of the clear blue said, 'Nobody in this room will say one word on behalf of – because I am representing State Farm. I have it from the highest authority. This case is not worth a plugged nickel. We're not paying a plugged nickel. Mandatory settlement conference over.'"

The meeting ended and the judge told the commission that he told the representatives he "needed time to go to the bathroom and put his robe on." He claimed he put his robe on and stepped into the hallway where he heard the attorney "telling [the adjusters] that they better back [him] up or else they wouldn't be in State Farm any longer." At that point the judge claimed he told the attorney what he was doing was improper and the attorney told him he was a "liar." And, here's where the commission disbelieved the judge's account of the hallway confrontation. "The [judge] testified [the attorney] said: 'Further, Judge Ross, you little bastard, if you fuck with me, I'll see to it that you're no longer a judge. And I've got State Farm's billions behind me.'"

The attorney denied making the remark and a company adjuster agreed that "there was no such discussion" between herself and the attorney in the hallway.

Stated the commission: "We are unpersuaded by [the judge's] testimony of his perception of the hallway events. We find the statements attributed to [the attorney] in the hallway did not occur."

The weirdest complaint against the judge was his peddling of a book he had authored on his ancestor, the outlaw Jesse James, titled, *I, Jesse James*. He was the great-grandson of the outlaw. Beginning in 1989 he sold the book from his office. At a profit of $2.95 a book, he sold them to jurors and others at the courthouse. And of course he was available to sign copies.

"In one case, a juror testified that a copy of Judge Ross's book was provided by the bailiff and passed among the jurors either in the jury box or the hallway," the commission stated. "Transcripts in one trial show that Judge Ross discussed the book with jurors in open court and told them it was for sale in chambers, and that he would autograph it. Other jurors testified that Judge Ross discussed the book from the bench. Some bought copies in chambers after the trial." After one trial the judge sold books to the attorney in the case. One juror in the case who bought a book told the commission "he was aware one of the attorneys had purchased a book and believed that the attorney had done it to 'suck up' to the judge."

Selling of his books was deemed misconduct.

As an aside, Judge Ross gained notoriety in 1984 when he ruled in a Disneyland case, finding that the amusement park violated the civil rights of two gay teens who were removed from the amusement park for dancing together. Afterward the park ended the discrimnatory policy against gay couples dancing together.

◊

The courtroom of Commissioner Mark Kliszewski of the Alameda County, California Superior Court was like a crude Romper Room for foul-mouthed staff disparaging juveniles and parents who came to court. As the Commission on Judicial Performance put it: "For many years, during his assignment to the juvenile division, Commissioner Kliszewski permitted court staff members to routinely make offensive and inappropriate comments, some of which related to race, gender, and sexual conduct, in the courtroom when court was not in session." The "pattern of derogatory comments" were made before court was in session, and "although the subjects of the remarks were not present, the remarks were made in the courtroom, often in the presence of Commissioner Kliszewski and other court staff. Staff members also made racial jokes and engaged in sexual banter."

Commissioner Kliszewski contended that he "spoke to the responsible staff members" several times to ask them to "tone down" their remarks. Apparently his actions were insufficient to prevent the remarks from recurring. Of course it didn't help that Commissioner Kliszewski "sometimes" laughed at the remarks himself. Perhaps it was inevitable then, that between 2010 and 2015, "Commissioner Kliszewski made numerous insulting and derogatory remarks about a court interpreter to other court staff [and] some of these remarks were made in the interpreter's presence," according to the California commission.

It was after Kliszewski learned that the court interpreter had complained to her supervisor that the commissioner had "spoken harshly to her in the courtroom." The discipline board said that at one point Kliszewski said, angrily, "That c[unt]! That f[ucking] bitch!" The judicial commission publicly admonished Mr. Kliszewski for making "profane and derogatory comments" that "violated his duty to maintain and enforce high standards of conduct." In calling his comments "at a minimum, improper action," the commission stated that Kliszewski's prior record of discipline was a factor. In 2000 the Alameda County Superior Court suspended him for 120 days for misconduct during his judicial campaign, which included making misrepresentations in his campaign literature. In 1996, the court suspended him for two weeks for discourteous and improper treatment of a female social worker who appeared in his courtroom. In both instances the court required Commissioner Kliszewski to participate in additional training. Whether he had flunked the training, the commission didn't say.

◊

Another potty-mouthed judge was disciplined in Kansas in 2020. In Coffeyville a judge's use of dirty four letter words like "fuck" and "cunt" and occasionally their five-letter brethren, "bitch," became so pronounced at the courthouse that one attorney called it "just routine," and a court clerk started keeping what he called a "swear journal" to document the judge's profanity. The clerk, Larry Carter, told the Kansas Commission on Judicial Conduct of a job review he had with District Judge F. William Cullins, in which the judge fumed, "Carter, go sit down in that fucking chair and don't say a fucking word."

The courthouse's chief clerk, Joni Pratt, who in 2016 was overseeing remodeling of the clerk's office, told the discipline commission that when she asked Judge Cullins whether she could use some carpet for courthouse elevators, he responded that he "didn't give a fuck about the carpeting." Additionally, a lawyer told the commission he heard the judge use "cunt" and "bitch" in referring to women.

Demonstrating what the judicial conduct panel described as the jurist's "unsound character," Judge Cullins wrote these words "in large print on the front page of [an] arrest warrant," which is an official court record: "This is a traffic case that needs to be filed in [Coffeyville court] or I need a better explanation. [signed] Cullins. Larry [Markle, the county attorney] said so, doesn't fucking cut it. [Signed] Cullins."

In his defense, Judge Cullins told the discipline commission that his speech – apparently referring to all of his profanity – was "protected by the First Amendment," which, he might be surprised to learn, really doesn't exist for people who sign up to serve on the bench. Judge Cullins contended that "cursing" didn't "impair" him from performing "duties of a judicial officer." Probably true, but it certainly showed low class. He suggested that he "needed a more effective management style." Also in his defense, a court official told the commission that Judge Cullins "ran a very efficient docket" and was "firm and held attorneys appropriately accountable."

The commission said that the judge's actions didn't warrant removal from the bench. However, it ordered him to get "professional coaching," and if he didn't, he could be suspended later. The discipline board suggested he seek "individual counseling or psychotherapy."

A bar of Lifebuoy stuck in his mouth might have helped as well, although the commission didn't suggest it.

◊

"Bull" is in there. In ecclesiastical law it is an instrument granted by the pope. Even "bull-headed" is listed, meaning headstrong or unreasonably stubborn. We're talking about *Black's*

Law Dictionary. But the word that isn't in the official language of law is "bullshit." Someone should have told Baltimore Circuit Court Associate Judge Pamela J. White. She was reprimanded for what she said to attorney Reverend Rickey Nelson Jones in 2014. During a hearing in a civil lawsuit, in which the defendant insurance company asked that the suit be thrown out, the judge raised her voice and said to Rev. Jones, who represented the plaintiff: "Are you telling me with a straight face, as an officer of the court, that the actions of an insurance adjuster from another company should be attributed to [the] defendant?"

Attorney Rev. Jones answered, yes.

"Do you have any legal authority that gives you the chutzpah to claim punitive damages in a negligence case for actions by an adjuster not employed by [the defendant] that would have allowed me to attribute ill will to [the defendant]?"

The Maryland Commission on Judicial Disabilities ruled that the judge "yelled and treated Rev. Jones in a rude, disrespectful, and unprofessional manner."

Several months later, things got interesting again. At a conference to set things ready for a trial, two judges met with the defendant and Rev. Jones, but his client, the plaintiff didn't show up as required by court rules. It was a fact not missed by Judge White about a month later. Judge White ordered Rev. Jones and his plaintiff client to show up in court and prove why they should not be held in contempt for his client's failure to attend the pre-trial conference. Before the contempt hearing, however, Rev. Jones and his client came to court and demanded Judge White remove herself from the case because of her "harshness" towards his client because she "had not shown his client consideration for her disabilities" and because she had "insulted" him, Rev. Jones, at the earlier hearing.

After listening to Rev. Jones, Judge White said, "I strongly believe that there was no insult and no basis or obvious prejudice as to Mr. Jones." She then launched the following long-winded statement before granting his demand that she remove herself from the case: ". . . Because I am incredulous, because I am in disbelief, because I find myself incapable of believing virtually anything that Mr. Jones has just told me, I'm in the unfamiliar territory of finding that I must recuse myself from any further proceedings in this case because I cannot believe anything that the Reverend Rickey Nelson Jones, Esquire – I'm reading off the letterhead – tells me. I think that 99 percent of what Mr. Jones has told me about his conduct on behalf of his client is pure bullshit!"

The commission stated that "Judge White's use of foul language . . . was undignified."

While she disqualified herself from hearing the trial, she refused to remove herself from presiding over the hearing she had scheduled to find Rev. Jones in contempt of court. The hearing went ahead, and predictably, the judge found Rev. Jones in contempt for not following court rules. She also ordered the lawyer to write letters of "apology" to the two judges he had met with at the pretrial conference for *his* "rude and uncivil behavior."

As the commission pointed out, in a damning factoid, the judge had already disqualified herself from the case but had heard the contempt matter anyway, and never mentioned it in her order holding Rev. Jones in contempt.

Unsurprisingly the lawyer filed a complaint against the judge with the Maryland judicial discipline commission.

At the hearing before the commission the judge refused to admit she "yelled" at Rev. Jones, preferring to characterize it as "I raised my voice and got his attention." As to the question of whether she could think of any reason why the contempt hearing should have been passed to another judge, she responded, "I can't conceive of any, no."

Calling her foul language in court "unprofessional," the commission said the judge violated the state judicial code of conduct by presiding over the contempt hearing "after admitting that she was biased against Rev. Jones and was going to recuse herself from the case." The commission also found that Judge White had a "stellar" record on the bench, and the maximum sanction should be a public reprimand, which should "preclude" the judge from repeating her misconduct.

◊

Anecdotally, records showed that judges become the most belligerent in mistreating litigants when they appear pro se or *propria persona* (pro per), which both mean without an attorney representing them in court. In such cases judges speak directly to them rather than through their lawyers. And as the Arkansas Supreme Court stated in a 2022 case of disciplining a judge: "Thousands of average citizens appear in [court] each year, and for many it will be their only experience with a judge . . . Non-lawyer litigants are more vulnerable in the courtroom setting, and the disparity of power requires judges to treat [these] litigants with courtesy and patience . . ."

No case better illustrates being discourteous to a pro per litigant than an adoption handled in Washington State by Judge Edwin L. Poyfair of Clark County Superior Court in 2011. The case involved the voluntary adoption of a six-week-old girl by a married couple. The birth mother had agreed to the adoption and the child's father had not been involved in the case. Before the birth mother fully gave up her parental rights she learned that the man who was adopting her baby had "a history of sexual misconduct with young girls." At that point she mistakenly believed that she had already relinquished her parental rights. Still, she no longer wanted the married couple to take her child. To that end, at a hearing before Judge Poyfair scheduled to terminate the biological father's rights to the baby, the birth mother talked the baby's father into coming to court and asking that the child be placed with him. In court, neither the birth mother nor biological father had attorneys representing them.

The biological father was of Spanish heritage and spoke Spanish. The judge immediately asked the biological father whether he was in the United States legally, and when the man said, no, the judge responded: "Well then, maybe we should call Immigration before you leave and find out if they wish you detained." The judge then called in a law enforcement officer who told the judge he could detain the man for an immigration issue. During the hearing, the judge mentioned the immigration status several more times. He said that he was "going to note for the authorities that he [biological father] is illegal, and that if in fact he should not be here then he should be picked up and he should be sent back." Later in the hearing, Judge Poyfair "required" the man to give him his identification. Later he returned it and said, "I don't know where Immigration is right now, I know that they, up in King County [Seattle], they're having a field day picking people up. I don't know down here what they're doing." At that point, the birth mother asked that her child be placed with the biological father rather than being adopted. To this, the judge said: "Ma'am, this isn't Walmart . . . and he doesn't get to go to the shelf and pick a baby off, all right?" He added, "It's not taking back a pair of shoes." When the birth mother tried to explain that she no longer wanted her child adopted by the couple because she had learned the prospective father had a history of sexual misconduct with young girls, the judge cut her off. He threatened her with contempt of court, saying, "You're going to spend the weekend here if you open your mouth again before I tell you to open it."

The Washington State Commission on Judicial Conduct, in censuring the judge, found various problems in the way he handled the hearing, which was the first of two for which he was punished. The commission said even though the judge had the case file in front of him he made "no effort to check the status of the case," which would have shown that the birth mother had not yet given up rights to the child. This meant she had every right to back out of the adoption at that time.

The judge told the commission that the statements by the birth mother and biological father "were verbal" and that they presented nothing in writing. The commission reminded him that they didn't require anything in writing, under adoption law. Worse still, the judge "did not inquire as to the allegations concerning the prospective adopting father." The commission stated that the judge also told the birth mother and biological father that "the court could and would authorize adoption of the child against their wishes, which was entirely incorrect legally and contrary to their fundamental constitutional liberty rights to parent their natural child. Instead, he urged these unrepresented litigants to talk with the prospective adoptive parents' lawyer, stating it would be best to try to work something out, strongly hinting that the best resolution would be for them to agree to the adoption." At the conclusion of the first hearing, Judge Poyfair set a date for another hearing on the adoption, and allowed the prospective adoptive couple to take the baby home with them. They would have had custody of the child for ten months when the date for the second arrived. He told the birth mother and the child's natural father that they needed to file "answers" in order to stop the adoption, and failing to do so would result in his finalizing it.

The misconduct commission took issue with the judge not informing either of them that they could get court-appointed lawyers, although they were "plainly legally entitled to such representation."

Date for the second hearing came, and the biological father did not return to court. The birth mother told the judge that he had "scared him" and that he thought he was going to "get deported." The judge replied: "He ought to be." The commission said the biological father was in fact later deported but it didn't know whether the judge's "inappropriate inquiry" into his immigration status had any role in it. At the second hearing, even though the parents of the child had filed "declarations" which said they wanted the adoption halted, the judge said they were not in proper form and added, in granting a one week extension in the case, "If you fail to get your response within one week, then I'm going to finalize the adoption." The commission noted that "there is no prescribed form which must be used by a birth [mother] to indicate her revocation of consent prior to termination of rights."

In other words, the judge was legally all wet.

In a final shot, Judge Poyfair told the birth mother that he "would not grant custody of a child to an illegal."

That really riled up the commission. "[The judge] did not return the child to the mother, a legal parent, and not having done so, he once more left the child with the prospective adopting couple without any inquiry into potential danger to the baby." Because the birth mother had never given up rights to the child, the commission stated, she had the absolute right to revoke the adoption, and the judge never explained the fact to her. On the father's immigration status, the commission said it was immaterial to the adoption. After the second hearing, the birth mother and biological father both hired attorneys, and about a month later, another judge returned the child to them. Stated the commission in announcing punishment of Judge Poyfair: "While there is not evidence that [the judge] intentionally or flagrantly transgressed his oath of office, he failed to explain and protect the constitutional rights of the litigants in the voluntary adoption case during the hearings at issue." Its language toughened. "Judicial intemperance can give the impression that the judge's ruling is based on personal feelings, rather than on the law and facts of a case. It is bullying conduct, in that a litigant is not free to respond in kind because of the power imbalance. This is particularly troubling in a case where such a fundamental and heartfelt interest as child custody is at stake."

In his defense, Judge Poyfair "explained his conduct by observing that family court can be frustrating and emotional" and said "his conduct stems from his strong concern for the well-being of children." The commission noted that the judge "acknowledged that the acts occurred and that his conduct was inappropriate." The judicial commission said that other than a discipline case in 1995 the judge had a clean record, and had a good reputation on the court.

The judge had planned to retire, and did so before the commission issued its final report. It said he had been a Superior

Court judge for 20 years and "has received several complimentary responses" on his service. He was named Jurist of the Year in 2008 by the Family Law section of the Washington State Bar Association.

◊

While attorneys know that taking a case to a jury is always a gamble, judges have been disciplined and removed from the bench for actually gambling. In Pennsylvania a former justice was disciplined for owning a business where people gambled, and in Rhode Island, a judge was removed from office for spending his days gambling rather than judging.

In Luzerne County, Pennsylvania Robert S. Chesna was elected as Magisterial District justice in 1987 and administered court for the Township of Hanover and the Boroughs of Ashley, Sugar Notch and Warrior Run. The judge owned a gasoline station, which secretly, proved to be a well-oiled gambling joint. In January 1991 the state Attorney General's Office launched an investigation into alleged illegal gambling at the business in Hanover, and on visits to the station, agents saw "video gambling devices in a back room of Chesna's Service Station as well as two additional machines located in a service bay of the station." On another occasion an agent saw the judge "cleaning" one of the gambling machines.

On one visit during the investigation, an undercover agent was allowed into the back room through a door which had a "punch number" lock. The agent had gotten the combination from an informant. In the room the agent saw eight gambling machines, and played one for a time. On the next evening, the same agent entered the back room and put two "marked" twenty dollar bills into a machine, which he played for about a half hour. At that point, the agent went to a worker at the station and told him he had won 102 credits on the machine. The employee paid him $25.50 in winnings. Leaving the business, the agent got a warrant to search the gasoline station, and seized the gambling machines. Ten machines with a total of seven hundred dollars inside and various gambling records were taken.

A day after the search the judge met with officials of the state Attorney General's Office, and later with an agent. According to court records the judge admitted he built the back room three years before; he owned "eight of the ten machines seized; that revenue from the machines amounted to about $1,200 a week, which he used to "put his kids through college"; and that he emptied the machines of cash every other day.

A few months later the judge was charged with possession of unlawful gambling devices and conspiracy, and a year following the raid of his gasoline station, he was placed in an "accelerated rehabilitation program and placed on probation for about two years. In exchange, he agreed to resign his judgeship, which he did in 1992, perform 180 hours of community service and pay two hundred and fifty dollars in restitution.

What? He said he put his "kids through college" with money from illegal gambling and he paid two hundred and fifty dollars in restitution? The machines paid out over $62,000 a year. Hmm. Be that as it may, the state wasn't done with him. In 1994 the Pennsylvania Judicial Conduct Board filed a discipline case to stop the judge from ever serving on the bench again, which is what the state Supreme Court agreed to do a year later.

Sad thing about the case of the Rhode Island judge addicted to gambling is when on the bench he was a great jurist by all accounts. That's the word from colleagues and co-workers when the Rhode Island Commission on Judicial Tenue and Discipline investigated Associate Judge John F. Lallo of the Administrative Adjudication Court in 2000. Seems the judge, who'd been on the bench for two decades, disappeared from the courthouse when he finished his cases and court duties, sometimes as early as 8:30 in the morning. On sixty-six "occasions" (days) over a four-year span you'd find him "gaming" at Indian tribe-owned Foxwoods Resort Casino in Ledyard, Connecticut, which was a one-hour drive fifty miles down Interstate 95 from the court's main offices in Providence.

Even not wearing a robe it wasn't news to any judge that there weren't many places to hide in a public casino during normal working hours.

"[He] always completed his caseload and often sat for other judges when they were on vacation or were otherwise unavailable," the commission stated about the quality of his work. "When his calendar was completed, however, whether in the morning or afternoon, [the judge] departed, apparently for the day," said the commission, adding, "the quality of [his] work was never questioned in any complaints filed with the commission in his twenty years of service as an associate judge."

Somewhere along the line the judge not only became "addicted" to gambling, he told the commission, he also had money problems because of a real estate venture going sour. He filed for bankruptcy and stupidly made false statements in the bankruptcy filings, for which, he was later charged and pleaded guilty. In late 2000 he was sentenced to two years of probation, which included that he not gamble or enter a casino.

After he was charged in the bankruptcy case but before his sentencing, the state's judicial discipline commission informed him that they were investigating him for violating judicial ethics, an investigation the judge readily cooperated in. In a settlement of the case, the commission recommended that the state Supreme Court remove the judge from office, which had already happened because he retired in 1998, and that he repay the state his salary for the days he gambled instead of worked. The amount was set at twenty-eight thousand dollars, which is about four hundred and twenty-five dollars a day.

The judge later appealed the commission's order that he repay his salary, arguing that the commission lacked the authority to levy punitive fines, such as in a criminal case. It was both an interesting and clever legal issue for appeal. The Rhode Island Supreme Court disagreed, upholding the commission's authority, and stating the money was "reimbursement to the taxpayers of the State of Rhode Island, who were deprived of his services while he regularly shirked his responsibilities and headed to Foxwoods during the work day. Accordingly, we conclude that the monetary sanction is civil and restitutionary in nature and is not punitive." The case was a precedent, giving the state judicial discipline commission more teeth.

◇

It was Oklahoma in 1999. But it could well have been a scene from Franz Kafka's novel, *The Trial*, written in 1914 about a man who is arrested and prosecuted for an unknown crime. Picture it, and put yourself in this sadistic judge's courtroom.

A man was arrested on a first-time rap of possession with intent to sell marijuana. He pleaded guilty in what amounted to a "blind" plea agreement which didn't list a specific sentence, apparently leaving it to discretion of a judge at a later date. As a result, the man was sent to an anti-drug program handled by the Seminole County, Oklahoma Drug Court. Seven months later the man was snatched from the drug program and hauled into the courtroom of Seminole County District Judge Jerry L. Colclazier. He sentenced the man to life in prison.

Allow repeating: life in prison for first-time pot.

Fairly Kafkaesque. I'm surprised the man didn't leave a stain on the courtroom carpet.

Here is the back story, and why, along with other complaints against him, Judge Colclazier was removed from office in 2002 by the state's Court on the Judiciary, as recommended by the Oklahoma Council on Judicial Complaints.

Apparently the judge listened to discussions the pot defendant had with drug counselors in the Drug Court program, and didn't like what he had heard. According to documents in the appeal of the man's life sentence, the judge heard the man "confess" to a "rape and murder," and also was told about a lie detector test the man had taken "which indicated" he "committed" the crimes.

That was enough evidence for the judge, and why he hauled the man into his courtroom, without notice, and sentenced him to life. The appeals court ruled that the harsh sentence was the result of the judge's "misplaced idea that sentencing is to be used to incapacitate offenders."

The appeals court also said the plea deal was faulty because it failed to spell out sentence if the man didn't finish the Drug Court program. In weighing the proper sentence, Judge Colclazier considered "mitigating and aggravating" facts, which is a standard way that courts determine what are called indeterminate sentences.

In court and on his own initiative, the judge offered the man's confessions to rape and murder as factors in aggravation. A prosecutor who seemed to know more on the topic than the judge warned him about using these "unsworn" statements in the case. The prosecutor stated that "there's not any proof of that; that he committed any murder . . . I would suggest and urge the court not to consider that in any way, shape or form."

The sadistic judge disregarded the prosecutor's legal wisdom.

Stated the appeals court in overturning the man's sentence and sending it back to be heard by any Seminole County other than Judge Colclazier: "Statements made by a Drug Court participant to supervising staff shall not be admissible in the criminal case pending against the participant."

The appellate court also didn't like the Kafkaesque way the man was yanked from the anti-drug program, saying he was "denied fundamental due process in the manner he was arrested, held without bail, not given any notice of what he was charged with, and never taken before a magistrate."

Because the judge was removed from office for "oppression in office," he argued in his defense that the phrase wasn't defined in the state constitution, which the Court on the Judiciary agreed with. The judge "contends that oppression in office sufficient to justify removal requires proof of illegality, bad faith or improper motive and that there was no such proof" in his case. And lawyerly, he argued if "oppression in office does not require such proof, then the constitutional provision permitting removal for oppression in office is void for vagueness." In rejecting the argument, the appeals court said the phrase has been defined by other states, and in *Black's Law Dictionary*, and boiled it down to a simple rationale: "A judge is guilty of oppression in office . . . when that judge intentionally commits acts which he or she knows, or should know, are obviously and seriously wrong and amount to an excessive use of judicial authority." Harkening back to the prosecutor's warning about using the rape and murder stuff in sentencing, it was a loud and clear message.

While the nine members of the Court of the Judiciary agreed that the judge had committed "oppression in office," which is basically acting beyond his authority, the court drastically split on removing him from office and barring him from ever running for judge again in Oklahoma. That vote was 5 to 4, with the minority seeking a lesser sanction than removal. He had been a judge for seven years, and was the district's chief judge until 2001. Booted from the bench in his mid-40s, the judge who had earned a law degree from Oklahoma City University, was still young enough to continue to practice law. Among his scholarly publications, which now seem strangely ironic, was 1999's, "Oklahoma Sentencing Laws," and 2001's, "Nuts and Bolts of Oklahoma Drug Courts."

◊

Judicial discipline agencies also consider cases of misconduct by attorneys who fill in for judges when judges take vacations or are otherwise unavailable. Attorney Nino F. Falcone served as a part-time judge in the Township of North Bergen in New Jersey, and had been a lawyer since 1984. He ran afoul of nor only the civil judge's misconduct committee but the cops in the summer of 2019.

According to records, a married woman who worked for a doctor friend of attorney Falcone came to the lawyer's office to talk about legal matters. The woman had been represented in "personal matters" by Mr. Falcone in the past. After they spoke, the woman got ready to leave and, according to records of the misconduct committee, Mr. Falcone "pulled" the woman "into him and began rubbing her back." When the woman tried to "push" him away, the attorney "held her arm, squeezed her breast and told her to 'let me touch you, let me play with you.'" Then, the records state, that he "grabbed her wrist" but let it go. He then allegedly "took out his wallet, and offered [her] 'birthday money.'"

The woman left his office and reported the incident to her husband and to police. Detectives had the woman telephone Mr. Falcone on a phone at the police station and recorded the conversation, in which, according to the records, the lawyer "admitted" that "he touched her inappropriately and apologized."

The attorney was then charged with low-level criminal sexual conduct, and later, entered a two-month "pretrial intervention program" which he completed and the sex charge was dismissed.

Along with it in July 2022, the state judicial discipline board censured the attorney and barred him from further service as a temporary judge in New Jersey.

◊

Of course judges pack.

When it comes to sheriffs and police chiefs approving concealed weapons permits it's nearly a slam duck that any judge who wants one gets one. And, why not? They try and sentence hardened, career criminals all the time, like members of the notorious and extremely violent MS-13 gang members who threaten revenge. California judges are even taught "gang calls" which are sounds street gang members shout when they see someone that want to kill. When a judge hears such sounds on the street he's taught to take cover immediately. I once counted seven armed cops inside a courtroom and four outside during a trial of two street gangsters who had boasted their "homies" would bust them out. So, of course, judges pack guns.

In modern courts, however, judges don't bring their pistols into the courtroom like Delaware Night Court Magistrate John O'Bier did in Sussex County in 2002. Worse than wearing his holstered weapon in the courtroom, he allegedly pulled it out and scared the crap out of two female court clerks, sometime after midnight.

In testimony before the Court on the Judiciary, which investigates misconduct by judges in Delaware, one of the clerks stated that she was leaving work when the "normally pleasant, friendly and easy-going judge" and another clerk had arrived for the graveyard shift, midnight to eight in the morning at the court in Georgetown, Delaware in January 2002.

It was a cold 35 degrees outside and the three of them talked in a warm courthouse office. It was 12:15 in the morning and one of the clerks was standing near a door and the other clerk was seated at a desk. The clerks said later that the judge seemed "tense" and "on edge" and mentioned a news story he had read about the father of a boy being beaten to death at a sporting event and "was talking non-stop and in an agitated matter." He also said he was suffering pain from a chronic back problem. "Suddenly," the clerk said, the judge "drew his weapon, pointed it a couple of feet to her left" and she "yelped." He "immediately returned the gun to its holster" but the woman said it scared her. In fact, even though she was supposed to leave the courthouse because her shift had ended at midnight, she was so frightened that she was "afraid to leave [the other clerk] alone with Judge O'Bier." She finally went outside and got into her cold car and thought about calling the other clerk, who was working the graveyard shift in the judge's courtroom, to make sure she was all right. She also considered calling the cops, but didn't.

Judge O'Bier's testimony about the gun incident was substantially different. He said he was "neither excited nor angry when he drew his weapon in the presence" of the clerks, saying, according to records, he "slowly and calmly removed his gun from his holster with one hand and displayed it in the palm of his other hand, possibly in response to" a "question about gun safety" from one of the clerks. He said it wasn't his intension to scare them, although, in hindsight, he "recognized" that he had made a "mistake in judgment when he removed his weapon."

In its investigation of the incident the state discipline court found that the judge hadn't slept much in the days before the incident because he suffered from a nervous system disorder – restless legs syndrome – which causes legs to feel like they are being poked with "pins and needles." This causes an urge to move the legs and disrupts sleep. Judge O'Bier testified that he was "extremely tired and exhausted" in the four days leading up to the gun incident and had probably only gotten five hours of sleep in four days before reporting for work.

There was also evidence that he had taken prescription painkillers for "moderate" to "severe" back pain after two back surgeries in 2000, which could have contributed to his poor judgment. In fact, medical records admitted into evidence suggested the judge reported to a physician that "he was taking OxyContin" on the day before the incident. The painkiller is an opioid drug, and the judicial court stated there was no evidence suggesting that he was addicted to drugs. The judge said he never took all of the pills he had been prescribed for pain.

The judicial discipline board found that the "evidence presented did not reveal that Judge O'Bier suffered from a drug addiction or that his competency was affected due to the use of medication. Rather, [it] found that [his] behavior resulted from a severe lack of sleep resulting from his diagnosed restless leg syndrome combined with the change in his work hours." The court ruled that it was "willful misconduct" for the judge to display "a weapon in a fashion that the two court clerks in his presence felt that their personal safety was threatened." He also committed misconduct by "Judge O'Bier's persistence in carrying his weapon on his person while at work in such a way that the weapon was clearly visible to the public and employees." Thereby the court suspended the judge for three months and ordered details of the case made public. It also ordered a "permanent ban on Judge O'Bier from carrying or displaying a weapon at work."

In a footnote the court pleaded for more money for security in the state's justice courts. "While we recognize that budgetary restraints have challenged court security in the Justice of the Peace Courts, we urge the [Delaware] General Assembly to provide adequate appropriations so that court security can be made available in the Justice of the Peace Courts during all hours of operation, thus obviating the perceived need of some magistrates to have firearms available." It also said the court system required "specific guidelines defining when, where and under what circumstances magistrates are authorized to carry weapons."

Today, it is wholly unnecessary for a judge to holster a gun under his robe while working. Court security at nearly every courthouse in America is tight, and courtrooms have adequate armed security provided by law enforcement. Even the U.S. Supreme Court, which arrived late to tight security, decided in 2010 to shut its six-ton bronze front doors to visitors and instead funnel them for weapons screening through side doors of the marbled columned building in Washington, D.C.

◊

Rudolph L. Mazzei, judge of Suffolk County, N.Y. Court said he was having trouble in his marriage over money and that's why he signed his mother's name to a credit card application. Oh, and there was a little factoid he neglected to share with the bank.

His mother was dead.

New York's judicial conduct commission opened its investigation in 1991 and after hearing the judge's side of the story voted to remove him from office, albeit with one member voting for a lesser punishment.

Judge Mazzei explained that his wife never opened mail addressed to his mother who had lived with them, and this is why he used her name on the card. He testified that "his purpose in signing his mother's name was to obtain a line of credit available to him that would not be known to his wife." And, well . . . Only days after receiving the card with a $5,000 credit line the judge used it at a casino in Atlantic City to obtain a cash advance of $2,000. A few hours later he sought another $2,000 cash advance – fourteen times, and it was rejected. He also tried getting half that amount and the bank refused. A bank employee then put a hold on the card so it could not be used. Over the next few days the judge spoke to bank employees, telling them he wanted the "matter cleared up so that his mother could use her card." But when he talked to an especially sharp employee who said he had noticed that his mother's Social Security number had been used to "file a death claim in April 1989," the judge had to think quickly. He "replied that his mother must have mistakenly used the Social Security number of his father on her credit card application."

The jig was up.

"Deception is antithetical to the role of a judge who is sworn to uphold the law and seek the truth, and cannot be condoned," the New York commission stated. "Over a period of several months, [the judge] engaged in a pattern of deceptive behavior which violated his ethical obligations as a lawyer and a judge."

The commission member who disagreed with firing the judge stated he repaid the $2,000 cash advance. The fact that he had other cards with higher borrowing limits tended to prove his story that he wanted to hide the card from his wife. "Though [his] conduct constituted, as the majority correctly states, deception, the deception was designed to receive a credit card without the knowledge of his wife and not to defraud the bank of money. While such behavior shows extremely poor judgment . . . it should not be considered as serious as an effort to deprive the bank of funds."

Is the member suggesting that it was all right to deceive his wife but not the bank?

◊

From a commonsense point of view it is difficult to see why the 28 members of the Ohio Board of Professional Conduct locked horns with Municipal Court Judge Edward Joseph Elum of Massillon, Ohio in the first place. In 2009, all he did was try to ensure police didn't whitewash an investigation of a cop who allegedly sent nudies to a woman suspect. Then, a few months later in open court, Judge Elum dressed down a young thug who needed it, using any angry father's salty language.

Sounds almost noble on both counts. But, the Ohio board looked askance at commonsense. It focused instead on law and nothing but the law. So, in 2012 Judge Elum, who had been on the job for 16 years was suspended for six months by the Ohio Supreme Court for breaches of judicial ethics. To its credit, the court set aside the penalty as long as he didn't screw up again. (Was the suspension "stayed" because the justices in their hearts sympathized with his actions, all be they unethical?)

Here's the background.

The first case involved a woman who was charged with driving while impaired, a couple of drug-related counts and failure to control her vehicle. The cop must have liked what he saw when he arrested her because he allegedly sent her 88 text messages, 15 nude and sexually explicit photos and a sex video afterwards. The woman reported him to the city prosecutor, and at a hearing in the case in Judge Elum's courtroom, the woman's attorney told the judge of the cop's conduct.

Hearing it must have riled Judge Elum, who, according to court records, had a "history of conflicts" and "disagreements" with the Massillon Police Department, and specifically, with its chief of police. In fact, in an interview with the local newspaper the judge was quoted as saying: "The chief doesn't like me and I understand that, okay? That's his prerogative. My position as a citizen-taxpayer and as a judge, I've watched that department go downhill since he's been chief. He is ineffective. Period. That's it." He also complained he was a target of police. "They are out to get me, but that's fine. That goes along with the territory here."

When Judge Elum was told about the nude pictures allegedly sent by the arresting officer it "alarmed" him, and according to Ohio board records, for "religious and moral reasons [he] did not want his name associated with the case." Meanwhile, the case against the woman lagged because her blood contained no alcohol when arrested, and the prosecutor asked for more time to do tests. At a hearing in the woman's case, the prosecutor again asked that the prosecution be delayed, and the judge was "afraid that the public might perceive further delay as the court's being unconcerned about the arresting officer's conduct." The judge was aware that the cops had started an internal affairs investigation into the cop's alleged misconduct. Records stated that the judge feared that the "police department's internal response might be to sweep the allegations against the arresting officer under the rug and nothing would be done." At the hearing in the woman's case, the judge took an unusual legal step. He said the police department was "delaying the prosecution of this matter," and ordered the cops, the prosecutor and the woman's attorney to "provide the court in a sealed envelope all transcripts and copies of the arresting officer's text and picture messages so" he, Judge Elum, could "review whether the prosecution has been compromised and [has] wasted the court's time." He ordered the goods submitted to him in five days. Later he explained he sought copies for the court so that they would be available to the woman in the event that the police department's internal investigation was "not resolved to [her] satisfaction." In other words, in case of a cop cover up. Five days later rather than turn anything over to the judge, the prosecutor asked him to reconsider his order for the materials, explaining that the woman's case had not been "compromised" by any misconduct by the officer, and that the nude pictures and texts did not tend to show the woman's innocence of the charges. Essentially he was arguing that the stuff was irrelevant in the case at hand. The prosecutor said the drug charges were being dismissed for lack of evidence, and the woman's attorney's had "no objection to these charges being dismissed without the sealed envelope being submitted for inspection."

  The judge said he was taking a break so the sealed envelope could be submitted to the court and announced that he was holding a hearing later in the day on whether to find anybody in contempt of court for not producing the materials as ordered. When court reconvened, the prosecutor told the judge she was unable to obtain all the texts and pictures. At that point, Judge Elum pointed out the "total neglect and disregard" of the police department and saved his harshest words for the chief of police who was in the courtroom: "I just want to make sure that everybody understands that the administrative justice at this point was jeopardized. I want the defendant to know and her family to know that the court was not a party of, nor did not participate in any cover up." He apologized to the woman on "behalf of the court" and let her know "that officer does not work for the Massillon Municipal Court. He is under direct control and supervision of [the] chief [of police]." The woman then pleaded "no contest" to the charge of failure to control her vehicle and the judge dismissed the more serious drug counts. The case being resolved, the prosecutor asked the judge to cancel his order for the sealed envelope of obscene materials, and he agreed.

In the discipline case against him, Judge Elum acknowledged there was no cover-up by the Massillon Police Department of the arresting officer's conduct, and that he used a "bad term" to describe the situation. He also admitted that his order seeking the obscene materials essentially "placed himself in the middle of an administrative investigation into the arresting officer's conduct and stepped outside his role as a judge."

The second case of judicial misconduct involved a teenager who was already on probation when Judge Elum found him guilty of underage drinking of alcohol, and another minor offense. The judge suspended his 180-day jail sentence and placed him on probation. True to form, the teen violated his probation two months later.

On a day when the teen was to appear at the courthouse to meet with his probation officer to find out whether he'd be sent to jail for failure to pay fines and court costs in his case, Judge Elum told the probation officer to bring him to his courtroom instead. In court, without either a prosecutor or an attorney for the teen present, although the courtroom had a host of people in the spectator's gallery, the judge conducted what he called a "probation review" and took it upon himself to lecture the lad about wrongdoing.

"Cody, quit screwing up," Judge Elum told the teen. ". . . Quit fucking up . . . You have a bad case of D.H. – Dickheaditis . . . You're screwing off. You can't keep continuing to screw off or you'll be like the rest of the dickheads at the Stark County Jail." The judge then issued an order allowing the teen more time to pay outstanding fines and court costs, which meant his probation would continue without jail.

The Ohio Supreme Court ruled that the judge's words and conduct were unethical. In the sealed envelope case, it stated, that he failed to "uphold and apply the law and perform all duties of the judicial office fairly and impartially." In the case of teenager he had failed to be "patient, dignified and courteous to litigants."

It failed to mention "Dickheaditis" isn't found in Black's dictionary of legal terms.

Chapter Seven

The story of Tulare County, California Superior Court Judge Valeriano "Val" Saucedo reads like a tawdry novel, showing sadly just how outrageously far an obsessive, aging judge will go to cozy up to his young, pretty and married courtroom clerk.

It all started with a mysterious letter, the soon-to-be infamous "anonymous" letter.

On September 17th, 2013 Judge Saucedo's wife found an envelope delivered to their home by the mailman. It was addressed to her husband. Marked "confidential," she didn't read it, and gave the letter to her husband when he came home. He opened it, read the letter, and handed it to her to read. Its grossly obscene contents shocked her. Ostensibly written to the husband of the judge's courtroom clerk, the letter stated: "You probably already know and approve. Your wife [the clerk] has been having an affair with [the bailiff] . . . She fucks him after work. He brags that she is a good fuck and you get sloppy seconds. He brags about her tattoos, and big boobs and tight ass. The only thing he complains about is her c-scar." The letter was anonymous, but carried a ring of truth because years ago the clerk had been separated from her husband and had had a romantic relationship with a courtroom bailiff, a topic of gossip at the courthouse. Adding credibility was the fact that the letter mentioned the woman's "c-scar," short for caesarian section, showing the writer had apparent familiarity with the clerk's naked body.

Someone must be "really angry at this woman," the judge's wife said after reading the four-letter-laced letter. Judge Saucedo told his wife he would take the letter to work and discuss it with his clerk, and added, with concern: "What if her husband gets this and beats her up?"

The next morning the judge called his clerk into his office and closed the door. He handed her a cover letter that said the anonymous letter he was about to show her "would be upsetting" and he said he would help her if she wanted him to do so. He also said the anonymous letter had been sent to her husband's work, a hospital. The clerk read the obscene letter, and shocked by its vile contents, broke into tears. She said she should "report the letter to

[the] court administration or law enforcement." She said she had no idea who would write such a gross thing.

The judge, however, balked at turning in the missive. He responded that she could not "tell anybody" about the letter, including her good friend, the courtroom's stenographer. Judge Saucedo told his clerk she could be fired if she reported the letter, according to documents in the case, and said that the "letter had to be from somebody in law enforcement because law enforcement would be the only possible source for his home address." In California, home addresses of judges are kept private. When his clerk "insisted" she report the letter to authorities, the judge said he would fix things by calling her husband's employer and intercepting the letter "if she trusted him completely," records show.

At some point around this time the judge had purchased a red Mercedes convertible. At the courthouse he asked his clerk and court stenographer to come outside and see it. Later he gave his clerk a short ride in the car and said, "Who knows, maybe one day you can own a car like this." In the days that followed Judge Saucedo gave his clerk money to buy a new cell phone because hers was broken. She said she did not need a new phone but he insisted. Later, when he learned she had not bought the new phone, he gave her more money for one. Relenting, the clerk bought a new phone and later she and judge exchanged text messages about it.

One day in court the judge handed his clerk a note that said he had called her husband's hospital employer and as far as the letter was concerned "everything was going to be okay," according to records. Later on the same day the judge met privately with his clerk in a room at the county law library and said the anonymous letter had been "shredded" at the hospital. In other words, the judge had fixed things, and her husband would never get the letter about her affair. At this private meeting Judge Saucedo again showed his clerk his copy of the anonymous letter, and suggested that the bailiff she had had the romantic relationship with wrote it. The clerk responded that the bailiff would not have written such a letter. She said they were now "just friends and were no longer romantically involved." When she told the judge she had visited the bailiff for "40 minutes" at his home recently, Judge Saucedo asked: "Are you sure you weren't intimate with him . . . at that time?" The clerk said she wasn't and told the judge that the bailiff was helping her pay for her sister's Jeep by giving her $200 a month. The judge then told her to stop accepting money from him, and that he would give her $200 a month, instead, to pay for the automobile. During this conversation she and judge cried, and when the clerk said she didn't want his financial help, the judge said she needed to take the money if she wanted his help. The following day he left $200 in an envelope on her desk, and she took it.

In the days that followed the judge continued to tell the clerk that the bailiff had written the letter and that he, Judge Saucedo, was "a very powerful man" who could get the man fired. Also the judge said he didn't have anybody to talk to, and began to cry. The clerk said she "wished" she could tell the court administration about the letter. The judge told her not to, and then, the judge "hugged" her and it made her "feel uncomfortable," according to records.

It was shortly after this that the judge's financial spigot really opened for her. In late September when the clerk arrived at work she found a bouquet of flowers on her desk, with an unsigned card that read: "New Day, New Week, New Beginning." The judge told her he had sent them to her so she could tell people at the courthouse that "they were from her husband" and that problems between herself and her husband were over. He told her that the bailiff would soon get the message to back off. His clerk said she did not "feel comfortable" with his sending her flowers and with his financial help; "and that although she appreciated it, she did not need help." To this, she would say later, Judge Saucedo responded that they did not have anyone else to talk to about the letter. If he told his wife she would ask why he did not report it to court administration, and that he thought of [his clerk] as a daughter so she should trust him."

Days later the judge left an envelope with $500 in it on his clerk's desk. She said he told her to "go shopping and she needed to change the way she dressed." She said later that he asked her to send him a photo of her shopping. Afterwards, the judge sent his clerk texts asking whether she was still visiting the bailiff.

It was the following Monday when Judge Saucedo handed his clerk a one-page typewritten note while she sat at her desk in the courtroom. The note stated: "I support you completely and unequivocally in all of your endeavors. Reflecting back on this last week, I am concerned that I have not yet fully earned your complete trust and confidence. Two examples come to mind. Last week, until I probed, you did not voluntarily tell me that you only had $10 in your checking account. Clearly, this was not enough money to make it through the rest of the week and weekend until Tuesday of this week, your payday. You should have voluntarily told me. Once I learned of your financial pressure, I initially gifted you $200 and then $500. I was happy to do so but what concerned me is that you did not voluntarily tell me. The second example is Saturday when I asked you about [the bailiff]. I again felt like I probed when we had agreed that you would voluntarily let me know if he contacted you . . . I truly want to earn your trust and feel badly that I have not yet done so. What else do I need to do? I voluntarily took a risk to protect you because you have earned my trust and respect. I have no regrets that I took the risk. It was absolutely the right thing to do. You have my utmost respect and trust and always will. I was upset with myself this weekend, notwithstanding your forgiveness, because sometimes I still feel that I am hurting and not helping you enough. This month and every month I will gift you $200 . . . However, I am happy to meet your other financial needs. As I've told you, from here on out, you will no longer have any financial worries. However, you must trust me unconditionally and voluntarily tell me everything. Don't be like my former clients. They didn't lie to me. Sometimes they forgot to tell me important things. Don't feel embarrassed or like a burden. I can handle anything. Looking at the future, I want to earn your complete trust and have you voluntarily tell me what is going on in your life. I am willing to do anything to earn your trust and confidence. I want to support your every endeavor but I cannot know your endeavors unless you tell me. In this connection, I find texting is fine but I find these notes and form of communication unsatisfying and incomplete. They do not fully inform me on what is going on. I prefer to talk to you and would like to know whether you wish to talk and when. Sometimes I feel like you would prefer to avoid me altogether and not talk to me. Perhaps, you don't even like me, want to talk to me or have me involved. I hope not. Let's work on these issues together, planning for your financial future (including a two seater [car] – although you seem skeptical about this promise). As you know, I do not make promises I cannot keep. Frankly, my biggest concern is how you would explain a two seater gift to [your husband]. (By the way, what did you say and what did he say about the flowers? Just curious.) Finally, I, too, am human and have an ego. Feel free, if you wish, to compliment me if you like things I do or wear, or, if you wish, you may treat me like the Maytag repair man. Please respond. Always your genuine friend and supporter."

This note made his courtroom clerk not only "uncomfortable" but "disgusted," especially where he told her to "compliment him on things he does or wears," she said later. When the judge asked her to return the note to him, she made a photocopy and returned only the original to him. Obviously at this point, she was in evidence-gathering mode.

In returning the original note, she again told the judge she didn't want more of his money, comments that apparently pissed off her boss. "What, do you mean you don't want my help anymore?" he said in an angry manner, according to the official record of the case. "So you mean the [anonymous] letter is true? So is it true about you and [the bailiff]? Maybe your husband does need to know about the [anonymous] letter." At that point, the clerk said, the judge left the court and she heard the door of a stairwell slam.

About this time the clerk felt "scared" by the judge's action and talked to her friend, the courtroom stenographer about both the anonymous letter and about the judge's one-page note to her. "This . . . is wrong," the stenographer reportedly told her. "This is not right. Something is going on with him." The friend reportedly told the clerk she needed to get a copy of the "anonymous letter."

That's when a daring black op was hatched. The clerk believed the letter was in the judge's desk. She said that after he left for the day, she would sneak into his chambers and look for the letter and make a photocopy. For her part in the op, the stenographer promised to "text" the clerk and tip her off when the judge left for the day. A 6:30 p.m., the clerk texted the stenographer to let her know she was then "snooping" in Judge Saucedo's office, saying she worried she was "going to be in big trouble." However, with the skill of a Navy Seals operation, the stealthy clerk found the anonymous letter, made a copy and carefully slipped it back into the judge's desk. Later that night, unaware the clerk had searched his office, Judge Saucedo texted her and said he was sorry for his behavior earlier in the day, when he reacted in anger.

The next morning, the clerk showed the stenographer the "anonymous" letter, and the court reporter who had worked with the judge for 15 years, immediately identified its author. "Judge Saucedo wrote the letter," the stenographer opined, based on "all these years [of] reading his pleadings and his rulings." When the clerk doubted it, the stenographer insisted, saying she was "positive; I know him too well." In fairness, when the stenographer was later asked about telling the clerk that the judge had written the letter, she gave conflicting statements. She denied to an official commission that she had said the judge wrote it, while telling an investigator for the same commission that she thought he had written it.

In the days that followed the judge learned that his clerk was having car trouble and offered to take her car to his auto mechanic, an invitation she accepted, even after her friend, the stenographer, advised against it, telling her in a text: "You really think it's a good idea to drop your car off tomorrow and be further into debt with him?" The clerk texted her friend and said: "I didn't ask for help, again he would not take no. I'm going to pay for it. Not going to say anything out loud any more. I'm seriously thinking of [asking] to be moved [out of the judge's courtroom]." Sometime in the night, the clerk had a change of heart. The next morning she met the judge at his mechanic's shop, her car was repaired, and Judge Saucedo paid the bill of $533.

The following month, October, the judge gave the clerk a note that stated: "Don't share with anyone any information. I assume you have not told anyone about [the bailiff] and the letter. Correct?" Still collecting items of evidence, the clerk copied this note and then told the judge of her silence on the letter. Later she said the judge told her he wanted her to return the original of every note he sent to her. He was unaware she was secretly making duplicates.

During this time in evenings, the judge and his clerk shared text messages. After he asked her if she had been shopping, she informed she no money for it. He asked for her bank account number so he could deposit money in her savings account. At first she resisted, saying she did not need his money. After he told her she "needed to trust" him, she gave him the account information.

It was about this time that big money gifts came her way. For example, the judge had overheard his clerk say she had always wanted to spend Christmas at Disneyland. The judge soon called her into his office and asked her why she doesn't go to Disneyland, according to records. She said she neither had the time or the money. "Judge Saucedo responded that she was going and it would be his gift to her," according to records. She told him she didn't want it but the judge insisted, and said, "Do you want your husband to find out about the [anonymous] letter?" In days ahead the judge spent $1,862 for a Disneyland trip for his clerk and her family and another $1,340 so her sister's family could come along. He said he'd even pay for meals and souvenirs. He allegedly provided her with a cover story, and reportedly told her to tell her family she was paying for the trips out of her "overtime" wages. The judge then deposited $500 in her bank account.

Once this trip was set, the judge asked his clerk to "reinstate" his "texting privileges." Apparently she had told him to stop texting her so much, in that he had sent her 445 texts over a two-month period. She said later that she had requested several times for him to stop texting her, and that he would "get upset if [she] wouldn't text him back right away or text him back at all."

In late October the judge talked about buying the clerk a new car, and they talked about a used BMW. While his clerk said she didn't need a new car she seemed hooked on the idea of getting a BMW. In a text message she told him she "looked" at "the car" on the Internet, adding it was "nice" but if "it doesn't work out, that's OK."

After the judge texted her and said she looked down, and then asked how she was feeling, the clerk wrote back: "Not to be picky but on the car issue I wouldn't mind a four seater sports car. . . . I don't mind a two door convertible . . . Hope that's not rude."

Yes, she was hooked all right.

To which Judge Saucedo responded: "Not rude at all. BMW makes a beautiful four seater convertible. I found one in L.A. . . . Did you have a particular model in mind?" He followed this up with: "I want you to be happy and I don't want to get a car that won't work for you. I am talking to three dealers. Hope to make this happen soon. As you know, I am serious about everything I do."

The next afternoon and evening there was a flurry of texts between them.

Judge: "It's silly but still feeling under appreciated. It's silly because you don't owe me anything. I am doing this for my own soul because it makes me happy."

Clerk: "I'm not doing anything different and I'm not sure why you are feeling that way. . . I truly do appreciate everything."

Judge: "I am feeling out of balance. I appreciate you are not doing anything different. Feeling today like a one sided friendship. My feelings are momentary and episodic. I'll be fine. Everything is on line and on course. No change. Just expressing my feelings. Said I am always honest in my feelings and dealings with everyone."

Later, after calling himself "just a silly man," in a text, Judge Saucedo said the car he had in mind for her was a four-door silver BMW sedan with "sun roof, blue tooth, black interior. Some wear and tear but not bad. 80,000 miles...." He added that the salesman said he could have it for $15,000.

Clerk: "When can I see the car?"

Judge: "When would you like to see it?"

Clerk: "Maybe tomorrow at lunch..." Then she asked if she would have payments to make on the BMW.

Judge: "I would make all of the payments. You would be responsible for an increase, if any, for insurance but I would certainly help. Remember this would be my gift to you. We would work out other reasonable accommodations. For example, if you decided you no longer wanted the car or wished to sell it we would decide what to do with the proceeds. It would be yours as long as you and only you owned it." Then he texted, "Have I not taken care of you without asking anything in return? Things would not change. You would just have to put up with my silliness like today." He then said, "You could have a new car within days."

When the clerk finally texted him back she said she was still worried about having car payments. The judge wrote back, saying, "I hope you trust me and that I have done enough to earn your trust... I would never hurt you financially or otherwise. I would never exploit you." Then he said, "I would also not want you to be nice simply because of our financial arrangement. That's why I sometimes ask whether you like me and respect me. It is important to have a friendship that extends beyond a financial connection."

The next morning the judge complained that his clerk had not responded to his last three texts. "True friends forgive each other for their mistakes and failures," he wrote. "I sincerely apologize for everything I said or did yesterday that was offensive or hurtful. I should not have communicated while off balance. Those are my worst moments. I wish to continue our friendship. I hope you will continue on this journey. In good faith, check your savings balance later today. Let me know if our friendship continues." He went on to explain that over the next year he planned to provide her with $26,400 in financial support. He said the car would be paid off in one year. "In sum, I am committed to helping you financially if you wish. I will make mistakes and so will you, including both of us being moody at times. But the test of friendship is overcoming these minor differences and reaching a better understanding. We cannot walk away over a simple misunderstanding. My goal is to help you succeed in your marriage and personal and professional life."

The judge and clerk then went to the BMW dealership for a test drive, and it was sometime later that the judge, according to the clerk, raised the issue of their having a "romantic relationship." (Now if this were a genuine story of red hot lovemaking in a dirty book, readers would have expected the scene where the man and woman characters talk about a possible "romantic relationship" in chapters well before this. But, after all, this is a 61-year-old judge in this real-life story.)

The clerk explained his unusual way of broaching the subject of a romantic relationship: "[Judge Saucedo] said that he had a conversation with his accountant . . . about having to cash stocks in to get the car or something like that, and his accountant asked him . . . who was I? Who buys a car for a person? Who gives them a Disneyland trip? And was he sure I wasn't more than just a special friend; was I his mistress? . . . And then [the judge] said that . . . if my husband didn't find out and his wife didn't find out, if he would consider having a romantic relationship with me.

"And I looked at him, and I said, 'What?'

"And he says 'If they wouldn't know about it, would you have a romantic relationship with me?'

"And I said, 'Is that what this is all about?' I said, 'No I wouldn't.'

"And he says, 'Why? Because of my age?'

"I said: 'I've never looked at you like that . . . I'm married, and you're my judge. I work for you. I would never look at you this way. And if this is what this is all about, then I don't want the car; just forget it.'"

She said the judge responded by hugging her and saying, "No. Okay. I'm sorry. I'm sorry. The car is yours."

Later before a commission looking into this case, Judge Saucedo denied this conversation ever happened. The commission said it believed the clerk's version, however.

In the days that followed the judge and clerk texted each other a lot, and the judge raised the issue of his relationship with her again. Judge Saucedo: "After reflection, I understand it. You think of me as an ordinary friend . . . Indeed, you have said in the past you want to go back the way it was. But I am not an ordinary friend. As you said 'a car and a trip who gets that'. No other ordinary friend has in the past given you or will give you in the future a valuable car, a trip for you and your sister and your families or a commitment to support you financially. Is this what an ordinary friend does? No. Only a special friend does this. An ordinary friend would provide only moral support. If you want me to be an ordinary friend like I was before September, I will provide only moral support. But if you want me for a special friend, everything is on line with full financial and moral support going forward. Special friend means you want to make time and effort to share thoughts and experiences with me." In a separate text he asked: "Am I an ordinary or special friend?"

It took ten minutes for his clerk to answer.

"Correct me if I'm wrong, are you once again asking for an emotional affair?"

"Absolutely not," responded the judge, and "why do you ask that question?"

In the next blast of texts between them, the clerk dropped a bombshell. "I think it's time I tell [my husband] absolutely everything from the letter, financial gifts, the trips, the car, I can't handle it anymore, I'm shaking, I'm sick, I'm an emotional mess and I have not bothered anyone in my life. I can't handle this no longer. The lies to my family and friends it's not worth how I'm feeling right now. I can't focus on my family since your texts yesterday ... They don't deserve this. I will also seek a therapist tomorrow just so you know. This has gone bad."

Judge: "Please calm down and think about this. Think before you act. What should I tell [the BMW salesperson]?" After two more of his texts went unanswered, Judge Saucedo, wrote: "Based on your text, I will resign as judge tomorrow. My career is toast. We can still save this. Please call."

The text must have jarred the clerk's senses because she answered the judge in a text three hours later, and stated: "I take it that you will follow through with the cost of my family trip [to Disneyland] and the car. I will not come out of this as a failure without either. I do not want to hear any more of our relationship status. Not one word. I am an emotional wreck as I text this. I will consider you a friend and nothing else ... I am still going to seek a therapist as damage has been done. I did not think this was going to end up this way."

Judge Saucedo responded, "Call me please."

"No phone calls. No more texts after this. Please" was her response.

"I understand but I am concerned about my career," wrote the judge, obviously sensing that this whole thing could blow up in his face. "It is toast unless you talk to me." Then in the same text he mentioned killing himself.

"In the garage committing suicide," he wrote. "Have the red car running with the door down. Please call."

The clerk answered that she would call police, and then said, "I'm not going to say anything. If you follow through with what I asked."

(Now if this were a real novel, the plot just twisted. Now we have the woman character essentially telling the male character if he follows up on all of the promises he had made her, she won't spill the beans about whatever secret she knows about him. Of course in this real-life story we are unsure what the clerk meant by his following "through with what I asked." Did she mean the part about just staying friends or the part about buying her a car and sending her to Disneyland?)

The judge's response? "Thank you for sparing my life and career. Absolutely I will follow through on the car, trip, and not another word as you request. Your text was timely because I was ending my life. Thank you for the gift of life."

On November 4th, 2013, Judge Saucedo called his clerk into his chambers and told her he had given a letter of resignation to the court's executive secretary. (Records in the case stated that the secretary later said she never got such a letter. The same records stated that the judge said he had actually mentioned retirement and not resignation to his clerk.) Meanwhile, the BMW had been held at the dealership, and the judge paid the balance of $14,000 and registered it in his clerk's name. He also deposited $200 in his clerk's bank account, which upset her.

"Why did you do that?" she said she had told him. "You said you were done."

In a text later to her friend the stenographer, the clerk said: "I'm sick of all this . . . why doesn't he just leave it alone . . . Just leave it alone already, ugh . . . It's sick . . . I'm disgusted . . . I want to so bad file harassment, but I know that's bad."

That day the stenographer planned to meet with the judge in an attempt to act, she said, as "go-between" to help the judge and his clerk repair their relationship. But just before this meeting, the stenographer texted the clerk, and said she had "a feeling once [the judge] knows the cat's outta the bag, he'll stop," but she added she was unsure whether he would "come clean." In this meeting the stenographer told the judge she knew about the text messages and the gifts, and that his clerk did not want him to send her any more text messages or give her any more money or gifts. In this conversation, she said she learned for the first time that the judge had paid cash for the clerk's BMW and about the judge's money deposits into her bank.

The next day the judge announced that he wasn't going to resign or retire, and acknowledged having gone "through something" in his life and things were better now and everything would be all right.

As they say, hardly.

On the following Monday the clerk arrived at work and told the judge that her Disneyland trip was coming up and she needed the trip expense money by Wednesday. She also told him that she was asking for transfer out of his courtroom. "Okay," said the judge, according to records. (This is not the version of their conversation he would tell to state investigators later.)

The next day, during a criminal proceeding in his courtroom, Judge Saucedo handed his clerk a typewritten note in an envelope while she was sitting at her desk. The note stated: "Yesterday, November 18th, 2013, you threatened to go to HR unless I deposited $8,000 into your savings account by Wednesday. The deposit slip for $8,000 is enclosed. Please stop. It is done. Enough is enough. It ends today. No more money will be paid out." That's the version of the story the judge told investigators. Rather than walking into his chambers and reminding him about his promise to send her to Disneyland, Judge Saucedo testified before the state judicial commission that she came into his office and threatened to report him to human resources unless he gave her $8,000 by November 20th. The stenographer testified that right after the clerk left the judge's office, the judge told her that the clerk had demanded $8,000 or she would tell HR.

The clerk denied the judge's allegation. But her real problem was that she saw the $8,000 in her bank account and made no effort to return it or to contact law enforcement. It is doubtful she was mentally equipped to realize what was going on. In essence the judge had accused her of extortion, and the money in her bank account amounted to "smoking gun" evidence. Unless, of course, she shut up.

The state's criminal code defines extortion this way: "Extortion is the obtaining of property from another, with his consent, or the obtaining of an official act of a public officer, induced by a wrongful use of force or fear . . . Fear, such as will constitute extortion, may be induced by a threat, either: to do an unlawful injury to the person or property of the individual threatened or of a third person; or to accuse the individual threatened, or any relative of his, or member of his family, of any crime; or, to expose, or to impute to him or them any deformity, disgrace or crime; or, to expose any secret affecting him or them."

In the days that followed, the clerk reported the whole episode to the court's managers who investigated and reported the case to the state Supreme Court's commission that disciplines and removes judges from office. Much to the judge's chagrin all of the notes he had written to his clerk and instructed her to return, instead were evidence in the case because she had secretly copied them. In addition, all of the text messages were admitted, and to be sure, 445. text messages make a thick pile of evidence.

The clerk told judicial commission investigators she "regretted . . . keeping the money, but at the time she thought if she gave back the $8,000, the judge would say she was guilty of all of this [extortion]." The commission viewed the $8,000 as hush money. "The examiner proved by clear and convincing evidence that Judge Saucedo deposited the $8,000 into [the clerk's] bank account for the specific purpose of seeking to ensure [she] would stay silent about his past behavior."

In his defense the judge denied wanting a "close" or romantic relationship with his clerk and said the gifts were his way of mentoring her and trying to resolve her marital difficulties.

In the end the commission ordered that Judge Saucedo be fired after 15 years on the bench.

One mystery remained. Who wrote the obscene "anonymous letter" left at the judge's house?

Judge Saucedo steadfastly denied writing the obscene thing, which if you recall, said the clerk was a "good fuck."

However, the commission had no qualms in saying the judge wrote it. When commissioners first read the vile letter, they were "highly skeptical that Judge Saucedo – a highly regarded, dignified, meticulous judge – could have possibly written the letter and then participated in a convoluted plan to persuade [his clerk] that she needed his help." Still, after hearing all of the evidence, the commissioners and its staff reached "the inescapable conclusion that Judge Saucedo did write the letter and mailed it to himself for this purpose."

And then his wife read it.

The investigation left no stone unturned, and even discovered that the judge was able to write that his clerk had a "c-scar" in the anonymous letter because he heard her talking to a friend about having a baby and requiring a caesarian section. What attention to detail, and it was fascinating how he deviously used this telling fact to enhance creditability of the anonymous letter.

At his hearing before the state's Commission on Judicial Performance, Judge Saucedo didn't fare well with examiners – two female and one male judge – who found him mostly uncreditable. This is ironic because part of his duties as a criminal court judge in Tulare County was weighing the veracity and creditability of people who testified in his courtroom. As example of his believability problems before the commission, when asked about the "suicide" text he wrote to his clerk, saying that he was in the "garage with the red car running," the judge's response was both lawyerly and pathetic: "I was in the garage, and that's where I kept my. – my Mercedes."

Known as a brilliant and hard-working jurist, also in his favor in the case, as his attorney told the Supreme Court, Judge Saucedo had never been disciplined before. He was active in his city of Lindsay, California, where he had served as mayor for four terms. He was Tulare County's first Hispanic judge when appointed in 1991. Yet before the dust finally settled in this strange affair, the California Supreme Court had refused to hear his appeal of being fired from his $190,000 a year job, details of the bizarre story had been widely reported, and the judge's clerk was left the richer.

And guess what. She never returned the $8,000 or the BMW.

Chapter Eight

Although cases of driving under the influence of alcohol or drugs in the population in California have fallen since the early 2000s, there are still upwards of 200,000 DUI cases a year. Back in the mid-eighties I knew a lawyer who had his-and-hers Ferraris parked in his garage. All this guy handled was drunk driving cases. He might have had Ferraris in the garage, but he operated like a Ford production line. Drunken drivers paid him $1,500 a pop. He pled them out and got the best sentence he could. Like lawyers today who advertise handling DUIs, he had struck legal gold because California has 35 million vehicles registered with DMV.

The public, and the state's Commission on Judicial Performance, deeply frown upon judges having anything to do with alcohol, at least in their official capacity. I actually once wrote a short news story on a judge who had bought a liquor license to sell booze in a restaurant he had an interest in. It was *that* unusual for a judge to own a liquor license. But it certainly was never unusual for judges to drink.

Each holiday season I used to watch a plump, waddling attorney who handled indigent criminal cases for the county walk down a courthouse hallway with an armful of various kinds and bottles of liquor, Christmas gifts for judges. You see, with a few bad words from the judges the county could have canceled the attorney's lucrative contract, worth many hundreds of thousands of dollars. I figured it was his way of keeping the machinery oiled.

Here is what the California commission says about drinking and driving and judges who get busted for it: "The offenses, driving under the influence of alcohol and driving with a blood alcohol level above .08 percent are high profile, heavily legislated crimes. This is so because these types of crimes, while having the potential for serious and fatal injuries to the innocent public on the roadways, are preventable and yet not uncommon. When a . . . judge is arrested for DUI, the arrest can often inflame the emotions of a community and often makes front page news. Thus, when a judge is arrested and convicted for DUI, it is prejudicial to public esteem for the judicial office."

Every first-year law student learns where the "bar" in the courtroom is. It's the railing or barrier which separates the gallery where spectators sit from the "well" of the court where the attorneys sit in front of the judge. This chapter is about another "bar," the kind where judges go to drink booze. Nationally judicial discipline commissions are so overrun with cases of judges busted for alcohol-related offenses that they could fill a beer truck. What is more, public records show that when judges get busted for driving snockered, they sometimes share a trait with other "important people," like movie stars and prominent politicians. It's what you might call, the "Do you know who I am?" syndrome.

It's understandable why they toss their prominence around when a cop stops them. A friend worked as a deputy district attorney in Los Angeles, and he told me he always kept his D.A. badge in his wallet, where it was visible when opened. He said that way when he was stopped for speeding, the cop saw his badge when he took his driver's license from his billfold. He said he never verbally mentioned he was a prosecutor and the cop didn't openly acknowledge it. Yet, he said cops always let him off with a warning, and he never got a traffic ticket. Of course if a cop stopped this D.A. for drunken driving, D.A. badge or not, he'd have been slammed in the pokey.

There is a big problem when a judge tosses around his or her "position" for purposes of influence when they're in hot water. Unlike movie stars and politicians, rules that govern judges such as the California judicial ethics code forbid it. Judges cannot tell police officers they're judges in efforts to avoid arrest for DUI. This is what happened to Judge Elaine M. Rushing, a longtime judge of the Sonoma County, California Superior Court, and the wife of one of the most prominent appeals court justices in the state.

By this time she had been a judge for 14 years, and in Santa Rosa in the summer of 2005 Judge Elaine Rushing drove with a blood-alcohol level higher than the state's legal limit for being intoxicated. Her blood-alcohol was .20 percent, which meant she was really three-sheets-to-the-wind. Legally drunk, she slammed her car into a wall, slightly injuring her head. Rather than stay and report the crash to the cops or property owners, she sped away. She drove another two miles and ran off into a ditch.

When a woman passerby stopped to help, the judge told her "to leave." When a second motorist stopped to render aid, the judge lied, saying that "we're fine," as if there was someone else with her. When this woman volunteered to call for help the judge said "not to call anyone." The judge then lied again, saying her "husband" was with her.

Fortunately somebody had called paramedics and police. When a firefighter arrived, he found the judge sitting in the driver's seat, and she lied that she had not been the driver. This is where the judge first played the "do-you-know-who-I-am card" by pulling out her official judge's "identification badge" and showing it to the fireman. Later the judicial commission that investigated her would state the obvious. She did so to "avoid being arrested for crimes related to her drinking and driving and to otherwise receive preferential treatment."

It is also where her cover story got so unbelievable that it never would have stood up to minor cross-examination in her own courtroom. "She said that an unknown woman had been the driver, and then that an unknown man had been the driver," commission records stated. "When [the firefighter] asked her where the keys to the car were, Judge Rushing said that the male driver had taken them when he fled the scene up a nearby hill."

About then a California Highway Patrol officer arrived – you know, the guy with police powers who can arrest you. "She repeatedly told [the officer] that she was a Superior Court judge in Sonoma County. She also repeatedly requested that [the officer] call her husband who, she informed the officer, was an appellate court justice."

The officer asked her what had happened.

"She falsely told him that she had not been the driver . . . [she] said that there had been two other people in the car with her, a man and a woman, and that the man had been driving. She said that she had met them at a friend's house, but did not know their names. She said that she had been sitting in the back seat (even though the car had no back seat) . . . When [the officer] asked Judge Rushing where the keys to the car were, she first told him that she thought they were in the car; then said that the male driver had taken the keys with him when he and the woman left the scene on foot, walking back toward the friend's house. She said that she had let the man drive her car because he and the woman were going to give her a ride home and then drive her car back to the friend's house."

There is no record of the cop's face, likely incredulous, as he listened to her drunken cock-and-bull story. Revealingly, the CHP officer asked the judge how much alcohol she had consumed. At first she answered "two bottles," and then changed it to "two glasses." When the officer asked her what kind of booze she had been drinking, "she asked him why he was asking, and again asserted that she had not been driving the car." When the cop told her that he had determined that she had been driving the car, and he needed her to answer some questions and perform a sobriety test, Judge Rushing responded to the effect, "But I'm a judge, and I told you I wasn't the driver."

At that point she refused to answer questions or take an alcohol test, and the officer arrested her for DUI. She continued to tell him that "because she was a judge he should not be arresting her." Once in the patrol car she began complaining that the handcuffs were too tight. She asked him if he had seen her judge's badge and said that "he did not need to be doing what he was doing and that he could remove the cuffs." The officer said that CHP policy stated she had to be handcuffed during an arrest. The cop even helped her out of the car and had another police officer check the handcuffs to make sure they weren't too tight. Records stated that the judge told the CHP that "in her courtroom she goes against court policies for CHP and other officers and that he should extend that courtesy to her."

A few months later after the judge pleaded the legal equivalent of guilty to drunken driving and was placed on three years of unsupervised probation, ordered to perform 10 days of work release, (which meant she didn't have to spend time in jail which could have been dangerous for a judge), and to attend an anti-alcohol abuse program. As a result of her plea, she issued a public apology in the newspaper to the residents of her county.

After the criminal case was resolved, the commission filed its judicial discipline case against her. However, before the commission finalized the case, and even before its "special masters" thoroughly investigated her drunken driven, the judge settled the case with a stipulation, or a legal agreement. She accepted censure for her actions, which probably was the same punishment she would have received anyhow after the investigation. However, commission members split seven to two in favor of the settlement. The two dissenters said they wanted a full investigation by the commission's examiners before deciding the case. Of course a full-blown investigation in which witnesses would have been called to testify would have likely added sordid details that Judge Rushing might not have wanted out.

Stating that she didn't have other alcohol-related offenses and had never been previously disciplined by the commission, it said:

"Judge Rushing's DUI, as well as the hit-and-run property damage incident involving the wall, and her resulting criminal conviction are utterly irreconcilable with minimum standards expected of a judge . . . [Her] conduct following her attempts to drive while drunk is particularly egregious. Falsifying stories to persons seeking to offer early assistance, and to emergency personnel and the arresting CHP officers reflects poorly on Judge Rushing's integrity and without doubt seriously negatively impacts the public perception of her, and of the judiciary in general." The commission called her efforts of avoiding arrest and seeking preferential treatment by blathering her position and her husband's – Sixth District Court of Appeal Justice Conrad Rushing – were "reprehensible." In her favor, the commission noted that she had gotten support from the legal community and had "modified her behavior."

◊

Commission records tend to show that judges who drink and drive and then commit additional crimes, such as hit and run, are punished more severely than for simple DUIs. Take for instance, Circuit Court Judge Kenneth L. Popejoy of DuPage County, Illinois.

A complaint against him in 2010 alleged that "while driving a 2003 Jeep Liberty [he] struck an unattended parked car and then, with willful and wanton disregard for the safety of persons and property, drove from the scene at a high rate of speed while the passenger-side front tire of his car was nearly off the rim, disobeyed multiple stop signs, and caused a 13-year old girl to move away from the road quickly in order to avoid being struck by his car."

In 2012 he was suspended without pay for two months. A common DUI would have warranted a reprimand.

Another judge, Lisa Guy Schall was admonished by the California judicial commission in a DUI case for driving a "vehicle in a reckless manner . . . She drove on the wrong side of a divided highway in Escondido, San Diego County. Specifically, she drove southbound in the northbound . . . lane." She was charged and convicted.

Plainly, she could have killed people in a head-on.

◊

Then there are DUI cases against judges in which you can see the same thing happening to you.

Take the discipline case of Arizona Court Commissioner Sheila A. Madden who in 2012 had had drinks at a casino and then got in her vehicle. As soon as she realized she was unable to operate the vehicle safely she pulled to the side of the road and called her husband to come get her. While waiting on the side of the road a cop stopped and ended up citing her for DUI after she took a breath test and it showed she had more than twice the legal limit for booze in her system. Two weeks later the court commissioner, who held a position in which she handled many tasks like any full-time judge, quit her job. She even reported the incident to the state Commission on Judicial Conduct so it could punish her.

She later pleaded guilty to the odd misdemeanor of being "in control" of her vehicle while drunk. She was then reprimanded by the judicial commission, which probably should have also praised her for being so damned honest.

Remember, in Arizona don't sit in your car, standing still if you've been drinking.

◊

It an oldie, a DUI case 1979. But I wonder if Supreme Court Judge William J. Quinn isn't still remembered by police officers around Warren County, New York. Least of all because upon one of his numerous DUI arrests, "in plain view" the judge "urinated on the police car."

When he got to the stationhouse he pulled out his checkbook with police employees present and asked what he would have to do to "get this straightened out."

Repeatedly in the seventies the judge was busted for driving under the influence of booze, a few times he was found drunk and asleep in his car.

In 1979 "his car stopped, blocking traffic" after he had "passed out at the wheel with the motor running and the car in gear."

When his DUI's began in the 1970s he was driven home by cops after his identity was known. By the late-1970s the police weren't doing that anymore. In 1975 he drove in the wrong direction on an interstate highway and was arrested. In 1977 Judge Quinn was admonished for his drinking "habits" by the New York Commission on Judicial Conduct, and by 1981, he was removed from office. During arrests the judge was often "belligerent," official records stated, once telling officers "My name is not Mr. Quinn; it's Judge Quinn and don't forget it."

◊

The California Highway Patrol caught San Bernardino County, California Superior Court Judge Donald R. Alvarez speeding and driving drunk on the freeway in 2003. He later pleaded the legal equivalent of guilty to misdemeanor driving under the influence of alcohol and the speeding charge was dropped. For punishment, he paid a fine, had to attend an anti-alcohol program and serve three years of unsupervised probation. After being charged, and later after his conviction, other judges reminded him that the state required him to "self-report" the case to the Commission on Judicial Performance.

He didn't, and about seven months after the incident somebody snitched him off to the "judge police." The judicial commission called him out on it four months after his conviction. The judge responded that the issue as he understood it wasn't if he "should" self-report, but "when." Said the judge: "It was never clear to me when the report should be made." Essentially, the judge argued that he was going to report after he completed "all post-disposition conditions of probation, including the alcohol program," in order as he put it, to "report the entire complete case to the commission." It was not clear whether his timetable included completion of probation in three years.

The commission found the judge's reasoning poppycock. It stated that the canons of ethics "clearly and unambiguously mandate a prompt report to the commission upon being charged or upon being convicted." The commission also reminded Judge Alvarez that a bench colleague told him he had to self-report early in the DUI case.

The commission stated that in cases involving a judge's use of alcohol it is the commission's "constitutional" responsibility to investigate and ensure alcohol use is not impairing the judge from administering justice. The commission labeled his failure to promptly report being charged with DUI a "minimum improper action."

◊

Judicial discipline files in most states include cases of judges driving drunk, getting stopped for DUI or crashing their cars because they're intoxicated. Few, however, talk about judges showing up sloshed at the courthouse for work. That is what happened to Iowa Judge Emily Susan Dean, a district jurist in May 2012.

"Judge Dean had been drinking a colorless liquid and fell asleep in the car while being driven by her court reporter," stated

Iowa Supreme Court records. "Upon arriving at the courthouse, Judge Dean swayed and was unsteady. Her court reporter recognized that she was not in a condition to take the bench and obtained assistance from an employee in the county attorney's office to persuade Judge Dean not to take the bench and to leave the courthouse." Later in the day, the judge was admitted to a hospital for three days of treatment for alcoholism.

Saying she "had very little recollection of that morning," Judge Dean wrote a letter to the state attorney general "admitting she is an alcoholic" and acknowledged she had unsuccessfully fought the disease for years. She stated that the May 2012 incident was "hitting bottom" in her struggle with alcoholism. An attorney witness claimed that in "February and March of 2012, there were occasions when Judge Dean appeared 'disoriented' and 'disheveled.'" An investigation by the Iowa Commission on Judicial Qualifications also showed that after "lawyers and litigants were assembled in the courtroom," the judge took the bench and stated, "Why are all of you here?" Judge Dean told the commission that she had "no recollection of . . . an occasion when she was confused by the presence of lawyers and litigants in the courtroom."

Additionally, the commission listed an allegation made by a "citizen" who said a "female driving Judge Dean's husband's car had urinated in a public street." The commission continued: "The citizen followed the car to a destination that fit the description of Judge Dean's mother's residence." In testimony, the judge said she knew about the allegation, but could not remember what happened and "could not deny it." She also "recounted the course of her alcoholism and her unsuccessful past efforts to address it." She asserted that other than [in May 2012] she did not come to work intoxicated" and had "handled her workload in a timely manner." Judge Dean testified she recognized she is an alcoholic and she "cannot allow herself to drink." She said her conduct "tarnished the reputation" of the judicial branch, but suggested her experience would give her "insight into her work as a judge."

After the Iowa Commission on Judicial Qualifications asked the Iowa Supreme Court to suspend the judge, she was suspended for a month without pay in 2014. The Supreme Court noted that "there was no suggestion . . . of inappropriate conduct on the part of Judge Dean . . . beyond her arrival at the courthouse in a state of intoxication." The court laid down a two-year treatment plan for alcoholism which included "regular attendance at meetings with a sobriety support group," and the judge agreed to follow it.

According to state records, the judge followed the plan and told the commission that she had "totally involved herself" in Alcoholics Anonymous (AA)" which had "become a focus of her life" since her suspension. She took five months off work to seek treatment, and in November 2012, she was reinstated to the bench. "She appears to have overcome the denial, recovered from the embarrassment, recognized the depth of the problem . . . and most importantly has been able to establish the kind of supportive framework associated with successful recovery over a lifetime," the court stated.

Appointed in 2006 and now in her fifties, Judge Dean received her law degree from the University of Tulsa in 1999. She also served on the board of the Iowa Lawyers Assistance Program, which helps attorneys and judges with drinking problems.

◊

Awarded the prestigious Scales of Justice gavel in 2012 by a judges association, Judge Richard M. Smith stepped knee-deep in legal do do eight years later.

It's when he threatened the sheriff of Linn County Kansas. He said he was going to "fuck up" the guy good, and he provided the best evidence against himself, himself. His talk with an investigator was tape recorded.

Later he'd blame devil drink for the screw-up, and in February 2021, the state Commission on Judicial Conduct banned him from ever being a judge in Kansas again.

The whole affair began May 6th, 2020 when Senior Judge Smith, who, after an untarnished 28-year career on the bench was working for the state Supreme Court to help reduce court backlogs. He unwisely called the sheriff's office in Linn County and told the female dispatcher to put divorce papers that were supposed to be served by the sheriff in a "drawer" so they couldn't be delivered.

Oh, and the cover-up. ". . . Trust me," he said in the phone call to the dispatcher. "And you've never had Judge Smith call you and say something like that."

It wasn't long before the Linn County sheriff, Kevin Friend, began an investigation. Here is how the local newspaper, the *Linn County News*, described the case. "Judge Smith asked the communications officer on duty to obtain paperwork that was filed for service in a local divorce case [and] he asked the communications officer to place the paperwork in a drawer and assure that the papers were not served . . . One of the parties was at Judge Smith's home and asking for assistance in the matter. As a favor for the subject, Judge Smith decided to use his authority as a judge to circumvent the system and stop a judicial process. It should be noted that Judge Smith does not practice as a judge in Linn County."

And, give the local newspaper credit for knowing right from wrong because it added, "This act is illegal and this activity should not occur."

While the judicial misconduct commission cited the act of trying to stop service of the divorce papers as the reason for its punishing Judge Smith, much happened after it to color the case.

In a taped conversation with the county's undersheriff in July 2020, Judge Smith made remarks against Sheriff Friend which couldn't be ignored by the judicial board.

Stated the Kansas Commission on Judicial Conduct: "[Judge Smith] threatened multiple times to 'fuck up' Sheriff Kevin Friend; [that] he would lie in wait and then go after Sheriff Friend; [and that] he would make up lies so that Sheriff Friend would be charged with crimes . . ."

Transcript of the "conversation" the judge had with the undersheriff in July 2020 is colorful, and according to the commission listed the following remarks by Judge Smith: "That smokey the bear hat I pretty sure I can shove that right up his ass . . ." And: "I could make all kinds of shit up. TV would love it. I'm not going to do that. I'm not that kind of person." And: "I'm gonna fuck him up before this is all over. Trust me. Just stay calm . . ."

In the end the only one who was "fucked" was the judge. In November 2020 he resigned as a senior judge for the Supreme Court. Three months later the misconduct board barred from ever serving as a Kansas judge for, it stated, using his position to benefit "the personal interests of others" in trying to stop service of the divorce papers.

To his credit, the judge underwent treatment for alcohol abuse. He told an investigator for the commission that "his mental and physical health had deteriorated significantly from excessive drinking in July 2020. He attributed his addiction problems with his divorce and resulting financial difficulties. He was found unconscious during a welfare check on July 15th [2020] approximately two weeks after the [tape recorded] meeting with [the] undersheriff." The judge told the investigator he "was diagnosed with acute alcohol poisoning" and was admitted for treatment.

◇

In 1984 Cook County, Illinois Circuit Court Judge Francis P. Butler allegedly "conducted a hearing while intoxicated and made intemperate and injudicious sexual remarks, which were insulting and demeaning to a 17-year-old girl and her parents." He was suspended for a month without pay.

In 1999 a judicial commission punished Judge Robert C. Bradley for his "appearance at the courthouse while under the influence of alcohol," which "impaired the integrity of the court and weakened public confidence in the judiciary."

◇

It amounted to a twofer. The interesting thing about the 2006 DUI of Circuit Judge Patrick Young, 58, of St. Clair County, Illinois was it yielded a two-for-one. Another St. Clair jurist, Jan V. Fiss, 64, was in the same vehicle with an open container. They were going home from a professional football game. Records stated that "Judge Young drove a car while under the influence of alcohol and was involved in an accident in which the driver of another car sustained injuries." Judge Fiss, meanwhile, a passenger in the car Young was driving, "was aware that Judge Young was driving the vehicle after Judge Young had been drinking alcohol for much of the day, and illegally transported open alcohol as a passenger in Judge Young's vehicle." Both judges were convicted of alcohol-related offenses, and reprimanded by the state judicial conduct panel.

Chapter Nine

It's oft quoted but here goes again. A couple of thousand years ago Socrates was asked what made a good judge of the laws. He answered in the brevity of pure wisdom. "Four things belong to a judge: to hear courteously; to answer wisely; to consider soberly; and to decide impartially." State files are full of cases in which judges either forgot or never learned the great philosopher's wise words. This chapter has stories of two such jurists, one in Michigan and the other in California.

The first case involves Oakland County, Michigan Circuit Court Judge Lisa O. Gorcyca, and frankly, no judge should ever have to handle a child custody case like the one that got her into a legal maelstrom.

If I were a judge I'd probably shy away from finding children in contempt of court. But that's what Michigan Judge Lisa O. Gorcyca did in 2015, the youngest a 9-year-old girl. The three siblings were handcuffed and hauled off to kid jail. The saving grace was they didn't go kicking and screaming for the television cameras.

The Michigan Judicial Tenure Commission, which recommends judge discipline to the state's Supreme Court, didn't think much of the Pontiac judge's actions, and recommended she be suspended for a month at a loss of $12,554 in pay. On the bench since 2008 and a former county prosecutor who handled rape, domestic violence and elder abuse cases, Judge Gorcyca had been re-elected in 2014 to a new six-year term. She graduated from the Detroit School of Law in 1993.

In truth, it was the kind of case that makes family law judges want to kick and scream themselves.

Judge Gorcyca had presided over the troubling and contentious custody battle over the children, filed in 2009, for five years before the hearing in June 2015 when she ordered the children taken to a juvenile detention facility for refusing to meet with their father. Along the way, over 40 court hearings were held in the divorce and custody case with 100 pleadings filed. The judge issued 78 orders, 30 relating to the children's custody and refusal to talk to the father. During this time state social workers and the father filed 13 motions against the mother for not cooperating in custody matters.

Parents of the children, two boys aged 14 and 10, and the girl, were granted a divorce in 2011. Even before the final decree the children refused to cooperate with court-ordered custody which allowed visitation by their father. Repeated attempts by Judge Gorcyca to give the father "parenting time" with the children failed because even though the children were placed in the same room with the father they refused to talk to him. "The children refused to respond to their father and even avoided eye contact with him," records stated.

The father complained that the children were being "manipulated" by their mother not to cooperate. This situation went on month after month and year after year until 2015.

Earlier, a typical unsupervised visitation at a public park in August 2010 went completely awry. The children called their mother and contended that their father had "made threats against them." According to records: "When the mother appeared at the park where the father and the children were located, the father allegedly began pushing her around. With their mother's encouragement, the children called 911, and the police responded. The responding police officers saw no visible injuries to the mother and concluded that there was no probable cause to arrest the father." The visit then ended.

The case was assigned to county social workers, and while the two boys claimed they were threatened by their dad, the daughter refused to talk about it. Thereafter the judge ordered that all visitations with the father be supervised. After the children continued to refuse to engage with the father the judge ordered "psychological evaluations" for the parents and "therapy" for the kids. This went on for years, and in 2015, the 10-year-old boy claimed his father had "abused" him. But after a full hearing and presentation of evidence, Judge Gorcyca found no abuse.

In this long and drawn out ordeal seven different therapists were assigned to speak with the children, and at a session in 2011, for the first time, "all three children 'huddled' in a mass, whispering to each other with no other verbal contact."

Around 2013, the parents, under threat of contempt of court by the judge, agreed to cooperate in visitations. But when the father was slated to pick the children up after school, the kids became "hysterical" and the school complained.

In August 2014 the children were ordered to meet with their father in the court's jury room. Upon arrival, they "sat in chairs in the hallway and refused to participate, linking their arms together and refusing to look at or speak to anyone." The judge went into the hallway to "persuade the children to participate in parenting time, explaining to them that they and their mother could be held in contempt of court if they continued to refuse to enter the jury room for parenting time" with their father. In fact, the children finally entered the room to be with their father after being escorted by armed deputies.

It was about this time that the judge first thought about declaring the kids in contempt. By the way, Michigan judges can find children in contempt of court.

About a year later the legal stuff hit the fan.

In June 2015, the two younger children were supposed to visit their father in the jury room but a court employee informed the judge that things "weren't going well."

The judge appointed an attorney for each child and conducted a contempt hearing.

At this point, let me give fictitious names to the children so the reader can keep them straight.

The 14-year-old boy is Harold.
The 10-year-old boy is Larry.
The 9-year-old girl is Jessica.

Harold, the eldest, immediately expressed "confusion" over what was happening, and apologized to the judge for not following court rules. "He admitted that he did not want to talk to his father, telling" the judge "that he believed that his father was violent and that he had observed his father hit his mother."

"All right," said the judge. "Well, the court finds you in direct contempt. I ordered you to have a healthy relationship with your father."

Harold: "I didn't do anything wrong." He then told the judge that it was his father who "had done something wrong, and that he thought there was like rules when – rules for like not, you know, not hitting someone." He then asked the judge why he was being punished.

Having already held him in contempt of court, Judge Gorcyca expressed her disapproval of Harold's actions. "You are a defiant, contemptuous young man and I'm ordering you to spend the rest of the summer – and we'll review it when school starts, and you may be going to school there. So you're going to be – I'm ordering you to Children's Village." That said, the judge continued: "You're supposed to have a high IQ, which I'm doubting right now because of the way you act; you're very defiant, you have no manners."

Then, the judge recalled something she had read in an official report, a report written after the children "huddled" together and "whispered" and appeared to communicate without "other verbal contact." In open court she told Harold that he "needed to do a research program on Charlie Manson and the cult that he has. Your behavior in the hall with me months ago, your behavior in this courtroom, your behavior back there, is unlike any I've ever seen in any 46,000 cases. You, young man, are the worst one. So you have bought yourself living in Children's Village, going to the bathroom in public, and maybe summer school, I don't know . . . You had very simple choices and you're clearly – clearly very messed up. . . So, I'm sentencing you to Children's Village . . . pending you following the court's direct order. When you can follow the court's direct order and have a normal, healthy relationship with your father I would review this . . . You are so mentally messed up right now and it's not because of your father." The judge turned to the father, and as she spoke she made a "circular gesture with her finger near her temple," and stated on the record: "Dad, if you ever think that he has changed and therapy has helped him and he's no longer like Charlie Manson's cult, then you let us know and we can do it."

Harold was handcuffed and removed by sheriff's deputies.

Charlie Manson?

The judge was parroting a report by a social worker who had assessed the children in November 2014. In the report the social worker likened the children to the murderous Charles Manson Family that slaughtered people in California in 1969. In the analogy to the cult, he wrote: "I advised mother that unless she gets these kids off the bench, there will be grave consequences – such as placement in (detention). Mother told the kids to listen; but to no avail. Mother believed the kids were traumatized because, according to mother, their therapist was threatening them with being detained, if they didn't shape up. The children would not answer any adult; they huddled together as if they were sending messages (and) vibes to each other in some sort of Manson-like behavior." The social worker said later that he was "using this Manson-like phenomenon to describe the kids as the girls that were associated with Manson indicated how he would be 'telegraphing' his 'vibes' to them. In fact, (a counselor) indicated that she saw the children tapping their feet under the table in the jury room as if they were sending Morse codes to each other."

The Manson Family? Really. You mean like Manson girl Susan Atkins who was sentenced to death for eight murders, including eight-months pregnant, actress Sharon Tate and others in the star's Los Angeles home? Atkins testified she stabbed Tate to shut her up when she pleaded for the life of her unborn child. Tate was brutally stabbed sixteen times, and after the murders, Atkins not only tasted Tate's blood but scrawled "PIG" with it on the front door.

You mean *those* Manson cult members?

(This judge never would have mentioned the children in the same sentence with notorious Michigan killer, Juwan Knumar Deering, who doused a house full of children with lighter fluid and burned six, aged 6 to 11 to death. Or, infamous Michigan murderer Andrew Kehoe known as the "Bath School Murderer" who killed 44 people by bombing a school. But, Charles Manson, one of the most infamous figures in the annals of crime? Hey, that's all right, those murders were way out there in California. No judge in his right mind anywhere in the Golden State would ever utter the name Manson in a family law case.)

That being said, let's continue. In the same memo to the judge, the social worker encouraged Judge Gorcyca to take tough action. "The court needs to consider, if there is to be any progress, a draconian approach. There has been no progress of any meaningful degree regarding father's parenting time (and) relationship with his children since August of 2010. In fact, the situation is, quite frankly, worse . . . What message would we be sending to these kids if we allow their behaviors to go unchecked – essentially condoning these bizarre, cult like actions?"

During the same June hearing, 10-year-old Larry, apparently having seen his brother cuffed and hauled away, tried to fix things. "Judge, I'm sorry for my behavior, and dad, I'm sorry for my behavior," said Larry in a hearing in court. At that point the boy's lawyer instructed Larry to "look in his (father's) eyes" and say it. "Dad," he said then, "the Judge wanted me to talk to you so here is something about myself. I enjoy soccer and I hope to be on the soccer team."

His attorney: "And what do you hope? – Do you mind, your honor?"

Judge: "Oh, it's impressive."

Attorney: "We talked about, what do you . . . you're going to tell the judge that you're going to be doing from this point forward when you get together with your dad, what was the 'c' word we talked about?"

Larry: "Communicate."

Attorney: "Communicate. That means dialogue, back and forth. Remember I told you not to be just a stick in the mud, your dad asks you a question, you respond. That's how one develops a relationship, starting through communication. Are you in agreement with starting to communicate with your father so that you can build a relationship?"

Larry: "Yes."

Attorney: "Look at your father's eyes and say that."

Larry: "Yes."

Attorney: "Look at the judge's eyes and say that."

Larry: "Yes."

The judge then turned her attention to the girl, Jessica, who apparently had a piece of paper with something her brother had written on it. "No, (Jessica), don't read what your brother wrote. You're your own person. Do you know what? I know you're kind of religious. God gave you a brain. He expects you to use it. You have a brain, you are not your brother. You are not your big, defiant brother who's living in jail. Do you want to live in jail? Just tell me this right now."

The girl's attorney: "Do you want to go to jail?"

Then, to the girl's mother, the judge said: "Mom, you must step away."

First deputy: "Go ahead and step over here, ma'am."

Second deputy: "Step away."

First deputy: "Step towards the back. Thank you."

Second deputy: "Step up. There you go."

Girl's attorney: "Okay, I'm urging you to apologize and say you will go and try to work with your father at visits. Can you do that?"

Jessica: "I'm sorry, I'll try to work with my father at visits."

Judge: "Well, you're going to stay here all day and it's going to be up to your dad. I'm going to see how you two act. Maybe the three of you should go to lunch in the cafeteria? If you have any hesitation at all you're living in Children's Village . . . You know what that would do to your mother, going home, riding down the elevator without you? Can you guys think about someone besides yourself? You should be thinking about your father and what your father has gone through unnecessarily because of I don't [know] why? . . . It's despicable to me what your father has gone through when he loves you . . . and he wants to be in your life . . . I'm so upset with you, I'm so upset with you. I'm even more upset with your brother, and I won't say what I think about your mother. I think your mom did something nice in the jury room for once. And I like your dad. And I – you have me as your judge for five and a half years. How old will you be (Jessica)? Let's see, you're going to be a teenager. You want to have your – you want to have your birthdays in Children's Village? Do you like going to the bathroom in front of people?

Attorney: "She said no, thank you.

Judge: "Is your bed soft and comfortable at home? I'll tell you this, you two don't have a nice lunch with your dad and make this up to your dad you're going to come back here at 1:30 and I'm going to have the deputies take you to Children's Village." The judge added that she had "wanted to do this to you all many times," but that their father had refused. Then Judge Gorcyca said, "Your mom didn't want me to either, but the ball is in your dad's court. Your dad is in charge. Unless you want to live in Children's Village. It's up to you. I have put other children in Children's Village. You guys can all hang out together."

At that point the attorneys and judge discussed where the two children could have lunch with their father, and then the judge cautioned the kids: "Everything's recorded (in the courthouse) and I'm going to watch. You walk – the minute you pull into this courtroom – courthouse, you're videoed. Outside, they can get you walking in, they can get you everywhere except in the bathroom."

Attorney for Larry: "What do you have to say?"
Larry: "I'll go with my brother then."
Judge: "Pardon?"
Larry: "I'll go with my brother."
Judge: "What does that mean?"
Larry: "Children's Village."
Judge: "So you don't want to have parenting time with your father?"

The mother's attorney then spoke up. "Do they realize that they would not be seeing their siblings?"

Judge: "You're not even going to be with your brother. That's cool. You won't be in the same cell. I'll put in there 'stay away from your brother.' All right, so you're admitting you won't have parenting time with your dad?"

Larry mumbled something the court stenographer couldn't hear.

Judge: "Okay. Is that a yes?"

Larry: "Mm-hmm."

Larry's attorney: "You want to go to lunch with your dad?"

Jessica: "No."

Jessica's attorney: "Now she's refusing because her brother is."

Jessica: "I'm not refusing because my brother is. I'm refusing because I want to refuse."

Judge: "That's ridiculous, I have to say. I've never seen anything like this. One day you can watch this video and realize that you two have been brainwashed. Your dad is a good man . . . And wipe that smirk off your face, Larry."

Larry: "It's not a smirk."

Judge: "I don't know what that is. I've never seen anything like it. You're a defiant, contemptuous young man and the court finds both of you in direct contempt. You both are going to live in Children's Village. Your mother is not allowed to visit, no one on your mom's side is allowed to visit. Only your father and therapist and (the social worker). When you are ready to have lunch with your dad, to have dinner with your dad, to be normal human beings, I will review this when your dad tells me you are ready. Otherwise, you are living in Children's Village until you graduate from high school. That's the order of the court. Good bye."

Handcuffed, the two children were led off.

When word of the contempt rulings were published in the media, the judge held another hearing and changed her orders, and the children were released from detention after 17 days. Finding the children in contempt of court, while perhaps overreaching to some, was understandable after hearing what happened. In fact the Michigan Supreme Court did not take issue with the spirit of her contempt ruling, calling it error to have granted the father carte blanche power to decide when the children would be released from detention. The justices also expressed sympathy and understanding for the judge's frustration in handling the nightmare divorce and custody case.

The Supreme Court disagreed with the judicial commission's recommendation for a 30-day suspension without pay for the judge. Instead the state's high court publicly censured Judge Gorcyca for her less than delicate handing of the children. The Supreme Court said the judge stepped over the line into judicial misconduct when she "mocked and threatened the children," and called them "mentally messed up" and "brainwashed." The court said the judge was generally hostile towards the kids and mother and even "lied about the conditions at Children's Village." But, the justice didn't think she disliked kids, generally. "Even though (judge's) misconduct involved children, it did not involve the unequal application of justice on the basis of a class of citizenship . . . Simply put, [her] conduct – though inappropriate – did not demonstrate an animus toward children, and there was no evidence that [she] treated children differently than she did other persons who had previously defied court orders," the court stated in its ruling in 2017.

The Michigan Judicial Tenue Commission investigators included the judge's stupid use of the Charles Manson Family when dressing down the young Harold from the bench, obviously believing it was improper. Shockingly, however, the state's high court didn't mention Judge Gorcyca having told the 14-year-old that he acted like a member of the infamous cult and should do some research on the murderous Mansons.

Yeah, judge, what a great subject for school paper. She really should have checked out the gruesome victim photos on the Internet before she opened her trap.

◊

The second judge who should have learned the wisdom of Socrates was Monterey County Judge José Angel Velasquez in Salinas, California. When lawyers walked into his courtroom in Salinas that December morning in 1995, they saw the 9-by-6 inch crucifix he had festooned to the wall behind the bench. It isn't clear what thoughts passed through the minds of the attorneys, but the biblical notion of "an eye for an eye" reciprocal punishment for wrongdoers as articulated by Jesus in the Sermon on the Mount might have been one. Because within a month the judge announced new very tough sentencing rules to punish drunken drivers.

First offenders would get up to 45 days in jail; second-time drunken drivers as many as 90 days; and third-time DUI losers would get 180 days in jail. Mothers Against Drunk Drivers (MADD) must of have loved his tougher stance on people who drive motor vehicles sloshed, but others didn't, and complained to the Commission on Judicial Performance. "The DUI policy, as announced, appeared to not allow for exceptions, and therefore created the appearance of prejudgment of DUI cases," the commission stated in a censure of the judge. "Judge Velasquez' actions . . . constituted conduct prejudicial to the administration of justice."

To his credit, after a public defender and a prosecutor complained about the crucifix, the judge removed it the same day. He said he "displayed the crucifix as an expression of his personal religious belief" and "did not intend to offend anyone."

Of course the discipline commission included the crucifix in its censure of the judge. Separation of church and state isn't a new concept, and the crucifix incident happened months after the judge first took the bench. So, it seemed to reflect the naivety of a new jurist. Soon, however, he started bad-mouthing colleagues.

Perhaps, given the background, it was inevitable. The son of farmworkers, he had been elected in 1995 in a tough election. He defeated a popular incumbent judge who had been widely supported by the county's lawyers and legal community. Then, as if to say more than metaphorically "there's a new sheriff in town," the judge was sworn in wearing a "fancy Mexican cowboy outfit" at a "novel ceremony that celebrated his heritage and the Latino community," a newspaper reported.

His harsh criticism of colleagues began after attorneys filed legal papers requiring removal of Judge Velasquez from hearing their cases. When this happens to a judge at any courthouse it means a lot more work for fellow judges who must pick up the slack. It causes friction, everywhere, every time.

In court Judge Velasquez accused his presiding judge of trying to make changes in his courtroom docket and not assigning him a regular clerk. He claimed that "it's being racially discriminatory." As the judge's repeated stinging remarks got louder, it attracted the media. In an interview dripping with paranoia he was quoted as saying in April 1996: "There's a conspiracy amongst local judges . . . They dislike me and will do anything they can to assassinate my character and disparage my reputation . . . There's tampering going on with my computer . . . and things being moved around my office. My fear is that these guys and ladies will come in here and plant something. In their quest to assassinate my character, they will do anything . . . We all make mistakes . . . but all these guys make it seem like I'm a total animal out of control." In a TV interview he accused several people including a judge and attorneys of being "racists." When a judge makes such comments they won't be missed by the judicial commission. Along with hanging the crucifix and his DUI sentencing policy, the remarks were among complaints that earned him the censure in 1997. A public censure is a step shy of removal.

This is speculation, but when Judge Velasquez answered the charges against him, and as a Hispanic judge, raised touchy constitutional issues, including "freedom of speech, freedom of religion, and freedom of expression" in his defense, the state commission freaked out. Politically, it wanted no part of it. Litigants who go against the First Amendment rarely win. A settlement was quickly arranged. The judge admitted the bad stuff, with the commission agreeing not to remove him from office.

Years after the discipline case, an attorney who had been the subject of vicious attacks by Judge Velasquez, said in a newspaper interview that the judge did become a "better judge" following the 1997 case. "But you are judged on what you did, not for what you promise in the future," he said. Judge Velasquez had promised to clean up his act. And after being slapped hard, you'd think that a judge would keep his head down, mind his judicial p's and q's and simply administer justice in a non-controversial way. Not Judge Velasquez.

It took a decade and he was back before the judicial discipline people. This time the commission handed him his walking papers in 2007 – likely what they wanted to do a decade before.

This time around with the commission, it was because the judge's courtroom had turned into a chamber of horrors for defendants. ". . . In an egregious pattern of misconduct that infringed the constitutional rights of numerous defendants and transgressed the limits of his authority, often in a capricious and malicious manner," the commission stated, summing up his conduct. "These incidents were not isolated; rather, they reflected a disturbing and persistent pattern of conduct that was completely at odds with the standard conduct expected of the judiciary."

Mistreatment of defendants was numerous, and a few are listed here. In a case of a drunken driver who petitioned the court to have his probation modified, the judge learned that the defendant had not installed a locking device on his car that stopped him from driving intoxicated, nor had the man shown "proof" that he had attended 30 Alcoholic Anonymous meetings as required. The man appeared in court without a lawyer and explained that he had been told to install the locking device after completing his DUI classes. Judge Velasquez told him that "he would be immediately taken into custody for a willful failure to comply with the court order to install the interlock device." Judge Velasquez then asked about the AA meetings.

"I am doing that," said the defendant. "I bring some proof here."

Without looking at the AA materials, the judge said: "Did the school tell you not to go to them [AA meetings]?"

As Judge Velasquez was ordering the man into custody, the defendant, who spoke Spanish, "started" to say something." But before the interpreter could translate, Judge Velasquez said: "Hold on . . . You continue to interrupt me, you'll be at 45 [days] in a hurry."

When the defendant tried to explain what the school had told him, Judge Velasquez warned: "I told you you're at 20 days, you insist, you'll be at 45 and you'll get to 60 in a hurry." The judge then imposed 20 days in jail for "willful failure to comply."

As he was being sentenced to the 20 days, the defendant asked if he could say something, the judge said yes, and when the man said he had been attending AA meetings and had been "given a completion date." The judge interrupted him, and upped his sentence to 30 days in jail. Then, he warned, "If you'd like to take more of the court's time, and you'll be at 60."

When the poor man said he "just wanted to explain," Judge Velasquez increased the sentence to 60 days in jail. Afterward, the defendant spoke again and before the interpreter could translate it, the judge popped him with an increase to 75 days, and, "threatened to increase the time to 120 days if he continued to speak."

The guy went from 20 days in hell to 75 – on a whim.

Hauled before the Commission on Judicial Performance, which was certainly more polite than the judge had been to DUI defendants, Judge Velasquez was asked, "Wasn't [the DUI defendant] entitled to present evidence and argument that he attended the [AA] meetings?"

The judge responded, "That's what the hearing was for." The judge admitted he had increased the man's sentence for "trying to offer a defense and for taking up the court's time." What a damning admission. The judge told the commission the defendant was "entitled to speak and inquire about sentencing." But, that's precisely what he didn't let him do.

Stated the commission: "Despite repeated efforts, [the defendant] was not given any meaningful opportunity to explain his position before Judge Velasquez summarily found him in violation of probation and remanded him . . . [The defendant] did not interfere with the court proceedings, and at all times was respectful to the court."

The commission agreed that "Judge Velasquez became fully embroiled with the defendant, increasing his time in custody for reasons unrelated to criminal punishment purposes."

In another series of cases, showing a strange pattern of conduct by the judge, he asked defendants cited for "exhibitions of speed" whether they liked the feeling of "peeling out" – meaning taking off fast and hearing their vehicle tires squeal. He asked this same question in repeated cases, so many that the commission stated that it tended to turn his courtroom into a "game show."

Here are three such cases.

Judge: "Listen to the question and I want you to be honest. That's whether you pay $200 or $800 depends on your honesty. When you peel out tires, because that's what you did, you spin your wheels? Did it feel good?"

Defendant: "Did it feel good?"

Judge: "Yeah. Yes or no?"

Defendant: "Yes."

Judge: "Are you sure?"

Defendant: "I mean it didn't feel good because I was in the water [after the accident]."

Judge: "Well no. The reason for peeling out is because there's a thrill to it. Right?"

Defendant: "Yes."

Judge: "So are you sure it feels good or it doesn't?"

Defendant: "No, it doesn't feel good."

Judge: "Okay. Now you're starting to lie."

Defendant: "No, I don't like it."

Judge: "I do. And if I ever peel out, I do it for a reason. But anyways. You answered straight. This will be your sentence. You'll be placed – and I just questioned you a little more, and then you weakened and went the other way."

Judge Velasquez imposed a $200 fine and wished the defendant good luck.

In a second case, before he accepted a plea in an "exhibition of speed" case, the judge told the defendant that his fine would be between $200 and $1,000, "depending on your answer."

Judge: "Does it feel good [to peel out]?"

Defendant: "No."

The judge then accused the defendant of lying.

When the defendant tried to speak, the judge cut him off, saying, "I didn't ask you if it was an accident, I just asked you a straightforward question. When we do that stuff, and I've done it, you peel out, you're just – you're showing off. You do it for a reason. Some girls are passing by, you wanted to get their attention."

The judge asked again, "if it felt good."

Defendant: "Not when you get pulled over."

Judge Velasquez fined him $800.

In a third case, after the defendant was told his fine would be $200 to $1,000, depending on "his answer to the question of whether it felt good to peel out."

The judge asked and the defendant said, "Yes."

"That's the answer I wanted," said the judge, and he fined the man $200.

In the brutal statement, the judicial discipline commission said that the judge's question of whether it felt good to hear your tires squealing "turned the proceedings into a game show with the defendant attempting to guess the correct answer in order to obtain the lower fine." It stated that "Judge Velasquez detracted from the dignity of the proceedings by announcing in court that he has engaged in the same criminal conduct as the defendant."

In his defense before the commission "Judge Velasquez maintained that determining whether a defendant is willing to own up to having intentionally engaged in exhibition of speed is within his sentencing discretion," and that "whether a defendant accepts responsibility for committing the offense is a proper factor for a judge to take into consideration in sentencing."

The commission found that "whether it feels good to peel out does not equate with accepting responsibility for the offense of exhibition of speed. The offense does not include a requirement that the defendant feel good." The commission agreed with their investigators that the judge to "some degree became embroiled in the process, acted in a way that might have suggested he had prejudged the case, and used his own experience as a young man as a factor in the ultimate sentence given."

Son of migrant farmworkers, the judge was called an important role model in the community. Apologizing for his conduct and saying he was learning to be a better judge, Judge Velasquez sought a similar penalty as in the 1997 case, a censure. The commission wasn't buying it.

The commission ruled his handling of these case was "prejudicial misconduct."

In more recent years Velasquez has practiced personal injury, criminal defense and worker's compensation law in Salinas. He mentioned his stint as a judge for 12 years on his public resume, but not his removal. He graduated from Santa Clara University School of Law.

◊

Honesty. Without it they court system would be a sham. It is why we have perjury laws on the books that can send courtroom lairs to prison for five years – a long stretch of eating cold, brown food for fibbing.

One of the worst cases of chronic lying by a judge involved California jurist, Patrick Couwenberg, who was kicked off the bench by California's Commission on Judicial Performance in 2001. The state's Supreme Court rejected his appeal a year later. His conduct of untruthfulness was so extreme, the commission stated it created "the appearance that he obtained his judicial office by deceit." Who did he lie to? To begin with, the state governor who appointed him.

Outrageously he even told the judge ready to introduce him at his "enrobing ceremony" after his appointment by the governor that "he was a Vietnam veteran who had received a Purple Heart," which was a lie. Embellishing himself as a warrior he claimed he had "shrapnel in his groin." The closest he had ever really come to war-fighting was in the Naval Reserve, from which he was discharged for a "liver" condition in 1967. Lying about his military record was an affront to the memory of more than 53,000 Americans who fought and died in the jungle war. Today, the federal Stolen Valor Act makes it a crime to falsely claim winning a medal in the military, for which punishment is a year in jail. The judge was crafty, telling a newspaper he had been in Nam in 1968. Anybody who lived through the war and the Communist Tet Offensive of 1968 knew it was one of the war's bloodiest years.

Judge Couwenberg, who served on the Los Angeles County Superior Court, also misrepresented other personal accomplishments, including his education (falsely claiming a bachelor degree from prestigious Cal Tech, in physics no less, and a law degree from prestigious Loyola University School of Law in Los Angeles). Not only did the judge lie about his law school, he lied about his date of graduation, putting it down on the official application for a judgeship as three years later than his true date in 1973. The misconduct commission alleged he did this to hide having flunked the Bar exam five times, and added, the judge attempted "to portray failing the Bar five times as something positive...."

The commission said that he added the false military record to his tissue of lies to "further the likelihood of a judicial appointment" because the Republican governor at the time, Pete Wilson, was a former U.S. Marine. Wilson appointed Couwenberg judge in 1997. "The reason for these lies is self-evident," the commission stated. "Seeking appointment to the bench is a competitive situation. Judge Couwenberg would have been competing with 20 to 30 applicants."

It didn't take long for things to unravel. In 1998 after a Los Angeles newspaper for lawyers published a story questioning Judge Couwenberg's military service, the state judicial commission opened an inquiry. The judge then lied to the commission about his lies. In a letter he stated: "At no time did I lie to the governor nor did I attempt to mislead anyone." But it was during testimony before the commission when things really got screwy. In what must have caused a chorus of raised eyebrows from commission investigators, the judge said he had been a spook for the Central Intelligence Agency during Vietnam.

Of all his lies, his use of false military credentials and medals to win a judgeship was the most reprehensible. In seeking a judicial appointment, Patrick Couwenberg had a luncheon with two judges, one of whom was considered influential when it came to judicial appointments. During the lunch this judge recalled asking Couwenberg about serving in Vietnam, saying, "You were in Vietnam and you were in combat?" One of the judges told the commission that Couwenberg "affirmed" it. The judge's question about "combat" was significant because as people who served know not all U.S. soldiers engaged in battle in South Vietnam, and many were stationed in much safer "base camps."

The influential judge then told Couwenberg that "it was critical" to let the governor know of his military service because both Governor Wilson and his judicial appointments secretary were ex-Marines. At the lunch, Couwenberg "indicated that he thought it was important, too." Afterward the influential judge took "several steps" to aid Couwenberg's quest for a judgeship.

A governor's judicial appointments secretary interviews candidates for judgeships and recommends them to the governor. John Davies, Governor Wilson's judicial secretary, told the discipline commission that he remembered talking to Couwenberg about his military duty. "Mr. Davies testified that a war record was a plus with Governor Wilson and that he recalled his interview with Judge Couwenberg because of his 'unusual war experiences.' He did not recall the details, but remembered that it involved 'undercover work' and that there was some 'sort of heroism involved.'"

Undercover work for the U.S. Army?

Sounds like a red flag.

In defending himself before the commission, Judge Couwenberg said he did not recall talking about his "military career" with the judicial appointments secretary during the interview. (Come on man, you were talking to an ex-jarhead! You want us to believe Nam didn't come up? Commissioners didn't say that, but they should have!)

Before the commission the judge "testified falsely that he had been involved in covert Central Intelligence Agency operations in Southeast Asia between June 1968 and December 1969, and had made a delivery of funds or documents to Africa for the CIA around 1984." The judge said he "went to Laos for a month in December 1968 and then went again for three or four weeks around June 1969."

The commission learned that during this time the judge was actually working full-time for "the Los Angeles County Department of Social Services."

To test the judge's bizarre testimony about living a double life, the commission won permission from the CIA to send a representative to testify. The CIA spook testified that the spy agency has "records of everyone who has ever been engaged in a clandestine or covert relationship with the CIA in an operational capacity. These records have been maintained since the mid-1940s and include anyone an operations officer has talked to and considered using." The CIA man said the agency had checked all records to see if Judge Couwenberg was named in any record and "he does not." Additionally, the spokesman spook said that "if someone were picked out, recruited in the U.S., and transported to Laos under our sponsorship, we would have a record of it." He also said there was no CIA record of sending the judge to Africa in the 1980s.

After the CIA official testified, blowing a large hole in the judge's assertions about his secret agent activities, the judge told the commission that "he never said he was with the CIA, but only guessed or assumed that the agency was the CIA." After the testimony the commission agreed with its investigators that the evidence showed "Judge Couwenberg testified falsely that he had been involved in covert CIA operations in Southeast Asia in December 1968 and June 1969 and had made a delivery of funds or documents to Africa for the CIA around 1984."

Predicably Judge Couwenberg offered a "mental defense." Judges in very serious discipline cases seem to plead medical maladies when all else fails. Specifically Judge Couwenberg said he suffered from a mental condition called "pseudologia fantastica," which for the lack of a simpler way of putting it, it is pathological lying. "Pseudologia fantastica is characterized by the creation of eloquent and interesting stories, sometimes bordering on the fantastic, that are told to impress others," wrote medical Professor Petra Garlipp in the book published by Oxford University Press in 2016, *Unusual and Rare Psychological Disorders*. "These stories may seem to be just on the verge of believability and often involve the patient assuming important and heroic roles. Patients react to questions or doubts with ad hoc elaborations in order to satisfy the listener. Thus, new lies are needed to supplement the old, and patients sometimes start to believe their own deceptions."

For his defense the judge presented a psychiatrist who told the judicial commission that "pseudologia fantastica is a description rather than a diagnosis," and that "objective medical tests that were administered to Judge Couwenberg did not reveal any suggestion of cognitive or psychological disorder." Nonetheless, the shrink testified for the judge, saying, "When we use the word lying, we generally mean that the person knows what he's saying is not true and is deliberately attempting to mislead another person. There's a two-part definition to lying. With the pseudologia fantastica it is really kind of an admixture of self-deception and trying to present oneself to other people in a certain way and not really related to a conscious intent to defraud or to lie, such as we might see in a person with antisocial personality."

The commission said it "recognized that there was evidence that Judge Couwenberg was in a detention camp as a very young child in Indonesia and (had) suffered racial discrimination in Holland in his youth." The judge's doctors testified that "these experiences caused him to have low self-esteem" which, one of them testified, "led to pseudologia fantastica." However, commission investigators "found little evidence of this connection," and "noted that none of the psychological tests revealed any evidence of a traumatic stress disorder," and that the judge "had never been treated for any psychological disorder . . . ." In effect, the commission rejected the judge's mental defense and ruled that "Judge Couwenberg did not have any mental condition that excuses . . . his misconduct."

(Perhaps the judge really did have this "pseudologia fantastica." His lies were so easily found out. A call to the law school would have quickly exposed he had never been a student there. His faked military record was also easily discovered. Even though military records are said to be "confidential" by the various branches, as a news reporter years ago I got a murderer's military record, including his mental health history from a Pentagon official on condition I used no names or titles in my story. His fabrication about undercover work for the CIA would have been a tougher nut to crack. Can you imagine the judge's "sinking" feeling when the CIA official walked into the commission hearing ready to snitch him off? All in all, his by-the-seat-of-his-pants lies had little depth of thought.)

In an aside, Mr. Couwenberg wasn't the first judge to have claimed military honors when none existed. In 1995 the Illinois Courts Commission censured Kane County Circuit Court Judge Michael O'Brien for "creating and allowing others to maintain the false impression that he is a recipient of the Congressional Medal of Honor." Curiously when this judge went for a faked military medal to pin on his chest, he grabbed the highest and most prestigious.

Chapter Ten

If the first story of this chapter had a title, it would be "Sex, Lies and Audiotape" because the sordid saga of Los Angeles Superior Court Judge George W. Trammell, III in the 1990s had it all. No "sex case" involving a judge ever put an uglier stain on the judiciary than this messy tale with the intrigue of a thriller, with "coded" messages and even the Asian mafia. In 1996. Superior Court Judge George W. Trammell III, then 60, initiated a sexual relationship with a woman after she had pleaded guilty and was given a lenient sentence by him. In 1999, the judge got censured by the judicial performance commission for his conduct, two years after he "retired" – a day after sheriff's detectives searched his home in Pomona, California, where he had bedded the woman twenty times. He had been a jurist for twenty-five years, and jeopardized his lucrative $90,000-a-year pension because of his bad conduct.

Here is the incredible story, which took six years to play out, from 1995 to 2001.

◊

For background, George Trammell graduated in 1962 from the University of Southern California Law School, spent time in the Long Beach City Attorney's office, followed by eight years with the Los Angeles County District Attorney before being named to the bench in 1971 by Republican Governor Ronald Reagan. By 1986 he had gained a reputation as a courageous and controversial jurist who battled Los Angeles police and ruled that closing criminal preliminary hearings was unconstitutional, a view the state Legislature later adopted into state law. A 1986 story about him in the *Los Angeles Times* stated that "while Trammell labels himself a moderate-conservative . . . he has made his share of rulings and statements that have aggravated law enforcement . . . Trammell was blasted by police and city attorney officials in 1977 when he ruled in what was described as 'a scorching opinion,' ruling that the [L.A.] city attorney's office improperly approved the shredding of tons of citizen complaints accusing police officers of brutality." The *Times* quoted Jeffrey Jonas, a deputy district attorney who worked in the courthouse with Judge Trammell, as saying. "He is intellectually astute – but sometimes his intellectualism gets in the way of good common sense."

What Judge Trammell did to end his judicial career lacked all common sense. Here is the incredible story, according to state and federal records and other sources, which took six years to play out, from 1995 to 2001.

◊

In the spring of 1995, three Taiwanese: Pifen Lo, 37, her ex-husband Ming Jin, and their live-in babysitter who was Jin's lover, Chang Chu, were arrested for kidnapping a couple and holding them for ransom. In a search of ex-husband Jin's home, investigators found plastic explosives, weapons and handcuffs. Investigators suspected Jin of having ties to Asian organized crime.

Overall, charges included counts of kidnapping for purposes of extortion and assault with a semiautomatic firearm; as well as charges of robbery, money laundering and possession of explosives, gun silencers and counterfeit computer software. While Jin and his lover, Chu, faced kidnapping for extortion counts, felonies punishable by life in prison without possibility of parole, ex-wife Lo faced lesser charges, including child endangerment, stemming from having her three children in the home with explosives. She faced a maximum of 12 years in prison.

The case was assigned to Judge Trammell.

On January 18th, 1996, Lo pleaded the equivalent of guilty to non-violent felonies of child endangerment, counterfeiting and money laundering. A month later, Judge Trammell sentenced her to probation for five years over objections of prosecutors, who wanted her sent to prison. He ordered her to pay a $100,000 fine, make restitution of $400,000, and undergo psychological therapy.

Several months later in July, a jury convicted Jin and babysitter Chu of kidnapping for extortion, and they faced life behind bars without possibility of ever being released. Judge Trammell, who presided over their trial, was set to sentence them. But, before her ex-husband's sentencing, the judge telephoned Lo and asked her to come to his office. "She went to the courthouse and waited outside Judge Trammell's chambers until he ushered her into his room," she told the judicial performance commission later. Lo had sent the judge a birthday card and they talked about it. They then talked about her ex-husband's case, and his possible life sentence. "He told me if I wanted my husband to come home early, I would have to pay a price," Lo told the state commission that keeps judges honest. While in his office, she testified, Judge Trammell complimented her, put his hand inside her clothes and fondled her breasts, and kissed her mouth. However, to add a little comedy to this sordid tale, the impromptu love-making abruptly ended "when someone sought entry into the judge's chambers and Judge Trammell let Lo out a side door." The woman further testified that a few days later the judge called her and invited her to his house, and on September 22nd, Lo went to Judge Trammell's home in Pomona. Again, they discussed her ex-husband's pending sentence. At this meeting, she claimed, the judge told her, "You know what I want." In his home they had sex. She claimed it was "over her objections," something the commission's investigators doubted. From September to December, Lo testified, she went to the judge's house once a week, sometimes three, to have sex. She said he warned her not to tell her husband, her lawyer or the prosecutor.

It is unbelievable that this seasoned judge didn't realize the career-ending fix he was getting himself into. Didn't he realize he was dealing with sophisticated criminals? The woman's ex was a reputed cardsharp with alleged connections to the Asian mafia in L.A. As it might be expected, after sex, Lo began secretly collecting the judge's "pubic hair" left on sheets as "proof of their sexual relationship."

To better communicate, Lo obtained a pager and Judge Trammell left numerous coded messages on it. His rudimentary "code" didn't rival World War II's Enigma Machine. The number "55" meant "I love you" and the number "1" substituted for "I want to make love to you." Lo and the judge spoke on the phone frequently. And, yes, like the gathering of public hair, Lo tape-recorded four of her phone conversations with the horny judge. She said she taped the calls because she feared the judge was going to send her to jail. Meaning: Revoke my probation, sucker, and send me to prison, and I spill our taped conversations about sex to the cops. Even worse for the judge, in their "conversations Judge Trammell allegedly discussed how he might be able to terminate Lo's probation after only a year," commission records stated. He also allegedly "advised her on how she might seek the return of property seized by the police, including a Mercedes automobile."

It was this Mercedes-Benz that landed the judge in prison on a federal rap later.

Both attorneys for Lo's ex-husband, Jin, and the live-in babysitter, Chu, filed requests to disqualify Judge Trammell from continuing to hear their cases. In other words, this would have meant another judge would sentence them. "On October 4th, 1996, the babysitter's attorney received a phone call from Judge Trammell's clerk instructing the lawyer to prepare a motion to reduce the babysitter's bail to $45,000." At that point, both the babysitter and her lover, Lo's ex-husband, withdrew their requests to disqualify Judge Trammell from sentencing them. Later in court and obviously without disclosing his affair with Lo, the judge "addressed" the requests to replace him and denied it. During this hearing, the judge tried a bit of subterfuge by telling the ex-husband Jin that he couldn't even remember "your wife or ex-wife's" name. Obviously it was meant to convey on the court record that the judge didn't know the woman well. It was laughable because by this time ex-husband Jin was aware the judge was screwing his former wife. At the hearing as well, Judge Trammell lowered the babysitter's bail to $25,000 so she could "attend a pottery class." At the time, in California it was an extremely low bail after being found guilty of kidnapping for extortion punishable by life in prison without parole. The bail reduction raised eyebrows at the courthouse, but of course, nobody knew of the judge's extra-judicial activities in bed with Lo.

That same month Judge Trammell's robed malfeasance for his lover Lo continued. On his own he telephoned a particular criminal defense attorney to represent Lo and replace the attorney who had been handling her case. He did this without telling Lo's current attorney. The judge then told the woman's new attorney that Lo had written a "letter to the court requesting the return of property seized in conjunction with the criminal case and he wanted the attorney to prepare a motion for return of property for Lo." As a result, "the [new] attorney filed a motion for return of [her] property," which included the Mercedes and some Rolex watches. Trouble was, the purported "letter written by Lo" was dated November 6th – days after the conversation between the new attorney and Judge Trammell, seeking the motion for return of the car and watches. If nothing else it proved judges make poor crooks.

During a hearing a month later, the judge heard arguments on the motion for return of the Mercedes and Rolexes. Before the district attorney arrived in court, Judge Trammell informed Lo's new attorney that "the district attorney intended to file amended forfeiture papers," which wasn't true. At the hearing over protests by the district attorney the judge ordered "return of most" of Lo's stuff.

In December the web of courtroom intrigue continued. This time Judge Trammell called Lo's probation officer. The judge had previously ordered the woman to undergo "psychological counseling." But now he called her probation officer and "told the officer that he thought the requirement of psychological counseling [for Lo] was no longer necessary" as part of her probation. Perhaps some fog had cleared from the judge's head, and he suddenly realized the bear trap he had laid for himself by requiring Lo to talk with a psychologist as a requirement of probation.

Can't you just hear this conversation in the shrink's office as Ms. Lo lies on the black-leather couch?

Shrink: ". . . Um, what was that you said, Ms. Lo?"
Lo: "I like to bake cookies."
Shrink: "No, before that."
Lo: "About the sex?"
Shrink: "Yes, that . . ."
Lo: "I said I was having sex with the judge who sentenced me."

Back to reality. In his telephone call to the probation officer, the judge suggested that the term of Lo's probation "need not continue for the full five years." In other words, Judge Trammell is sleeping with a female defendant who is on probation and must report monthly to a probation officer, and her secret lover, the judge, is hinting that he might now lop time off of the sentence he gave her before he became her sex partner. To accomplish this, the judge then called Lo's new attorney – the one he selected for her – and "told the attorney that when Lo approached the one-year anniversary of her probation, he wanted the attorney to file a motion to terminate probation, which he would be inclined to grant." Lo's attorney later told the judicial performance commission that Judge Trammell also "told him that Jin and Chu had filed motions for a new trial based on ineffective assistance of counsel, that he thought they were well taken, and that he believed Lo's case had been 'over-filed' [by the D.A.] and that she had 'over-pled.'"

So, for a moment, dear reader, let's recap this ugly but true courthouse drama.

It must be understood that Judge Trammell declined to testify at a judicial commission hearing, citing his fifth amendment right against self-incrimination by being forced to "witness" for himself. This meant his side of the story cannot be fleshed out in official records. He knew his actions might lead to criminal charges against him.

For a moment consider Judge Trammell's original sentence of Lo. She faced a maximum of a dozen years in prison for the crimes she admitted to. Over the objections of the district attorney's office, which wanted a prison stay for her, the judge gave her probation – an extremely soft slap on the wrist. We'll never know whether, gazing at her from the court bench, Judge Trammell had fallen for this small, lithe and pretty woman in the months before her sentencing. Did he believe by giving her a lenient sentence and sparing her from jail, it'd ingratiate himself to her, and make it easier to get her into the sack?

Aristotle is credited with a famous quotation in jurisprudence: "The law is reason free from passion." As leavened by Judge Trammell, the law was anything but dispassionate when it came to his lover.

During the span of months in which he had sex multiple times with Lo at his house, the judge allegedly did the following: (1) Told Lo that her probation could be reduced from five years to one. (2) Told her attorney to file a motion to have her Mercedes and other seized property returned, apparently made up a story that the D.A. was revising the property forfeiture, and then ordered Lo's property returned. (3) Granted bail to convicted kidnapper-extortionist Chu, the babysitter, and set it at an obscenely low amount for the crime. (4) Essentially replaced Lo's attorney with another lawyer, this one of his own choosing, and paid for this attorney with a check. (5) Told Lo's probation officer that four years could be trimmed from her probation period, and suggested she no longer needed psychological counseling as part of her probation. (6) Told Lo's new attorney he should file a motion to terminate Lo's probation, a motion he was "inclined to grant." (7) Told Lo's attorney that ex-husband Jin's and Chu's motions for a new trial based on incompetence of their attorneys were "well-taken." Folks, a new trial would have cost many thousands of dollars. We don't know the judge's sexual proclivities. But his actions while presiding over the case of a woman he was secretly screwing was a perversion of justice.

What the judge didn't know was the whole sordid affair was about to crash down on his receding hairline and chubby cheeks.

◇

On January 2nd, 1997, deputies belonging to the county sheriff's anti-gang unit at the jail "intercepted" a letter written by Jin to his ex-wife, Lo. Included in the "correspondence" was a "petition alleging sexual misconduct by Judge Trammell." Jin also mentioned that "Lo had collected pubic hair from the judge as proof of their sexual relationship" and that the judge had "fallen in love" with Lo, and had offered to "take care of her and her three children when Jin went to prison." This petition was to be filed with the court of appeals. In a note to his ex-wife, Jin wrote: "Wife: make one copy and send it . . . and please keep the original." It is speculation, but perhaps the ex-husband believed that Judge Trammell was going to sentence him to life in prison so he could have his ex-wife all to himself. Anyways, with the capture of Jin's jailhouse letter, the jig was up.

Four days later three Los Angeles County Sheriff's investigators met with Judge Trammell and showed him Jin's "petition." In this conversation, "Judge Trammell admitted that Lo had been to his house once or twice, that he had called her four or five times and had taken her to dinner. He admitted telling her that he loved her, but denied having had sexual intercourse with her." The judge explained he had "invited Lo to his home" so he could "get close" to her because he feared he was being stalked by her ex-husband Jin's organized crime buddies. Judicial commission's files include some "evidence" that supports Judge Trammell's assertion that he was "being stalked." For instance, in August and early September of 1996, after Jin and Chu were convicted at the trial presided over by Judge Trammell, he reported a series of "unusual occurrences which he felt were designed to intimidate him." He told a deputy sheriff that Lo, Jin and Chu sent him "birthday cards" and he "wanted to know how they knew his birth date." The deputy sheriff offered to install a surveillance camera at the judge's home, but the judge declined, "stating that he and a prior live-in girlfriend had purchased a camera." Later, the judge's old girlfriend said they never bought a security camera. Judge Trammell also told the deputy that someone posing as the judge had deactivated his daughter's residential alarm; that he had prowlers at his home; and that one night he "discovered a shotgun that he had purchased . . . lying in the middle of his bed with . . . a [shell] in the chamber, and he normally did not leave it that way for safety purposes."

On the same day Judge Trammell met with the three sheriff's investigators he issued an order canceling the probation condition requiring Lo to receive psychological counseling. This was done without telling either her attorney or prosecutor in the case.

Three days later, sheriff's investigators served a search warrant on the judge's home and courthouse office. The following day, Judge Trammell "retired" from his $133,000-a-year job. California law bars a judge from collecting his retirement benefits if convicted of a felony involving his judicial office. The judge's benefit was $90,000 annually. As soon as he retired he moved to Florida. With the judge's retirement, the ex-husband sought a new trial for kidnapping, and another judge granted it based on Judge Trammell's suspected misdeeds. In granting Jin a new trial, Orange County Superior Court Judge Frank F. Fasel said it was possible that Jin had set up Trammell. But, he said that even if Jin had offered his ex-wife Lo as bait, a judge "shouldn't be biting." Jin then pleaded guilty to a lesser charge and was sentenced to prison. Think of it, Trammell's relationship with the man's ex-wife caused a jury verdict of guilty of kidnapping for ransom to be set aside. Then as a result of Jin's plea deal, he skated from the possibility of spending the rest of his life in prison. Talk about a horned-dog judge totally screwing up the system of justice. As a prosecutor involved in the case put it: "The entire post-trial proceeding has been an embarrassment to the legal system."

◇

In an investigation that concluded two years after Judge Trammell's retirement, the California Commission on Judicial Performance stated it would have removed the judge from office if he had not already quit. It found "clear and convincing" evidence" that "Judge Trammell had a sexual relationship with Lo from mid-September 1996 through early January 1997," ruling that he "engaged in willful misconduct in carrying on, and actively concealing, a sexual relationship with Lo, while she was a probationer under his supervision and he was presiding over the criminal cases against her two co-defendants, and in using his judicial office to further his relationship with Lo." Evidence against him included Lo's testimony, telephone billing records showing numerous calls between Judge Trammell and Lo, four of which were tape-recorded by the sneaky woman. The commission stated the obvious: "Judge Trammell had served on the bench for 25 years when he first met Lo. He clearly understood not only that the relationship was improper but also that he could not ethically continue to preside over her case and those of her co-defendants." However, the commission found the evidence insufficient to say he coerced her into sex. In fact, in a 2001 civil case filed by Lo against the state of California, in which she sought $20 million in damages for the judge's actions, jurors heard a tape of the judge and Lo having sex. On the tape, Lo "sounded happy and more the aggressor in the relationship," jurors said. Judge Trammell is heard saying, "I love you" at the end of the tape he had recorded without Lo knowing. The jury rejected her claim, and said a female juror, "We thought [the sex] was consensual." She said Lo wasn't a credible witness, adding, "There was so much evidence that pointed to the judge [being] not guilty based on the evidence we had." Accusing Trammell of sexual battery, her suit sought to hold the state liable as his employer. The heart of the case was ripped away when an appellate court ruled that "a judge cannot, as a matter of law, be supervised by the state." An attorney who defended California in the suit said Lo and her ex-husband "used the judge's attraction for her to achieve something they needed." Jin had warned Judge Trammell that his sexual relationship with Lo would be made public unless "you take care of me," said the lawyer, adding that "it's pretty clear the intent was blackmail."

◊

For you quick-witted readers who wonder whether the judge committed "crimes" in what he did, the answer is yes, but not the ones you might think. After the L.A. district attorney failed to charge the judge, claiming they could not build a solid case against him for rape, federal prosecutors stepped in as they often do when states fail to act. The U.S. Attorney's Office in Los Angeles charged the former judge with abusing his authority by arranging for Lo to reclaim the Mercedes and Rolex watches seized in her arrest. Because he used the U.S. mail to send a check to Lo's attorney who wrote the motion for return of the car, prosecutors charged the judge with "mail fraud." He faced 10 years in prison and a half-million dollar fine. "This individual, entrusted with the most sacred of responsibilities, abused his power and corrupted the administration of justice," a federal prosecutor said. "This is a crime of the worst kind." In the federal criminal case against the former judge, Lo claimed Trammell forced her to have sex by threatening to send her ex-husband to prison for life if she did not comply. Trammell countered that he was set up by Lo and her gangster ex-husband. In 2000 at the age of 64, the disgraced judge pleaded guilty to two counts of mail fraud and was sentenced to 27 months in federal prison. The sentence was harsher than the 18-month prison stay prosecutors had agreed to in Judge Trammell's plea bargain. His sentencing judge said Trammell's actions were a "betrayal of the public's trust." U.S. District Judge A. Howard Matz told the man now in the dock rather than on the bench that he was punishing Trammell because of the "inherently coercive" nature of his relationship with Lo, saying Trammell "definitely pressured her to have sex."

In 2016, at the age of 80, former Judge Trammell died in Long Beach, California. It appeared the last 15 years of his life were spent in relative contentment, and his troubled past had disappeared. Wrote an acquaintance in his mortuary prayerbook: "I am sad to hear of his passing. I met him in 2014 at his daughter's house . . . and spent two days with him. I have nothing but respect for how he changed my life meeting him . . . May his family know that he was loved by many and I wish them love and many years of happiness. God bless George, he was truly an angel here on earth."

◊

It was inevitable given the quantitative evidence. In 2023 a *Forbes* magazine survey showed that six of ten people have had romances involving a person they work with, and 40 percent of these cheated on a current partner, husband or wife.

So, yes, this happens to jurists as well. Take the case in Illinois of Judges Scott D. Drazewski and Rebecca Foley, which began in 2010 and wasn't litigated before the Judicial Inquiry Board until 2014 because, well, nobody wanted to talk about it.

The two McLean County circuit court judges had worked at the courthouse, and had served on committees together. In December 2010, both married with children, the judges attended a conference in Washington, D.C., where they began an extramarital affair, according to Illinois Courts Commission records. And, if it matters, when the married judges got together they apparently weren't playing Scrabble because the inquiry commission contended that between December 5th, 2010 and February 17th, 2011 the affair "had been sexually intimate." The affair stayed somewhat quiet, although people around the courthouse, including attorneys and other judges, began to notice that the two jurists spent a lot of time together in their respective offices "behind closed" doors.

That's always a tip off in the workplace.

In Bloomington, Illinois, others noticed that at meetings Judge Drazewski and Judge Foley would sit and text each other on their phones and seemed "flirtatious" with one another. As the courts commission noted the affair "became a matter of public knowledge and concern to, among others, the legal community, judges and court staff." True, workplace romances generally amount to private affairs, however, with married judges hopping in bed with each other it gets complicated. Just so happened that Judge Rebecca Foley's husband was an attorney and as it would also happen at a community courthouse, her lover presided over "a number of pending cases in which Foley's husband, Joseph Foley, represented various parties."

That's really what got Judge Drazewski into hot water with the judicial discipline board.

On December 13th, 2010, Mr. Foley, an insurance attorney, represented a client in a three-day trial before his wife's boyfriend and essentially lost the case. Judge Drazewski decided against Mr. Foley's client and awarded the other side $40,000. Now there wasn't evidence that the judge ruled against his girlfriend's husband because of the sexual affair, and in fact, Mr. Foley said later that if he thought that were true he would have put it in court motions. The inquiry commission found it interesting that on the first day of the trial Drazewski and Judge Foley exchanged 105 text messages, although Judge Drazewski later told the board that the texts were about "their respective lives" and not about cases before him. However, Judge Drazewski also told the commission that he understood, in light of the affair, how his "impartiality might be questioned."

In mid-February of 2011, possibly because of hearsay around the courthouse, Mr. Foley confronted his wife about having the affair, and she admitted it. Obviously he had a lot of things to say, but one of them, according to the Illinois commission, was that she tell her paramour to "recuse" or take himself off all cases being handled by Mr. Foley in Judge Drazewski's court. The records state, Mr. Foley told his wife that if Judge Drazewski did not remove himself from hearing his cases "[Mr. Foley] was going to notify Mrs. Drazewski." (That's something like an appeal to the highest court in the land!) After Judge Foley spoke to Judge Drazewski he took himself off Mr. Foley's cases.

However, later when the chief judge of the court asked Judge Drazewski why he was recusing himself from Mr. Foley's cases he did not volunteer it was because of his affair with Judge Foley. It might sound strange to non-judge and non-lawyer readers, but the Illinois commission believed that Judge Drazewski should have come clean about the affair at that time, while the judge maintained that he didn't have to do it. Also, a bit weird, was that when the court's chief judge asked for a legal opinion on whether she was required to report the affair between the two judges, she told the commission "she had been advised by legal counsel that it was not a reportable violation." Obviously this was a relief because she had known both judges for many years and respected them, and had given Drazewski a promotion in 2009.

Meanwhile the affair became courthouse gossip, with some attorneys saying it was "a black eye" for the local judiciary. It also spilled over at a meeting of judges celebrating retirement of a judge. As assembled judges listened, the retiring judge slipped this gem into his speech: "When two judges start a relationship that's going to affect the rest of us." The court's chief judge said she was so upset by the remark that she walked out of the meeting. Talk about an 800-pound gorilla in the room.

As respected Illinois Judge Jennifer Bauknecht told the Illinois commission, "Judges are to maintain the highest degree of professionalism and conduct both inside and outside their professional lives, and in Central Illinois it's still a big deal when somebody had an affair. And these were two judges that were having an affair . . . everybody knew about it . . . and I think the public lost confidence in the judiciary."

In 2014, after someone reported the affair to the Illinois judicial commission, it began investigating. As one might suspect, the inquiry board focused on the legal ramifications of the affair rather than the affair itself. The commission concluded that both judges had a duty to disclose their relationship during the time Judge Drazewski was hearing Mr. Foley's cases. "We conclude that under the circumstances when a judge presides over a trial involving the attorney/spouse of a person with whom that judge is having an undisclosed marital affair, and the judge does not disclose or recuse, that conduct not only has the appearance of impropriety, but is an impropriety."

In the commission's order in 2016, six years after the affair began, Judge Drazewski received the harshest punishment, a rare four-month suspension without pay, while Judge Foley got censured. Judge Foley, according to the commission, never "acknowledged any violations of the canon to the commission." Both Judge Drazewski and Judge Foley apologized for the "pain, suffering and humiliation" the affair caused their respective families.

By the time attorney Mr. Foley testified before the commission he and his wife had divorced, as he is referred to in records as "the former husband of Rebecca Foley." Additionally, in 2021, years after the discipline order, 63-year-old Circuit Judge Drazewski retired after 22 years on the bench. At that time it was reported that he had "faced ethics charges related to an undisclosed romantic relationship with another judge, Rebecca Foley, to whom he is now married." Also in a strange bit of irony, one of the applicants to replace retiring Mr. Drazewski as judge was the attorney he had replaced as husband of Judge Foley – Joseph Foley.

◊

The California judicial ethics code is mute on the specific question of judges having sex in their chambers, although one might suspect that a judge ought to know he shouldn't being do that. Still, after the disciplinary cases of Orange County Superior Court Judge Scott Steiner and Cory Woodward, a judge in Kern County, the state might want to add a specific ban on "judge office sex." Both judges engaged in sex in their private chambers. Now we know why judges' offices usually have comfy sofas.

Shockingly, neither judge lost his job over the indiscretion. Where but in government and in a porn-film factory can you have sex in the workplace and not be fired? (I worked at a newspaper where a couple had sex in the newsroom. Yeah, they had to hit the pavement. I also knew a guy who screwed an editor in the photography darkroom. Sorry, there were no pictures.) Judges can be clever devils. They know when they are caught red handed – say in a sex scandal – all they have to do is "stipulate" to sanitized facts in the case. A stipulation is a legal term meaning both sides agreed to what is said. Thus, it spares the judiciary from a lengthy, painstaking and costly investigation of prying evidence out of people who would rather not talk. As a result, once a stipulated censure is announced the barest of factual information on the judge's indiscretion is released to the public by the judicial discipline commission. Both of these sex cases – California Judge Scott Steiner and California Judge Cory Woodward – were resolved by stipulation. Therefore, while these disciplinary cases were mostly about issues of judges having sex in their offices, the public record is threadbare of juicy and titillating facts, and in fact, hardly reveal enough to rate a single X, if it were a pornographic film.

For instance, while the commission reports that a judge having sex in his office is a bad idea because others might see or hear something embarrassing, it doesn't tell the public how these acts were discovered, whether by a cleaning lady walking in on them while they thumped and bumped, or by a female court clerk outside the door hearing moans and an exhilarating scream of sexual climax.

So, from the official file, here's judicial soft porn.

Orange County Superior Court Judge Scott Steiner, then 38, was censured but not removed from office for admitting that he had sex with two women in his office in 2012. He admitted having sex once with one woman at night and twice with the other woman during the day, but not when court was in session. The women were both former law students of Judge Steiner, a former prosecutor and teacher at the Chapman School of Law. He had a "personal relationship" with the women at the time of the intimacy. The fact that the women were once his students probably wasn't a fact ignored by Chapman's administrators. Surprisingly, even after disclosure of having sex in his office, which of course wasn't equipped with a bed – chambers usually have a nice big sofa for judges to nap on – he was re-elected as judge in 2016.

Here is the official version of his sex with "Ms. A and Ms. B.," as the official record referred to them. How about if we call them, instead, Ms. A. for "Ms. Arraignment," and Ms. B. for "Ms. Bifurcation."

"Judge Steiner engaged in sexual activity in his chambers on multiple occasions, with [these] two women with whom he was engaged in personal relationships," the official account of the activity stated. "This included engaging in sexual intercourse with 'Ms. Arraignment' in his chambers on one occasion in the evening in early 2012, and engaging in sexual intercourse with 'Ms. Bifurcation' in his chambers on two occasions during the work day, although not while court was in session, in May 2012."

(The judge showed good judgment in not having sex in his office during court sessions because jurors probably would have wondered what all the moaning and bumping was all about on the other side of the mahogany wall.)

"Ms. Arraignment" had been an intern working for the judge, and "Ms. Bifurcation" was an attorney practicing at Orange County Superior Court. One can see there wasn't a lot of steamy action in this stipulated settlement report.

Oddly, the Steiner sex case would play a major role in another judge being admonished publicly by the judges' discipline commission. Near-rookie Judge Jeff Ferguson of the Orange County Superior Court supported Judge Steiner in his successful re-election campaign in 2016. Steiner was opposed by Deputy District Attorney Karen Schatzle, and during the election Schatzle decided to make some political hay out of Steiner's in-chambers sexual escapades. She posted the following on the Facebook page of the North Orange County Bar Association: "Scott Steiner uses his office for sex and yet so many aren't concerned; crazy politics!"

Judge Ferguson shot back, posting: "Karen Schatzle has sex with defense lawyer while she is D.A. [district attorney] on his cases and nobody cares. Interesting politics." His Facebook page was open to all local attorneys who were members of the local Bar Association. Candidate Karen Schatzle and the defense attorney denied "any intimate involvement while they were appearing on the same cases," and Steiner supporter Judge Ferguson removed the post.

The judicial commission ruled that Judge Ferguson's post, claiming Schatzle was "having sex at the time or had sex in the past, with [a] defense attorney while she was prosecutor on his cases was made with knowing or reckless disregard for the truth."

Meantime, the in-chambers-sex case against Judge Cory Woodward of Kern County involved his married court clerk, and they had sex during business hours. He stipulated to findings of the commission and was publicly censured. "From approximately July 2012 through mid-May 2013, Judge Woodward was involved in an intimate relationship with the clerk," the records stated. Even after the judge changed jobs by moving to another courtroom in another division of the court, he insisted that the clerk come along with him. (Hey, why wouldn't he?)

"During Judge Woodward's intimate relationship with the clerk, he engaged in sexual activity with her in [his] chambers," the state commission stated. "He also engaged in sexual activity with her in public places." Sometime in early 2013 the judge was leaving the bench during a break and he "made an inappropriate sexual gesture toward the clerk while a member of the public was present in the audience (unbeknownst to the judge)." The commission did not disclose what the "sexual gesture" was. The commission also disclosed that the judge passed notes "during court proceedings" of "a sexual nature" but failed to say what they said. The judge also allowed his sex-partner clerk to address him informally by a "longstanding nickname" used by other judges for him in front other court employees. (Wasn't it law professor Anita Hill who told Congress that U.S. Supreme Court Justice Clarence Thomas mentioned the nickname, "Long Dong Silver"?) The commission doesn't disclose the pet name for Judge Woodward. (Wonder if it was "Woodie"?)

In February 2013, more than a half of a year into their affair, the local court's executive officer told Judge Woodward that the "clerk's husband had reportedly expressed concern . . . about the judge's relationship" with his wife. The exec suggested that the clerk be reassigned and the judge said he would talk to her about it. Thereafter, "Judge Woodward called" the executive "and said that he would not be making any change to the clerk's assignment," and said the "clerk had talked to her husband, that they may be separating, and that her husband was angry with her." The commission failed to disclose whether it was the judge's affair with his married clerk that was causing the end of her marriage.

A month later a supervising judge met with Judge Woodward and told him another clerk had complained that his clerk was calling him by his nickname and was engaged in "flirtatious behavior" towards the judge. This judge suggested Woodward reassign his clerk and the judge declined. "He stated she was a good clerk." However, when another complaint came in about his clerk's behavior, the court reassigned her. The court executive "explained that the court was reassigning the clerk in response to reports of inappropriate behavior toward Judge Woodward, including the use of a nickname." When Woodward acted like he didn't know what it was all about, another judge put it to him bluntly. "The problem is people think something is going on between the two of you," the judge told him, to which Judge Woodward did not respond. Then the other judge said that the court "can't be reacting to something when someone thinks this is a Peyton Place when this isn't."

Judge Woodward did not respond to the comment.

In May, a couple of months later, Judge Woodward met with the presiding judge and assistant presiding judge to address "possible security concerns raised by the fact that the husband of Judge Woodward's clerk had contacted the court." During this meeting Judge Woodward misled the two judges about the nature of his relationship with the clerk, according to commission records. Later in the month, however, he came clean and confessed that he had an "intimate relationship" with the clerk.

As Judge David M. Rothman stated in his California Judicial Conduct Handbook, when a judge's sexual conduct is not conducted in private or "takes place on public property or by use of public resources, the conduct moves from private to public concern and demeans the judicial office." Here is what the California misconduct commission wrote about judges having sex in their offices: "Engaging in sexual intercourse in the courthouse is the height of irresponsible and improper behavior by a judge. It reflects an utter disrespect for the dignity and decorum of the court and is seriously at odds with a judge's duty to avoid conduct that tarnishes the esteem of the judicial office in the public's eye. In addition, by engaging in sexual activity in chambers during court hours . . . risk[s] exposing court employees who might overhear or otherwise become aware of the libidinous conduct to a hostile work environment."

◊

Sexual misconduct by a Buffalo, N.Y. judge who resigned in 1993 was especially appalling, and a case instructive in how members of official bodies that discipline judges wrangle over punishment. At age 53, Erie County, New York Family Court Judge Anthony P. LoRusso had been on the bench for 16 years when he suddenly quit for "personal and professional reasons" – among them a three-year-old investigation by the New York State Commission on Judicial Conduct for workplace sexual harassment, including having sex in his chambers with a court stenographer more than a decade earlier. The record has numerous examples of misconduct, involving a handful of women who worked at the courthouse. In 1988 a woman known only as "Ms. D" in commission records claimed the judge came up behind her when she was sitting, breathed heavily and kissed the top of her head, whispering that he had just been talking to attorneys about "delicious and delectable blow jobs." She said he did the same thing again a year later. Another woman alleged he touched her ass, and she warned him, "Don't do that!"

It was years before in 1978, moreover, when the married judge was 37 years old and had engaged in repeated seemingly "consensual" sex acts with the stenographer in his office that caused the commission its intellectual dyspepsia. The judge didn't deny he was "intimate" with the woman. The woman, described as "unworldly" and sexually naive, was 19-years-old when the judge hired her with her proud papa's approval – "we'll take the job" – fresh out of stenographer school. For two years she worked as

Judge LoRusso's court reporter and secretary in Buffalo City Court. Then when she was 21, the judge overheard her tell court clerks that she felt "bloated" after eating so much during the holidays. Judge LoRusso called the woman, identified as only "Ms. A" in commission records, into his office and told her that "he could check to see whether she was 'retaining water.'" He told her to go into his private bathroom in his chambers and to "remove her pantyhose." He then "lifted her skirt above her knees, pressed his fingers on her thighs, rubbed her legs and told her to get dressed." The woman did not protest the prurient "examination." Weeks passed and the judge told the woman that he should again check her for "the problem." Back in his office, and having locked the door, he "directed" her to remove her pantyhose. This time he touched her thigh, and "pulled down her underwear and touched her vagina." Ms. A told the commission that "she had never been touched there before," and that over coming months as the judge's "sexual activity" "escalated," she was "subjected to conduct with which she was totally unfamiliar."

Three weeks after first touching the compliant woman's private parts, the judge called her into his office. She "found him in the bathroom with his penis exposed." The judge put her hand on his dick, and said "he would 'teach' her." Weeks later the old letch called "Ms. A" in again, and this time told her to take off her pantyhose and sit on the couch. "He removed her underwear, rubbed her vagina and performed oral sex," commission records stated. Two weeks later in his chambers, the judge "took her hand and placed it on his clothed crotch. He then exposed his penis and pushed Ms. A's head down toward it and had her perform oral sex." It was, in his own words, one of those "delicious and delectable blow jobs." A few weeks later, the judge had sexual intercourse with the woman while she laid on her back on his desk. In other acts he had anal sex with her and at some point, "administered an enema" to her. During the anal sex after the woman complained of pain, the judge stopped. After that, no further sexual contact took place between them.

The sex acts took place near the end of the workday after court sessions. "There was little, if any, conversation" beyond the judge's "directions to Ms. A," and during these encounters she referred to him as "judge." The woman told the commission: "I did whatever he told me to do." The court stenographer also testified that while she didn't protest having sex with the judge, she sometimes "cried" afterwards and "experienced physical discomfort during the activity and afterward." She said that "after each incident, she hoped the contact would end." Asked by commission members if she feared losing her job if she didn't do what the judge directed her to do, she replied: "I didn't know what he could do. I didn't know if he could arrange for me to lose my job. I did not know." Once the sex stopped, Ms. A worked with the judge another decade and attended family and social gatherings with him.

The commission ruled that the judge "took advantage of her innocence, her submissive nature and her inferior position in the workplace to subject her to a series of sexual indignities," adding that "once he learned that she would submit without protest, he escalated the nature of the activity in each successive encounter." The woman only revealed the sex after she learned about another woman's sexual harassment complaint against the same judge. The female court employee had brought cookies to the courthouse to share in 1988, and testified that after he ate some the judge whispered: "I had an orgasm eating your cookies."

Obviously seeing the writing on the wall, the judge resigned from office days after he attended the commission's final session on his discipline case in March 1993. While the commission voted to remove him from office, it was on the issue of sex with "Ms. A" being consensual that caused member dissent. The majority agreed that the judge's sexual harassment of female employees established "a pattern of conduct prejudicial to the administration of justice, warranting removal from office." It also stated that his "sexual encounters with Ms. A constitute misconduct. By his own admission, Ms. A was an immature 19 year old when he gave her a job . . . The record demonstrates that she was still unworldly, docile and submissive two years later when [he] directed her in a series of passionless sexual experiments in his locked chambers over an eight-month period."

The majority addressed the issue of consensual sex. "A woman who does not protest does not necessarily acquiesce. There is a power imbalance between employer and employee that often makes a worker in need of her job feel she must swallow such indignities." Although the judge "never explicitly told the women who were subjected to his unwelcome conduct that their jobs were at stake . . . there was always the implicit threat that a person in his position could impair their job security."

One commission member, a judge himself, said he disagreed that the sex with "Ms. A" "constituted" judicial misconduct because it was consensual. The judge "never in any way communicated to Ms. A that her court position would be at all affected if she did not consent to sexual activity with him," the member wrote. "Conversely, Ms. A never in any way communicated or indicated" that "his advances were unwelcome or that she preferred not to engage in sexual activity with him. Rather, the evidence . . . reveals that she was a willing, albeit passive and inexperienced, participant in the sexual activity . . . I do not find misconduct from a sexual relationship between two consenting adults in private – regardless of the relative positions, ages or marital status of the participants, the degree of passivity or enthusiasm of one of the partners, or the choice of sexual activity."

Of course this member and another, a judge who didn't buy Judge LoRusso's sex with the young stenographer as "judicial misconduct," somehow overlooked the fact that the sex took place in the courthouse in the judge's private office with the door locked, and at least once on his desktop. Having sex in in the judge's office was never framed as an issue. You mean, really, having sex in a judge's office isn't judicial misconduct? If not, what is? It's doubly troubling when a member of a judicial misconduct commission states that a judge who has had "consensual sex" in his chambers isn't doing anything wrong. Plainly this dirtbag judge had to be fired.

◊

The matter of a judge in Tucson, Arizona is an example of what disciplinary commissions across the nation loathe most. That a judge's bias will influence his decisions. In the case of Tucson Municipal Court Judge Theodore Abrams that appears to be what happened, because a very young attorney refused to have sex with him. It is also a case in which a reasonable observer is forced to wonder whether the judge even had the intelligence to serve on the bench, if only because he became "harsh" with the attorney after she declined his sexual overtures. A judge since 2002, Judge Abrams was sexually involved with a female criminal defense attorney in the summer of 2008, an affair that lasted into the next year. Often, according to the Arizona Commission on Judicial Conduct, the attorney appeared in the judge's courtroom on cases and the judge "neither disqualified himself nor disclosed the relationship to the parties or other counsel." The affair ended, and the attorney introduced the fortysomething Judge Abrams to a young assistant public defender fresh from law school, Sharolynn

Griffiths, whose name appeared in separate court records because she later sued the city of Tucson for sexual harassment.

For more than a year afterwards the judge tried to get his hooks into the younger woman, and she rebuffed his unwanted advances. At one point she told him that "a sexual relationship would be improper because of his position as a judge, her routine appearances in his court, and the fact that he is married."

Still the judge's apparent unquenched sexual appetite persisted. "Between November 2009 and October 2010, Abrams left" the young attorney "at least 28 voicemail messages and sent her at least 85 text messages, many of which included sexual innuendos or explicit sexual content," the commission's investigation found. "In December 2009, Abrams left [her] a voicemail message that even he [later] characterized as 'obscene.'" In the message the judge "described a sexual act he wanted to perform on her." The following day he asked the young attorney to come to his office "to pick up some paperwork." While there he asked her if she had gotten his voicemail message. He then said he wanted to "take her to a friend's condominium for sex." When the woman declined, the judge "inappropriately touched" her and later called and repeated his "obscene" voicemail message. At about this time the judge "reminded" the new assistant public defender that she was still on "probationary" employment status and of "his connections in the community."

Implicitly, the message was clear: he could have her canned.

At some point the judge "groped" the young attorney "under a table at which they were sitting with others after work." He also made "slurping noises" to her.

For more than a year, Abrams repeatedly pursued a sexual relationship with her.

Unknowingly functioning as a would-be pimp, his old girlfriend, the woman he had carried on the affair with, also had introduced the judge to a second woman attorney, a prosecutor. True to form Judge Abrams began hitting on her, sending her "sexually explicit emails."

Well after assistant public defender Ms. Griffiths had declined all of the judge's sexual overtures, she appeared in his courtroom for her very first trial. Once the prosecution finished its case against her defendant-client, the young attorney properly asked for a dismissal. "[Judge] Abrams became upset in the courtroom and accused [her] of wasting judicial resources, violating her duty of candor, and committing a fraud on the court," the commission found. "He denied the motion and declared a mistrial." Calling his comments to her "uncharacteristically harsh and inappropriate treatment," a county Superior Court investigator would later state the opinion that "Abrams' actions against" the female attorney "were in retaliation for her rejecting his sexual advances and telling a mutual friend about them."

In a statement of apparent denial, according to an investigator assigned to look into the case, "Abrams claims that [the attorney] did not necessarily object to [his] sexual comments," and "continues to maintain that he does not feel he was harassing her."

Other than that, to his credit, Judge Abrams was forthcoming with the state commission. He told the commission that "his misconduct arose from personal and emotional problems." He said he had undergone open heart surgery in 2007 and "became addicted to pain medication and developed severe depression." He contended that "these problems made it difficult" for him to "control his impulses," "affected his judgment" and "led to inappropriate relationships and communications."

The commission didn't buy it, though, saying that there was no evidence to show one caused the other. The judge also claimed that "he sought psychiatric treatment before the allegations of sexual harassment came to light." And, once the allegations came out, he "admitted himself to an intensive substance abuse and psychiatric treatment program." The judge claimed he lacked a "dishonest or selfish motive" in his actions, a claim the Arizona Supreme Court disregarded, stating that "clearly [he] displayed a selfish motive by pursuing his own sexual interests without regard for his oath and duties to the legal system."

The investigative commission recommended his firing, which both the state Supreme Court and the judge himself agreed with. The city council of Tucson also voted to terminate his judgeship.

◊

Here's a question for female attorneys. What do you say when you're alone with a judge in his chambers and he tells you he has the hots for your body and kisses you, sticking his tongue deep into your mouth?

"Hey, I'm not French!"

Little weak.

Kick him in the nuts?

That'd be cool . . . and effective.

Or, you just stay the heck out of the office of Judge Arthur S. Block, a judge of the old Riverside County, California Municipal

Court until it was merged with Superior Court in 2000. Once censured, Judge Block retired when the judicial discipline commission finished its investigation of his "alleged inappropriate sexual conduct" and other allegations.

Judge Block might not equal an all-star groper like actor and former California Governor Arnold Schwarzenegger, who was accused of groping and sexually humiliating women for three decades on movie sets, and finally admitted that he had "behaved badly."

Yet Judge Block did his share. During a juvenile hearing in February 2001, Judge Block called a female lawyer for the county up to the bench for a "sidebar" conference, but failed to invite the opposing party's attorney, which was highly irregular. While she was in front of him and close, the judge "reached out as if to fasten a button on the front of her suit."

The woman said she was "startled and offended" and backed away, buttoning her suit herself.

A couple months later during a juvenile dependency hearing the same female attorney went into the judge's office during a break, along with attorneys for the parents of the juvenile. "After discussing certain issues in the case, the attorneys began to leave chambers to return to the courtroom to resume the proceedings," the California Commission on Judicial Performance wrote in its findings. "Judge Block asked the female attorney to remain and to close the door. Judge Block was seated behind his desk, with the woman seated across from him. Judge Block told her that he was attracted to her. Judge Block walked around his desk and had her stand. Judge Block kissed her, putting his tongue in her mouth. When Judge Block released her, she left his chambers and returned to court." The commission lambasted the judge for not "disclosing what had happened in chambers" when he returned to the bench. (Come on. When I read that line in the official report, I laughed. Yeah, right, the judge is going to come back into open court and say, "Oh, for the record, I just sloppily French kissed the county's attorney in my office. Let's proceed.")

Another sex-related allegation against Judge Block involved a Spanish interpreter who translated in his courtroom for juvenile litigants. During a hearing the interpreter was "leaning over a juvenile defendant" and the judge made a remark, saying in effect that he knew why so many young defendants were asking for her services as an interpreter. Later the commission wrote, addressing the judge personally: "You then asked the interpreter to approach the bench, and when she did, you said, in substance, that she knew why, and gestured toward and looked directly at her breasts."

The interpreter said she felt "embarrassed and offended." She later asked not to be sent back to his courtroom.

◇

In one of the stiffest fines ever levied against a judge for misconduct, the Indiana Supreme Court not only prevented Delaware County Superior Court Judge Joseph G. Edwards from ever running for judicial office again in the state, it body-slammed him with a $100,000 fine, essentially a refunding of his judge's salary to the state.

He had been elected to the Superior Court bench in 1996, took office in January 1997, and resigned 13 months later in the thick of a misconduct investigation by the Indiana Commission on Judicial Qualifications, which recommended the high court fire him. While the main charge against him occurred in 1991 when he was an attorney, from 1989 to 1996 he also worked as a part-time probate judge, which is why the state's judicial discipline body investigated him. It's a case which must have rankled the sensitivities of the Supreme Court justices because the main charge of misconduct was his handling of the divorce of an 18-year-old whose husband was arrested for murdering a Muncie cop. Because the woman was penniless, she and Joseph G. Edwards, the then-attorney agreed to trade sex for his legal work on her divorce and child custody case.

In 1991, then-attorney and part-time judge Mr. Edwards filed her divorce petition in Delaware County, Indiana Superior Court, and the woman had "sexual relations with [him] in exchange for [his] representation," commission records stated. "She continued to have a sexual relationship with him until sometime in 1994," records said. During this relationship, the attorney gave her "cash in exchange for sex" and sometimes gave her money, without having had sex. He told her to use a fake name when she called his office, and instructed her to tell others that her "father" had paid her legal bills.

But, shortly after filing the woman's divorce petition the attorney asked that it be dismissed. He apparently had extra-judicial things in mind. Because her divorce was mentioned in a newspaper story about the police officer's murder, along with the attorney's name, he told the woman he would refile the divorce in nearby Henry County, which was about 25 miles south of Delaware County. Significantly, attorney Edwards served as a part-time probate commissioner of the Henry County, Indiana

Circuit Court, and also as a temporary judge on the same court. In other words as an on-again, off-again employee at the Henry County courthouse he had access to such things as clerk's stamps and other items used to authenticate court records. According to commission documents, in March 1992 the attorney gave the woman "what appeared on its face to be a legitimate divorce decree from the Henry Circuit Court. The document purported to grant her a divorce" and give her "legal custody of her child."

The document was fake.

"File stamps were generally accessible to officials and employees of the Henry Circuit Court, to the Henry County Clerk's office, and to [attorney Edwards]" in his capacity as a part-time judicial officer at the courthouse. A handwriting expert testified at the commission's misconduct trial of Edwards that the date on the faked divorce decree was the same handwriting on documents in court files at the courthouse which had been signed by Edwards when acting as part-time judge. Stated the Indiana Supreme Court: "We agree with the conclusion of the [commission] that [then-attorney Edwards] was responsible for the preparation of the fraudulent dissolution decree."

But, wait, we're getting ahead of ourselves, because the woman's legal headache was just beginning. The attorney told her that the Henry County Circuit Court document meant she was legally divorced and that she had been awarded custody of her child, and of course, she believed him. She followed up by informing her jailed "ex-husband" of the divorce. Later, the faked divorce document showed up in an adoption case in Delaware Superior Court. The State of Indiana had initiated a suit to strip the woman of her parental rights and allow her child to be adopted, which was ultimately approved. The woman stopped her relationship with attorney Edwards when she lost her child. At the adoption hearing the woman told a judge that her attorney Mr. Edwards, had handled her divorce. When the judge then asked him if he had represented the woman, Edwards said "he did not know" the woman and "never had a connection with her," according to commission records.

It was in the adoption case that truth about the faked divorce decree reared its ugly head. When a judge asked Edwards about a phony stamp on the document, the attorney lied, explaining that "someone" had taken and misused the signature stamp. When another judge asked Edwards whether he had ever represented the

18-year-old woman, his lies continued. Edwards said he had not. Only later did he admit to a judge that she had been his client.

When the woman learned that her divorce decree wasn't worth the paper it was printed on and had absolutely no legal validity, she called Edwards on it. "He advised her that there may have been a glitch in the computer system causing the decree to become lost." He then "dictated" what she should write down to "put the divorce back in the computer." Edwards then took the paper written in the woman's hand, and tried to file it in court. When an eagle-eyed Henry County deputy clerk "inquired" about the "propriety" of the attorney who was a "part-time" probate judge filing a "pleading in Henry Circuit Court," Edwards promised he would "get out of the case." When the same clerk looked at the handwritten divorce petition and called it "junk," he said, "Maybe so, but . . . she [woman] really needs to get it filed."

The handwritten document was a clumsy effort to fix the fake divorce decree, with an actual divorce petition in the woman's handwriting, one without the attorney's name mentioned anywhere in it.

The Supreme Court stated in its findings that Edwards faked the divorce decree and "he provided it to . . . his client, with the false representation that she had obtained a divorce and legal custody of her child when in fact neither event had occurred. [He] lied to [two judges] about his representation of [the woman]. And [he] performed legal services . . . in exchange for sexual favors." There were other charges of misconduct against Edwards. Given the details of the sex and faked divorce, the Supreme Court had little leeway to have done anything else but fire him as a judge. As is often the case, he resigned three months before the final decision by the court, in May 1998, which stated: "Joseph G. Edwards is permanently enjoined from ever seeking judicial office of any kind in the State of Indiana. He is disbarred from the practice of law and permanently enjoined from seeking reinstatement as a lawyer." Both actions were serious enough, but it was the big fine that was most startling. "We further fine [him] $100,000," the court stated. "The fine will be suspended if Edwards documents to the satisfaction of the commission that he has reimbursed the State of Indiana for all judicial salaries he received as part-time probate commissioner in the Henry Circuit Court during the time period [and] he was the full-time judge pro tempore of Delaware Superior Court" from 1983 to 1994.

The trial before three "masters" or judges on his misconduct lasted three days, heard from 32 witnesses and had 55 exhibits. To pour salt on an open flesh wound, the justices "further assessed [Edwards] with the costs of these actions." These justices must have been really offended.

As a footnote, the woman's husband was convicted and sentenced to death for shooting and killing the police officer in 1990 as he was being taken to jail for public intoxication. Another officer patted him down but had missed a gun the husband's pocket. He was executed by lethal injection in 2007.

◊

Judge W. Jackson Willoughby of the Placer County, California Superior Court had this habit of staring at his bailiff's breasts and touching them, apparently through her uniform. He even asked if he could see them up close and personal. After investigating, the commission stated: "The judge's touching of his bailiff's breasts as well as his staring at her breasts and asking to see them constituted conduct prejudicial to the administration of justice that brought the judicial office into disrepute." The commission noted that while his conduct was inappropriate he could still be reformed after they censured him in 2000, when he was 65 years old. Of course a judge who touches things that aren't his is probably likely to run afoul of rules in other ways.

The back story on the breast-touching is interesting. In 1998 the judge's female bailiff had breast-implant surgery and told the judge that she would be off a couple weeks and told him why. The judge asked her if the surgery was safe, and told her that "she was sexy just the way she was." The woman said she was losing weight at the time, and as the judge told her how nice she looked she didn't find the comment offensive "because everybody was telling her that." Then, "following the surgery" the judge "frequently stared at her breasts and on more than one occasion asked when he would get to see her breasts." After the surgery the woman got an infection in the surgery area, and one day, while she was out of uniform and the judge was "walking out of the restroom" he called her over. "He gave me a hug and told me he hoped that I was feeling better," she said. Afterward, she told commissioners, "[Judge Willoughby] just open-handedly grabbed both of my breasts and started rubbing."

Another time in his office, the woman said that she "made a number of complaints about her personal life" and Judge Willoughby comforted her, telling her to "hang in there." Here is what Judge Willoughby testified happened next: "Well, we, I hugged her, we hugged each other actually. So I had my arms around her and I was kind of patting her on the back . . . Well, what happened was probably the biggest mistake of my life. My hands went from holding her and it came around the side and I apparently caressed her left breast for a moment and then when I realized what I'd done, I immediately took my hand away." How did he think it made her feel? "I saw someone whom I thought felt better, was less upset than she was when she came into the chambers . . . She looked up at me and said, 'thank you for caring about me.'"

The commission investigators, however, found that there was "no credible evidence she was then or ever thankful for being grabbed in the breast area." Stated the investigators: "Judge Willoughby did not need any training on avoiding sexual harassment to know that it was wrong to touch his bailiff's breasts." The misconduct commission also said the judge's statement that his touching her breasts was not done "out of a sexual impulse" was not believable. The commission noted that the judge "recognized the impropriety of his touching his bailiff's breasts and issued a public apology."

In another instance, a bailiff was changing her shirt in a hallway where she had a locker and under her uniform shirt she wore a t-shirt. When she looked up she saw Judge Willoughby watching her, and she asked him if she was blocking his way. "I could stand here and watch you undress all day," he responded. The judge told the commission that he could not recall saying that, but if he did, it was in a "facetious or sarcastic fashion."

Judge Willoughby had a special name for a female deputy district attorney who practiced in his courtroom. "Old Iron Tits." At least that's what his clerk and bailiff told the commission. The judge told the commission he didn't remember calling her that, but "probably referred to the attorney in the derogatory fashion alleged."

Judge Willoughby said the deputy district attorney did a fine job in his courtroom, and that "the nickname did not originate with him." He said he had "heard the phrase at a judges' meeting," but he declined to rat out any other judges who might have used the derogatory sobriquet.

In another incident, when his female clerk asked him if she could leave the court, the judge remarked, "I just want you to sit there and look pretty." She also said he would "pucker" his lips and blow air kisses at her.

The judge's wife backed up her husband by saying he "often" blow kisses and hugged people.

Considering the touching of his bailiff's boobs, calling the deputy district attorney "old Iron Tits" and blowing kisses at his clerk, investigators stated that it all "constituted a pattern of inappropriate conduct in the workplace towards female court employees . . . ." As a result, the judge was publicly rebuked by the commission.

◊

Oh, yes, and then there is the judge who had sexual "fantasies." Los Angeles County Superior Judge Robert S. Stevens was a state senator in California when he was appointed as a judge by Democratic Governor Jerry Brown in 1977. In 1979, press reports began circulating that the judge, while a member of the state legislature, had talked about his sexual fantasies with a married couple who worked for the legislature.

After an investigation, the state commission censured Judge Stevens in 1981. He left the bench in 1983, retiring on disability.

According to records: "From January 1975 until August 1979 Judge Stevens repeatedly initiated conversations with [the married couple] . . . in which he discussed his sexual experiences and fantasies and proposed that [they] engage in various kinds of sexual activity with him and with other persons, all in explicit, vulgar, and offensive language. His purpose in doing so was to gratify his own sexual desires."

In an interview later in life he said he acknowledged having engaged in sexually explicit conversations with the couple, but said they also made statements. "It wasn't a case of [their] sitting and listening," he said. He said using the word "fantasy" was incorrect for the phone calls. "It was never a serious intention about anything," he said. "No offensive actions were ever anticipated or engaged in."

Apparently word about the judge's calls to the couple became public after they "sought help" in trying to stop him from talking about his desires. "Judge Stevens . . . should have known there was a substantial likelihood that his conduct would become known to many persons and thereby bring the judicial office into disrepute," the commission stated. The state Supreme Court censured him for "conduct prejudicial to the administration of justice."

The case was also interesting because Judge Stevens was censured for activity before ever becoming a judge. Rules of the California Supreme Court state that the court can punish a sitting judge for "actions occurring not more than six years prior to the commencement of the judge's current term." Obviously this case was unique because the judge's sexual remarks made newspaper headlines and the commission had to "do something" to prove its reason for being.

◊

Hands down this is one of the weirdest cases to come before the California commission on judge misconduct.

While in his office and putting on his robe, Judge John B. Gibson allegedly "wiggled his fingers through his robe in the area of his groin and said [to the female clerk], 'Say hello to Mr. Bobo.'"

Things like that soon get the attention of discipline people, and in later testimony before the commission the San Bernardino County Superior Court judge was asked, "Who is Mr. Bobo?"

Judge Gibson: "I'm told by my attorney who had his paralegals go on the internet, Mr. Bobo is one of those plastic blow-up clowns that has sand at the bottom of it. And if you strike it, it will rock back and then come to an upright position again. Until you told me that, I did not know."

Commission: "Did you ever know that Bobo has a Spanish origin?"

Judge: ". . . No, I did not."

Commission: "It means a boob, doesn't it?"

Judge: "So I'm told."

Commission: "Do you use the word or the phrase 'Mr. Bobo' in reference to yourself?"

Judge: "Yes."

Commission: "What do you mean when you use 'Mr. Bobo' in reference to yourself?"

Judge: "It's a name that implies a comedic small, diminutive figure."

Commission: "Round?"

Judge: "I hadn't thought of that. I suppose."

Commission: "Something that somebody beats on once in a while?"

Judge: "No. I never gave it that punching bag analogy."

Commission: "Did you ever say to [the clerk] in words or substance, 'Say hello to Mr. Bobo?'"

Judge: "Not in the context she's put it. If I did something that stupid, I would refer to myself by that name. Like, 'Mr. Bobo really blew that one.'"

Commission: "So you'd use it as a way of putting yourself down?"

Judge: "Yes."

Commission: "Did you ever stick your finger out of your robe when you were putting on your robe and say, 'Say hello to Mr. Bobo?'"

Judge Gibson: "No."

Commission: "Did you ever do that in substance?"

Judge: "I don't follow you."

Commission: "Did you ever say words to that effect and make such a gesture?"

Judge: "No."

Despite his denial, another court employee also told the commission that she saw Judge Gibson "in the hallway stick his finger out of the opening in front of his robe, below waist level, and say, 'Say hello to Mr. Bobo.'"

The commission found the judge's testimony on the "Bobo" issue wasn't "credible" and it investigators "found that the incidents occurred."

"Mr. Bobo" wasn't the only character to have gotten the judge in judicial hot water. In 2000 Judge Gibson was admonished by the Supreme Court for a "pattern of inappropriate conduct" towards "female court employees," mostly involving a courthouse clerk supervisor who worked closely with the judge.

The commission issued its weak punishment because the judge and the supervising clerk had known each other for a long time and had what it called an "unusual" and "unique joking relationship."

Additionally, the judge apologized for his actions.

Here is some background. While a deputy district attorney in the 1980s the judge, who was appointed to the court in 1990, had struck up a friendship with the clerk who had a good sense of humor and liked joking around. After his judicial appointment, the commission stated, this "casual" joking relationship continued, "unfortunately."

The commission found that in response to a memo from the clerk which suggested that she and Judge Gibson meet to "discuss administrative matters," the judge wrote back:

"I have received your memo of September 4th, 1991. I can't imagine anything that would please me more than implementing new procedures with you. Naturally I would consider it a great personal honor to implement you, old or new. However, as you point out, my schedule is tight and I would attempt to squeeze you in, but we can forget about Mondays. Mondays are my meetings with the Royal Pelican Society and, as everyone knows, Monday Night Football must take priority over everything else. Tuesdays and Thursdays aren't any good as anybody can tell you. That leaves us with Wednesdays and Fridays. Fridays would be good. Oh, I'm sorry, I forgot we were implementing new procedures. Fridays wouldn't be a good day for that. Maybe we could work something out on Wednesday. No, can't do Wednesday. That's lunch with Judge Ashworth and Hodge. It's important I attend these lunches with them for often they discuss all of the new procedures they have been implementing with Francine, due to their close contact with her. Oh, well. In all seriousness, I would cancel all of the appointments to reverse my vasectomy to have a meeting with you to implement new procedures. Tell me when and where. Should you actually desire to eat lunch I will have solid substance as opposed to mere coke. Love and Kisses, Buggs."

The clerk said the "suggestive sexual references were offensive."

Judge Gibson denied "any sexual innuendo in the memo" but the commission disagreed, noting that "a reasonable and objective person would consider the memo sexually suggestive."

In the presence of the female clerk and a friend of the judge, Judge Gibson said: "Isn't that the best looking pair of legs and ass you've ever seen?"

His remark embarrassed her, the clerk said.

His friend said, "John, you're a judge now. You shouldn't be saying things like that."

Judge Gibson responded: "I can say whatever I want to her."

The judge told the commission he should not have said it.

The clerk stated that the judge made other remarks, such as: "Those are nice shoes you have on, and your legs look very nice in them"; "That's a beautiful blouse you have on. Do you have a slip on or a camisole?"; and "That's nice material. I wish I could be that close to your skin." The clerk stated that while she "did not attribute any sexual innuendo or intent to these remarks," she was offended because she did not believe the judge was "sincere" in making them.

In another instance, when a woman with large breasts walked into his courtroom wearing a tight sweater, the judge said to his clerk that he "really enjoyed seeing [the woman] walk in the door with her light-colored sweater on and her 46DD bra and her nipples showing . . . I really get excited when I see that." The judge denied making the statement and said that he told his clerk that the attire worn by the woman who worked for the clerk was "not appropriate for the court." The commission believed the clerk's version.

The clerk told the commission that on "several occasions in 1991 and 1992 Judge Gibson tugged on [her] bra strap" and on one occasion the judge said, "I'm an expert at undoing these." Again, the judge denied doing that and the commission believed the clerk's version because it "fell within" their "joking relationship."

The commission stated that a "judge must refrain from speech, gestures, or other conduct that could reasonably be perceived as sexual harassment."

Some California judges had more than one discipline case before the commission, apparently showing they did not always learn a lesson in the first go-round. Judge Gibson was one. A decade after the admonishment for his "Mr. Bobo" antics, the judge was again admonished for telling a female attorney and another attorney in his office that a male attorney who appeared on her behalf in a case was "incompetent." The female attorney told the commission that the judge said either, "He was incompetent and just stood in the courtroom scratching his balls and picking his nose," or he said, "He was incompetent and just stood in the courtroom scratching his ass and picking his nose." Either way, she testified that Judge Gibson "accompanied" the remarks "with gestures indicating the aforementioned actions." In other words, he scratched either his balls or ass, and picked his nose.

◊

For three years a judge in Michigan allegedly sexually harassed his secretary who told him she had no romantic interest in the married judge. The situation got so bad that she filed a sexual harassment complaint with the labor board. Once the Judicial Tenure Commission got wind of her complaint, it filed its own discipline case against Judge Gregg P. Iddings of the Lenawee County Probate Court in 2016.

After the commission investigated, it entered into a deal with the judge, who had correctly alerted the commission about the woman's harassment complaint after it was filed by her. The Judicial Tenure Commission agreed to a two-month suspension without pay. It stated the judge is "extremely remorseful over these matters, he has cooperated throughout the investigation, and he is desirous of resolving these grievances."

The state's Supreme Court, however, rejected the deal in 2017, and upped the penalty to a six-month suspension. In reading the long list of alleged harassment it is clear why. The woman who had a son began working as the judge's secretary in 2010, and sexual harassment began, according to commission records in 2012.

Here is what the commission contended the judge did:

1. Sent her "after-hours text messages . . . in which he discussed his marital problems and his personal feelings."

2. Offered to purchase "expensive items" for her for Christmas and invited her to "Rhianna [and] Eminem and other high priced concerts."

3. Suggested she "accompany him to exotic locations for court-related conferences where they could share a hotel room."

4. Showed her "a sexually suggestive YouTube video of a high-priced lingerie web site, Agent Provocateur."

5. Made "comments which he admits" she "could have reasonably interpreted as an invitation to have an affair with him."

6. Wrote her a "letter of recommendation" which referred to her "professionalism and dependability" and the phrase, "besides, she is sexy as hell," which he deleted at her request.

7. Inputted the words "Seduce [woman's name] on a court computer and invited her to view it.

8. Told her that outfits she wore to work were "too sexy."

9. Mentioned that "she owed him" for allowing her to leave work early to attend her son's after-school activities.

10. Stared down the front of her blouse.

The woman said that early on in her employment she told the judge that she had "no sexual attraction towards him." She also said she told him that his "wife would not appreciate his comments and actions." The woman also said she was "very upset" when a rumor started at the courthouse "that she was having an affair" with the judge and asked him to "shut it down."

After she left his employ the woman filed a complaint that alleged the judge's harassment caused "an enormous amount of stress, anxiety, discomfort, nervousness, mental breakdowns, mood swings and disruptive sleep." In the summer of 2016 the woman settled her sexual harassment complaint against the county, her employer the probate court and the judge. The settlement amount was reportedly $100,000.

Appointed to the bench in 2009 and re-elected in 2012 to a six-year term, the judge told a newspaper that he accepted the court's six-month suspension. "As a judge and a decent person, I have admitted what I have done and take full responsibility for my actions," he stated. "I should be held accountable for them."

◇

Talk about a judge with poor judgment, this Illinois jurist tried to kiss a female Chicago police officer in his chambers. When she used a "police maneuver" to stop him, he asked her instead to "touch his butt."

Let this be a lesson to all inexperienced though horny judges, don't try to kiss a self-described "tough cookie" cop unless it's your sister.

For three separate incidents of improper actions involving women at the courthouse, Circuit Court Judge Mauricio Araujo was charged with bringing his judicial office into disrepute, and as a result, he resigned in 2020 after a dozen years on the bench.

The judge told the Illinois discipline board that his "actions were not sexual," but friendly. The board stated that he "further testified that his gesture of physical affection, to give a female friend a hug and kiss on the cheek, was part of his Columbian culture. He stated that there were about five female officers he felt friendly enough with to give them a hug and kiss on the cheek. He believed there were two or three male officers he was friendly enough with to give hugs to as well."

Here is the account, the police officer gave to the board about the 2016 incident.

She said he needed a search warrant signed and texted the judge about approving it for her, and he told her to come to his office in the courthouse about one in the afternoon, which she did. Dressed in civilian clothes but wearing a bullet-proof vest, she said she knocked on the judge's door. He told her to come in and she did. She said he "came around his desk to greet her and she stated that he immediately invaded her personal space and tried to kiss her on the lips. She was in shock and used a technique she learned in the police academy, referred to as a 'back sir,' which involved extending her arm out, and stepping back to re-evaluate the situation and create distance from" him. She said she "admonished" him by saying, "aren't you married?" He responded that he was, and she said she walked to a window to get the attention of her partner waiting in their squad car outside. She said she then asked the judge whether he wanted to talk to the "informant" who was providing the probable cause for the warrant, and the judge said yes, bring him inside. She said the judge was standing between her and the office door and when she tried to pass him, he reached for her hand and said, "here touch it."

"Touch what?" she said, startled.

"Touch my butt," she quoted him as responding.

In disbelief, she pushed the judge out of the way and returned to her squad car. She told her partner about the judge's actions, and she said the officer "just laughed." She said she made him return to the judge's office with her to get the warrant signed by Judge Araujo. The unmarried female officer said she considered herself a "tough cookie" who had worked in Chicago's toughest neighborhoods and she wasn't going to "give" the judge "that power over her."

In another incident, a court stenographer complained that she was alone in an elevator when Judge Araujo got on the elevator and begun looking her up and down. She said he then asked, "How much?" She said she took the comment to mean how much money did she want for having sex with him. In a second incident that followed on the same elevator, the court stenographer said the judge asked her "if she had thought about what he had said before," and the woman said she "told him she had a boyfriend so that he would understand that she was not interested, and she also mentioned" that he was "married." She told the discipline board that he "shrugged his shoulders and said, 'so what?'" The woman said she began using the stairs at the courthouse so she wouldn't run into the judge on the elevator.

Judge Araujo told the discipline board that the incidents never happened. Still, after evidence of these encounters were detailed at a hearing attended by the judge, he quit the bench.

◊

Sometimes determinations against judges, especially those dating back many years, offer few details and only a sanitized overview of the facts of the case. The case involving Associate Judge Oliver Spurlock of the Cook County, Illinois Circuit Court is one. He was removed from office in 2001 for allegedly engaging "in a pattern of sexually intimidating and inappropriate conduct, made a variety of sexually intimidating and inappropriate comments, and engaged in sexually intimidating and inappropriate physical conduct toward female attorneys who appeared before him in his capacity as an associate judge. In addition, it is alleged that the [judge] failed to [remove] himself from cases handled by a victim's assistance coordinator with whom he had a romantic relationship; he improperly used his judicial chambers to engage in sexual acts with a court reporter, and that he refused to answer any questions by the Judicial Inquiry Board concerning the proposed charges."

◊

Allegations of sexual improprieties also happen at the federal court level, and in 2017, federal Judge Alex Kozinski in San Francisco became the poster boy for improper sexual conduct in the federal judicial system. But more than three decades earlier, he was a legal wunderkind when on August 10th, 1982, in the windy 91-degree muggy capital, President Ronald Reagan nominated him to a 15-year term on the U.S. Court of Claims. One of the president's White House lawyers, Kozinski had clerked for U.S. Supreme Court Chief Justice Warren E. Burger. In those days his face was aglow with the feverish beauty of a prodigy in law. What the president never knew, and Kozinski's resume obviously didn't mention, was the new jurist apparently saw himself as a sexual athlete.

A clerk on the 9th Circuit Court of Appeals told *The Washington Post* that Judge Kozinski, a 1975 grad of UCLA Law School, showed her "a chart that purported to depict women with whom he and his college classmates had sexual relations." Kind of a sexual scorecard.

For decades on the surface the affable Kozinski served with scholarly distinction on both the Court of Claims and later as Chief Judge of the ultra-liberal U.S. Court of Appeals for the 9th Circuit in San Francisco. But, privately, he was apparently dogged by the misguided notion that every woman wanted him.

Retired U.S. Court of Claims Judge Christine O.C. Miller experienced the judge's private side. She alleged that in 1986 – a year after Reagan elevated him to the appeals bench – "Kozinski grabbed" her "breasts as the two rode back from a function in Baltimore." This happened, she claimed, after declining "his request that they stop at a motel and have sex."

It would take another 30 years for the stuff to really hit the fan, however, largely because women stayed shut up.

In 2017 Judge Kozinski, born in Bucharest, Romania in 1950 in the midst of the Cold War, was caught up in the "#Me Too" movement. At least 15 women accused him of sexual misconduct, which included kissing and groping. The allegations spanned decades and included former law clerks who complained that he showed them dirty pictures in his office – pornography that had nothing to do with any legal cases they were working on. Former clerk Heidi Bond who worked for Judge Kozinski for a year in 2006 told *The Washington Post* that the judge called her into his chambers "at least three times to show" her pornography. She claimed he asked her "if it was digitally altered or if it aroused" her. Another clerk for a different 9th Circuit judge, Emily Murphy, complained that when she and other clerks were talking about exercising, Judge Kozinski "talked about her working out naked." She told the *Post*: "It wasn't just clear that he was imagining me naked. He was trying to invite other people — my professional colleagues — to do so, as well. That was what was humiliating about it."

After the spate of allegations, a formal investigation was launched. As a consequence, at age 67, Judge Kozinski retired and pocketed his $200,000-plus annual pension. He issued this apology: "It grieves me to learn that I caused any of my clerks to feel uncomfortable; this was never my intent. For this I sincerely apologize."

Chapter Eleven

In one of the strangest "otherworldly" courtroom comedies ever, a California appellate court overturned the verdict in a civil lawsuit after Orange County Superior Court Judge James M. Brooks and two attorneys entered, well, another dimension.

During the 2005 trial in which an employee had sued a company for discrimination, the plaintiff was testifying about his emotional stress by saying, he "felt like, he was in a white room without doors or windows that had no boundaries."

After his testimony, the defense attorney questioned the man by asking, "Have you ever heard of 'The Twilight Zone?'"

Plaintiff Witness: "Yes, sir."

Defense Attorney: "Goes kind of like this, do- do, do-do."

Plaintiff's Attorney: "Your honor, would just object. This is argument."

Judge Brooks: "Your objection's on the record, ma'am."

Plaintiff's Attorney: "Also improper argument."

Defense Attorney: "You're traveling through another dimension, dimension not only of sight and sound, but of mind, journey into wondrous land, whose boundaries are that of imagination; that's sign post up ahead, your next stop, 'The Twilight Zone.' Do-do, do-do. Do-do, do-do."

Judge: "That was terrible. Get to the question, please."

Plaintiff's Attorney: "Noting for the record, counsel was singing 'The Twilight Zone' theme song."

Judge: "And how the jurors left it will be reflected on [the] same record."

Defense Attorney: "Endless white room with no doors or windows. Is that where you got your idea of this white room theory?"

Plaintiff Witness: "From where?"

Judge: "Twilight Zone. That's his question."

Witness: "No, sir."

Defense Attorney: "Do-do, do-do. Do-do, do-do."

Plaintiff's Attorney: "Request that counsel stop singing. As entertaining as it is for the jury, it's mocking my client and mocking the trial."

Defense Attorney: "Ever heard of 'The Twilight Zone,' the show?"

Witness: "Yes, sir."

Judge: "For the record, he [defense attorney] hit few notes of 'The Twilight Zone' theme song which don't seem as mocking. He was off color."

Defense Attorney: "Go through life tone deaf and colorblind. This is tough."

The California Commission on Judicial Performance stated that although most of 'The Twilight Zone' material came from the defense attorney, the "judge encouraged" it, and "gave defendant's lawyer free rein to deride and make snide remarks at will, and at the expense of [the] plaintiff." An appellate court later found the stupidness so appalling it overturned the verdict and sent the case back for a new trial by another judge.

The weirdness in the trial didn't end with the singing of the theme from 'The Twilight Zone,' although it certainly felt like it was still in the Twilight Zone.

When an attorney expressed an objection to something the other side had done Judge Brooks held up a sign with one word on it written by his own hand.

"Overruled," the sign he held up said.

One can only imagine the laughter coming from the jury box when jurors saw this courtroom caricature.

The following day, the defense attorney who performed "The Twilight Zone" theme so out of tune, presented the judge with a neater looking sign that said "overruled" on it, and said, "Your honor, want to help you if may. This is a much nicer version."

Judge Brooks then turned to the plaintiff's attorney, agreeing. "Better than my homemade one," he said.

Stated the plaintiff's attorney: "Plaintiff objects to [defense attorney] presenting another 'overruled' sign to the court. The court's sign was adequate enough."

Judge: "The court will await receiving 'sustained' sign from plaintiff's [attorney] so we can split the benefits here."

Plaintiff's Attorney: "How many [objections] do I get?"

About a week later in the same trial, the judge again used the defense attorney's overruled sign, and plaintiff's attorney objected to its use.

Judge Brooks: "It's lightening things up."

The appellate court justices who overturned the verdict after the trial weren't amused, calling the use of the overruled sign held up by the judge as part of the "sideshow in the overall circus atmosphere, mocking [a] serious proceeding important to the parties." The court said "it cast the judicial system itself in a bad light in the eyes of the litigants and the public at large."

In 1991, Judge Brooks made headlines in Southern California after he fined members of an anti-abortion group for blocking traffic at a Planned Parenthood facility, and dozens of the group's members camped on the front lawn of his home over several days.

First elected in 1987, Judge Brooks who earned a law degree from Southwestern University School of Law in Los Angeles, was a zany character on the Orange County bench for over two decades. His supporters called him a "hardworking public servant" whose humor livened gloomily boring legal proceedings. For instance, a newspaper reporter wrote that while she was in his courtroom a plump bailiff walked in, and the judge quipped: "What's he doing in here, we're not giving away Twinkies?"

His courtroom was always full of laughter.

However, often his wit could be trying and crossed the line into crude sarcasm, insults and perceived racism. For instance, in 2006 he held a hearing on whether to toss a couple in jail for failing to show up to be questioned by attorneys. The husband told Judge Brooks that on the day before the meeting, "I woke up about 3:30 on the morning, with a very intense pressure in my chest. I went over to my doctor and they did an EKG and found abnormalities in it. So he asked me to immediately go to the nearest hospital." To which Judge Brooks quipped: "Gee. I wonder what's going to happen when we put you in jail. Your little ticker might stop, you think?"

Afterward the judge ordered the wife to attend a new session with the attorneys, and told the woman's lawyer: "Tell her to bring a check for $5,000. That's the sanction I'm imposing for her contempt and contemptuous conduct towards the court . . . I'd mention jail but it might give her a heart attack."

The commission admonished the judge for his "humor," saying it violated his ethics which "requires that a judge be patient, dignified and courteous to litigants and others with whom the judge deals in an official capacity." The commission called his remarks, "sarcastic, demeaning, and intimidating."

The same year, 2006, the judge presided over a civil case in which business assets had been transferred to a woman from Syria, and he said, ". . . in her native Syria [she] probably wouldn't be allowed to own property."

In looking into the complaint the commission also noted that the judge had been previously warned about expressing "ethnic bias" by referring to Hispanic defendants as "Pedro" and telling an "undocumented Hispanic" man that "you have more names than the Tijuana telephone book." He also issued an arrest warrant for an Asian defendant for "ten thousand dollars or twenty thousand yen."

In 1999 Judge Brooks was warned again by the commission for telling a defendant that he would have handled "an assault on his family" differently. "I would go down and punch [his] lights out," the judge said, adding that instead of calling police, it would be, "touch them, you die."

In 2003, Judge Brooks called "operators" of a mobile home park "Nazis" and compared their actions with "Nazis during the Holocaust." In another court case the judge pontificated about the costs to taxpayers of undocumented aliens and said they receive "benefits to which they are not entitled."

Despite the various complaints against Judge Brooks the harshest punishment he ever got from the commission was a public admonishment in 2006. He resigned from the bench in 2008 at the age of 71.

◊

Literally of thousands of pages of documents outlining judicial misconduct, including disturbing words uttered by judges in court, what an Orange County, California Superior Court judge said in 1997 about a criminal defendant about to go to jail was reprehensible. This was also a case that showed it is often hard for attorneys who must appear in the future before judges that are under investigation by discipline commissions to testify against them.

In the case Judge Susanne S. Shaw ordered a criminal defendant into custody after his bail amount was increased, and the slightly built man later testified what the judge said to him. "She looked right at me and asked me if I knew what they do to skinny little white boys in jail," the man said. The state's Commission on Judicial Performance said the comment was "understood to suggest that the defendant might be subject to unwanted sexual activity in jail."

There was no official transcript of the proceeding, and the judge denied making the statement. Although others in court said they heard it, too. In fact, the most compelling evidence came from the man's defense attorney, who was reluctant to testify against the judge, whom by all accounts was respected for her legal acumen. The commission's investigators who interviewed the attorney stated, "It was plain throughout his testimony that he would rather have been anywhere but in a courtroom testifying in this matter. Even though he made no effort to mislead, it was plain he would rather have walked through fire than say anything to harm Judge Shaw. At times, his testimony had to be pulled from him." Of the attorney's testimony, the commission stated in its report: "Ironically, it is this reluctance that makes him very convincing and turns his concession that Judge Shaw 'may' have made such a comment into a most powerful bit of evidence."

The investigators said they believed much of what the judge said about the incident and had doubts about some witnesses who spoke against her. Still, the investigators found that the "comment" was prejudicial misconduct, noting that it "personalized the situation" of the man's "race, gender, and physique." Giving her benefit of the doubt, the investigators who were also judges stated that "Even if Judge Shaw meant no sexual reference, such a comment could only be taken as intimidating by any reasonable observer. It was discourteous and undignified."

They were too timid. Her comment not only suggested that the "white boy" might be raped in the jailhouse, it inferred his attackers would be of a different race. Think of the outrage if she would have said, "skinny little black boys." For her "white boy" remark and other offensive statements and actions, the state commission barred the judge from ever sitting as a fill-in for judges on vacation.

She retired in 2006.

◊

Generally judicial ethics codes in all states say that judges "shall be patient, dignified, and courteous to litigants . . . ." The same applies to jurors. Whether a judge agrees with the verdict of a jury in a trial he is presiding over, the judge isn't supposed to berate it. It was one reason why Lake County, Illinois Judge John R. Goshgarian was suspended from the bench without pay for three months in 1999. After a verdict he berated a juror who happened to work in the courthouse. Because he disagreed with the jury's not guilty verdict Judge Goshgarian called the jury in a loud voice "stupid" and "gutless," stating that it was the "worst verdict [he] had seen in years." And, they wonder why people say jury duty sucks.

◊

The unorthodox judicial antics of Los Angeles Municipal Court Judge Mario P. Gonzalez were both disgusting and bemusing, and got him fired in 1983. While the discipline commission allowed him to continue the practice of law, it's doubtful there'll ever be another character quite like Judge Gonzalez on the California bench. It wasn't really the severity of his offenses. It's the number and "diversity" of his offenses that was remarkable.

1. In the middle of a jury trial he stood, told the attorneys to continue without out him and left the courtroom.

2. He openly advertised a "Bargain Day" in court in which traffic ticket violators could get their fines reduced by pleading guilty.

3. When a person was cited for violating L.A. County's dog-leash law, the judge wrote a "press release," announcing the law was unconstitutional, without giving the county a chance to defend its ordinance.

4. During jury selection in a criminal trial a black woman said she worked as a supermarket checker, and he asked, "What is the price of watermelon per pound?"

That's just a flavoring. The list of alleged misconduct is long and varied. It is the latter fact, of having so many different kinds of misconduct that's so unusual. Normally a judge has one or two ethics lapses or repeats the same offense. Not with Judge Gonzalez. Each offense was distinctive.

Even the judge's defense was interesting, although not unheard of in judicial discipline cases. He alleged that he was a conservative jurist and liberal attorneys who testified before the Commission on Judicial Performance were out to get him. "I've never had a rapport with what I consider to be liberal-minded-orientated individuals, and [the three complaining attorneys are] those kinds of people," he told the judicial commission. "And a person of my background and philosophy could never cut it with [them]." The Supreme Court found that "he persists in his theory that his adversaries conspired to record his every misdeed and regards virtually every allegation as personally motivated."

The ex-judge died in 2017 at the age 91. His obituary stated he started work after serving in WWII as a cab driver and "with the encouragement of a passenger he decided to go to school and pursue a career." It said he worked as deputy sheriff, fireman, defense investigator and attorney, and "finally [as] a municipal court judge." The obituary went on to say, "He would want to be remembered for his integrity, love for his country and community, and the deep love he had for his family . . . He was a good, honorable man who made his family proud."

The former judge hasn't fared well with online judicial headhunters. Listing his misconduct, including an allegation of "sexual harassment" which the Supreme Court found unproved, a web site whose self-styled role is to "expose dishonest" judges, attorneys and public officials, called Judge Gonzalez a "racist, misogynist, idiot," and complained he was still practicing law.

From his "office" in the cemetery?

Let's let his misconduct speak for itself, although, Judge Gonzalez certainly spoke and acted more like a cabby than a jurist at times. For instance around 1978 the judge left "the bench abruptly during proceedings in his courtroom" and told the attorneys to continuing questioning witnesses. He told them to write down any "objections" they wanted to make and he would rule on them later. While the commission said this conduct happened "several times," the discipline record mentioned a jury trial and preliminary hearing, in which testimony was given. "As was customary in petitioner's chambers, on most of these occasions there was no court reporter to help reconstruct the questions asked or the objections taken," the Supreme Court found. Judge Gonzalez denied the allegations of his leaving the bench. He called his accusers "liars." In addition, his court clerk and bailiff backed him up. However, the Supreme Court, noting that the standard of evidence was the lower threshold of "clear and convincing," found that his accusers had no reason to lie. It said for a judge to leave the court in the middle of a trial was "so unusual that even the casual observer would have remembered it plainly." The court ruled: "By leaving the bench during judicial proceedings Judge Gonzalez has demonstrated a flagrant lack of respect for his judicial office, in violation of . . . the Code of Judicial Conduct. If only for a few moments at any one time, on these occasions he abandoned his role in the adjudicative process in utter disregard for his obligation diligently to perform the duties of his office. As such, his unjudicial behavior rises to the level of willful misconduct." The record failed to say why the judge left the bench.

In another example of strange misconduct, Judge Gonzalez announced in open court that he would be holding a "so-called half-off sentencing bargain day" for people who pleaded guilty. The judge admitted he announced the "bargain day" as a way to clear the court's heavy backlog of cases and to bring in more money to public coffers. He contended "bargain day" only applied to traffic ticket fines. The Supreme Court said evidence showed half-off day also applied to some misdemeanors, which are more serious offenses than traffic tickets, which are infractions and not subject to jail sentences. In fact, the court said, public defenders who represented criminal defendants "advanced" cases on the court's docket to take advantage of "bargain day." The court called his actions willful misconduct. "By his wholesale plea bargaining scheme Judge Gonzalez has deliberately misused his otherwise lawful power to reduce sentences and fines in individual cases," the court stated. ". . . Even the admirable goal of expediting judicial procedures cannot justify the court's abrogation of its duty to determine each case on its own merits." It also lambasted him for saying his intent was to bring in additional money for the county, which conflicted with rules of sentencing. "Judge Gonzalez certainly should have known that his "bargain day" sentencing offer – even if limited to vehicular offenses – contravened the principle of individualized sentencing embodied in our Penal Code."

The judge was also criticized for "occasionally" going into the room where juries were deliberating verdicts. Inside without the defense attorney or prosecutor present he would discuss aspects of the case with jurors. This just isn't done in a modern courtroom, where when jurors have questions about a case, a judge and all attorneys involved will discuss it in court before taking any action.

The commission also accused the judge of another weird practice, even though it might have been done with charity in mind. Judge Gonzalez was active in such groups as the Boys and Girls Club and other civic organizations. In a few cases where he denied a defendant's request to be released from jail on his promise to return to court, he told the defendant's attorney that he would grant the so-called "OR" release if the attorney wrote a check for $25 to charity, which the judge would hold, and if the defendant returned to court the attorney's check would be returned. It is assumed, that if the defendant skipped and didn't return to court the check would be donated to the charity listed on the check. The judge "apparently reasoned" that defense attorneys "could best prove trust and confidence in their clients by risking their personal funds," the discipline court stated. The judge explained that his purpose was "both psychological and educational." The court called the "impropriety" of the judge's actions "obvious."

(The strident web site cited before stated that the judge was "extorting money from attorneys." Extortion? Attorneys should have called the cops. The site, which states it has no political party preferences either way, is flush with anti-Trump stuff, including a satire piece on the former president pushing a line of "petite" condoms. Like much "journalism" on the web today, the site is quick to name-call, and you're soon drenched in it. Pejoratives for judges and attorneys who have been disciplined include "perverts," "ethical gremlins," "certified morons," "die-in-the-wool bigots," "Dumbos," "losers," "racists," screwball nutcases" – you get the idea.)

Other misconduct by Judge Gonzalez included a habit of starting court proceedings and questioning defendants even though a defendant's lawyer hadn't arrived in court. Around 1976 a Los Angeles County deputy public defender was delayed in one courtroom, which happens many times a day in courthouses. When he finally entered Judge Gonzalez' courtroom he "discovered his client seated in the witness chair giving testimony in response to questioning by either" the judge or the prosecutor. When he objected, the judge sent the case to another courtroom. He did this more than once, which violates court rules of conduct. "[My] court was busy," Judge Gonzales told the state discipline commission, and the public defender had "not responded to" his "summons" to be in court, "so [I] had started without him."

In a move that the state Supreme Court labeled "almost farcical," but one the local media must have loved, Judge Gonzalez issued a press release, disclosing that Los Angeles County's dog leash law was unconstitutional because it singled out a specific animal owner. "In an almost farcical misapplication of constitutional law, Judge Gonzalez declared that the dog leash [and] license ordinance violated the equal protection clause of the Fourteenth Amendment because it applied to dog-owners but not to owners of 'Canaries, Chinchillas . . . Mynah birds . . . Squirrel monkeys, Steppe legal eagles, Toucans' and so on," the disciplining court stated. Announcing his "opinion in the form of a press release," without allowing the county to appear in his courtroom and present reasons why the law was not unconstitutional "exceeded the bounds of his judicial authority" and devoid of "minimal . . . fairness." The Supreme Court also questioned his motives, hinting they were political. Noting the judge was a candidate for Superior Court at the time and "was motivated by a desire for pre-election publicity," the court said, "though his press release opinion may indeed have earned him a certain political notoriety, such a blatant exploitation of the judicial office for political ends seriously and impermissibly undermines public esteem for the impartiality and integrity of the judiciary." His action was "willful misconduct as a matter of law," and the California Supreme Court ruled that "The record further reveals that Judge Gonzalez has engaged in a continuous course of overreaching and abuse of judicial authority."

Perhaps worst of all, words he contended he spoke in "jest" is where Judge Gonzalez deserves to be called names. Like the "watermelon" remark, the man lacked basic racial or gender sensitivities. Even in the context of the 1970s when most people treated these social issues with less ferocity, his remarks were offensive, especially comments that were every bit as crude and disgusting as his "watermelon" comment to the black female juror. In 1980 an African-American deputy district attorney (who later became a judge himself) confided to Judge Gonzalez that his wife had just had a miscarriage. "Oh, good," responded the insensitive judge, "one less minority." Realizing his crudeness the judge "thereafter" said he was sorry. Judge Gonzalez made the remark in front of another judge of Spanish heritage. Also, at a courthouse Christmas party the judge said to a deputy district attorney who was Jewish: "Tell me something . . . with all the interbreeding that your people do, aren't you afraid that they will produce a race of idiots?" The woman told the commission his "tasteless" remark made her "very angry," calling it "anti-Semitic." Also, in questioning a Japanese-American man about "inflation" during jury selection, Judge Gonzalez said he "did not know why he was speaking to a Japanese juror about inflation because, 'what do fish heads and rice cost?'" Also, at sentencing of a "tall and large" Hispanic man for "beating his wife" who was a small-built woman, the judge told the defendant that "such a course of conduct may be tolerated in Mexico and Africa but would not be tolerated in America."

Stated the Supreme Court: "The record reveals that both in open court and in private communications with persons associated with the court, Judge Gonzalez improperly engaged in personal verbal attacks, indulged in indelicate sexual and ethnic remarks, and made comments that cast doubt on his appreciation of the nature and importance of his judicial duties."

Apparently Judge Gonzalez didn't get along with some other judges at the courthouse in the East Los Angeles Judicial District. Talk about the fast-lane to being booted from the bench. "We also find ample support in the record for the conclusion that Judge Gonzalez has made insulting and derogatory comments from the bench and in chambers, impugning the character and competence of his judicial colleagues," the high court stated in its ruling of terminating his judgeship. ". . . On several occasions [the judge] made grossly unflattering remarks regarding the physical appearance, impartiality, and work habits of his fellow judges. He insinuated that one judge had accepted a bribe and admitted to calling another judge a 'coward' to his face."

Finally the Supreme Court decided it believed "three attorneys" who testified before the commission and complained about the judge's actions, such as leaving the bench while court remained in session, and did not believe Judge Gonzalez. "In a tone that rapidly grows tiresome, he reiterates a conspiracy theory typically raised as a defense in judicial misconduct investigations, and contends that the three attorneys simply fabricated their stories. As he does with virtually every allegation, Judge Gonzalez fundamentally misperceives the nature and gravity of the charge and instead views the entire matter as one of political disagreement or personality difference."

The judge did not offer the kind of "remorse" or depth of thinking the court wanted to hear. "In the final analysis Judge Gonzalez utterly fails to grasp either the substance or seriousness of the numerous charges levelled against him by the commission," the court wrote. "Despite multiple admonitions . . . Judge Gonzalez has treated this investigation as an attack on his character. Thus he boasts he is opinionated, outspoken, hardworking, and extroverted, but never prejudiced and always impartial . . . While he concedes there may be certain minor irregularities in his judicial manner and procedures, he denies he has ever deliberately abused his judicial office and generally refuses to admit he has done anything improper."

The court fired him but allowed the judge to keep his license to practice law because it found that none of his misconduct rose to the "level of moral turpitude, dishonesty, or corruption." Besides the court admitted, ethical standards of conduct for judges are higher than for lawyers. Hmm.

◊

This discipline case has its strange, humorous aspects. But, really, it wasn't funny at all.

In August of 2016 Illinois Judge Valarie E. Turner was handling minor traffic tickets in her courtroom when she saw a woman she thought had been elected a judge in Cook County, Illinois. At a break in court, Judge Turner introduced the woman to a prosecutor, calling her "Judge Crawford." Rhonda Crawford, a law clerk, had made it through the primary election but still faced the general election unopposed for a vacant judgeship. She should have, but didn't say that she wasn't yet a judge.

When court resumed, Judge Turner made this startling announcement: "We're going to switch judges." She took off her robe, handed it to Crawford, and she put it on. Ms. Crawford, an attorney, sat on the bench and Judge Turner stood behind her as "Judge" Crawford presided over some minor traffic ticket cases being handled by a prosecutor. At one point, "Judge" Crawford asked Judge Turner if she could deny the prosecutor's request to delay a case, and the real judge told her that she could. "Judge" Crawford then denied the prosecutor's motion for a continuance.

That same afternoon the prosecutor learned that Rhonda Crawford wasn't yet a judge, and he ran to the presiding judge to complain. When the chief judge asked Judge Turner about the incident, she said she thought Rhonda Crawford was a new judge and was observing her courtroom for tips on being a jurist.

The ticket cases handled by Crawford had to be litigated again, and the incident was reported to the Illinois judicial discipline commission. What the courts commission learned was sad, and likely why Judge Turner mistakenly believed Ms. Crawford was a judge. Judge Turner had been "recently . . . diagnosed with Alzheimer's disease" and was suffering loss of memory, the courts commission said. The disease disabled her, and essentially disqualified her from being a jurist. Realizing her illness, Judge Turner told the board she would stop being a judge and asked for disability benefits. She also sought dismissal of the board's complaint. After an exhaustive investigation by the commission in which the state's judicial retirement system also got involved, and fifteen rounds of seemingly pointless jostling between the board's legal staff and the judge's attorney, in 2017, the commission ordered Judge Turner's retirement.

But the story didn't end there. It got even sadder.

Rhonda Crawford, as expected, went on to win the judgeship. However, prior to the November 2016 General Election, prosecutors charged her with "official misconduct," a felony, and "false impersonation," a misdemeanor, for donning Judge Turner's robe and presiding over the minor traffic tickets. She pleaded not guilty. Because of the indictment, an appellate court ruled that she could not be sworn in as a judge. In April of 2017, three days before her trial on the two charges, Ms. Crawford committed suicide, according to *The Chicago Tribune*. The paper quoted a medical examiner's report, saying that "police found a gas-powered generator in Crawford's enclosed bedroom and three bottles of prescription drugs – two used to treat pain and one a muscle relaxant – that she had taken." The records said she died of "carbon monoxide poisoning." Aged 46, she left a note, stating, "I have decided to end my life."

◊

A few years before the above tragic case of Illinois Judge Valarie E. Turner and Rhonda Crawford, another sad discipline case involved a female Illinois judge.

Cook County, Illinois Circuit Court Judge Cynthia Y. Brim, who according to records, "pushed a Cook County Deputy Sheriff" outside Chicago's Daley Center in 2012. The shoving took place a day after the judge, in office since 1994, went on an hour long "rant" in traffic court about race, justice, and of all things, "kahoonas." Now it wasn't clear whether she was referring to "the Great Kahoona" in the 1957 novel and later surf movie "Gidget," or that she was talking about large testicles, but whatever she meant it sure sounded weird coming from her mouth in her courtroom. (Perhaps she referred to the Chicago media and attorneys who opposed her re-election after being supported by the city's Democratic establishment.) After the courtroom outburst, she was led away and barred from returning without an escort. Later suspended, she continued to collect her salary of $180,000 a year.

In any event, Judge Brim was subsequently charged with battery for shoving the deputy, and a non-jury trial was held. At the conclusion of evidence the trial court judge ruled that "evidence against" Judge Brim "satisfied the elements of battery beyond a reasonable doubt," but that she was "not criminally responsible because she had been legally insane at the time of the battery." Evidence apparently showed that Judge Brim "had and continues to have schizoaffective disorder," a serious bipolar mental illness.

After the state judicial commission investigated the case it reported that the judge "had been hospitalized for psychiatric episodes five times" since becoming a judge. The commission reported that she had admitted that she "hadn't taken" her antipsychotic medications for years before her 2012 courtroom meltdown. However, she told the commission that "I can serve as a judge with full capability as long as I continue to take medication as prescribed."

The commission refused. In 2014 the Illinois Courts Commission removed her from office.

Even though media reports told of many attorney complaints against the judge, among them being tardy in making rulings and being late for court, it's remarkable she managed to work as a judge all those years while suffering from severe mental illness.

◊

Judge Christopher J. Sheldon was on to something. That judges are unnecessary in courtrooms.

No wonder the California commission in business to scold judges, with a few million in its yearly budget to spend on it, shut him up pronto by issuing a public admonishment of the judge who had been on the bench six years.

Riverside County, California Superior Court Judge Sheldon handled a heavy calendar of pretrial misdemeanor cases, estimated at a hundred a day in 1995 and 1996. For six months during this span the judge didn't take the bench to hear all minor cases and left the bench while other cases were still being heard. Instead, he let prosecutors and defense attorneys work out these minor offenses and allowed court clerks to "enter pleas and execute court documents imposing sentences, enter continuances agreed to by the attorneys and set hearing dates."

Where was the judge? Well, occasionally he'd be outside the courtroom, "jogging on the stairs next to his chambers."

Hey, what the hay, Judge Sheldon had instructed the attorneys and clerks to come get him if they needed him for a ruling. But, then, it was reported that he also left the courthouse altogether while his courtroom was in session. They had cell phones, didn't they?

"The conduct gave the appearance that the judge was not interested in courtroom proceedings and that he was using court time for personal matters," stated the commission, probably scared senseless that the judge's radical idea of courtrooms not requiring judges might spread. The commission said that when a person walks into a courtroom he expects a judge to rule on his case, not a clerk. Yet here is how the judicial watchdog commission described it, showing just how well-oiled it worked. "Judge Sheldon's misdemeanor pretrial calendar was conducted Monday through Thursday. It was scheduled to begin at 1:30 p.m. and usually lasted until 4 p.m., although it occasionally ran as late as 6 p.m. The number of cases on each calendar was frequently more than 100. Judge Sheldon decided that it would not be necessary for him to be on the bench to handle each case during the misdemeanor pretrial calendar. He met with deputy public defenders and the deputy district attorney assigned to his pretrial calendar and with one courtroom clerk to explain to them his new procedure. He asked the attorneys to handle routine things and to let him know if they needed him. He did not personally explain to [all] the courtroom clerks how to handle the cases in his absence. Judge Sheldon, starting in July 1995, took the bench only to handle the in-custody defendants at the beginning of the calendar, some private attorney cases, cases in which the attorneys could not agree upon a disposition, and driving under the influence cases reduced to alcohol-related reckless driving charges. He also took the bench to issue bench warrants at the end of calendars. The large majority of cases on the pretrial calendar were adjudicated in Judge Sheldon's absence and without his participation. On the vast majority of cases on the pretrial calendar, the defendants' attorneys and the prosecutor agreed on a disposition. For those cases, [the judge] did not take the bench. Most of the cases on Judge Sheldon's calendar had out-of-custody defendants. Judge Sheldon had no involvement in . . . 95 percent of the out-of-custody cases. The sentences were determined by the deputy district attorney who sat at counsel table in court and talked to defense counsel who lined up to talk to him."

Streamlined judgeless justice? Seemed to have run smoothly, all right, while the judge took a jog.

No wonder the commission freaked out.

◊

Like many who are in government service, judges must file so-called "statements of economic interests." For officeholders like city council members it's important because it sheds light on whether they are voting on an issue that will help them financially, say voting for their city to buy land they own. For a judge it is just as important because disclosing their holdings ensures that they won't rule in a case that benefits them financially.

One of the most blatant examples of a judge hiding assets led to his resignation in 2015. The discipline case against Merced

County, California Superior Court Judge Marc A Garcia involved work as a defense attorney for poor criminal defendants before he became a judge. He worked with other lawyers on what is called a "conflicts panel," and when the partnership dissolved, the judge continued to receive income. "On Judge Garcia's Statements of Economic Interests for the years 2008 through 2012, executed under penalty of perjury, he failed to disclose the $250,000 in income he received," the state commission reported. When he was a lawyer Judge Garcia had worked under a contract with the county to defend indigent criminals. The money was paid in $4,516 monthly installments, beginning in January 2008, months after Garcia was appointed to the bench in October 2007 by Republican Governor Arnold Schwarzenegger. The money was deposited, the records stated, into a "blind trust account established by Garcia."

Here is a quick explanation of what an attorney on a conflicts panel does. Two bad dudes are arrested for the same murder and neither can afford an attorney. The court assigns a public defender for one of the killers but law won't allow the public defender's office to represent the second killer because it would have a conflict of interest in defending both defendants. That is where a conflicts panel attorney, already under contract with the county, is appointed by the court to defend the second killer.

In 2004 the conflicts panel the judge worked for won a five-year contract with the county of Merced worth $5.6 million, ending in 2008. It wasn't long after the contract was signed that the partnership dissolved.

Another problem for Judge Garcia was that during a three-year period the judge also allegedly heard criminal cases in which an attorney who had been his former partner handled cases in his courtroom, and failed to disclose he was getting monthly checks from the old partnership.

"Judge Garcia disputed that there was any intent on his part to conceal . . . [the monthly] payments . . . but admitted that his conduct could give rise to an appearance of concealment and thereby violate the Code of Judicial Ethics." He agreed that his conduct was "prejudicial to the administration of justice that brings the judicial office into disrepute." The commission levied the maximum punishment on the judge, who retired when the case was settled, by barring him from ever sitting as judge again in the state.

◊

Arizona Justice of the Peace, Judge Jose Luis Castillo apparently recognized the jerk the moment he walked into his courtroom. After recognizing an attorney who had entered his court on a case, Judge Castillo bowed out, or recused himself from hearing the matter.

"I remember you," said the judge in open court. "I recuse myself from your cases . . . you are the gentleman who yelled at the lady who is now my wife."

The judge didn't stop there. He went on to "state that the attorney was disrespectful to other women based on rumors he had heard in the community," and said he was "concerned" that the lawyer was a "misogynist."

The judge "brusquely ordered" the dude to leave his courtroom.

The Arizona commission found that the attorney had been polite and wasn't given much time to defend himself. On the other hand, it found Judge Castillo's "tone . . . accusatory" and "aggressive" while he "expressed disgust with the attorney's alleged conduct."

In 2016 the judge was reprimanded for misconduct.

◊

Petty court politics got the best of a New York Village Court of Liberty judge in 1994, when the state's Court of Appeals agreed with the State Commission on Judicial Conduct to kick him off the bench. Apparently Judge David Schiff was upset when another judge dismissed traffic charges against a driver who had been involved in an auto accident with Judge Schiff. When the judge heard of the dismissal, he told a police officer, "It's a wheel. It goes around, and maybe someday I can do the same for him." He also told a prosecutor, according to commission records, "I'm hung heavier politically" than the other judge.

If he really intended to retaliate, and this point is unclear in the official records, he got his chance in a case in which a plaintiff in another case sought a judgment in his courtroom against a defendant who was being represented by the other judge's law firm. In New York lawyers served as part-time Town Court justices. The judge ruled in favor of the plaintiff and against the defense in the case.

Judge Schiff's own court clerk testified before the Commission on Judicial Conduct that she "overheard him remark to an attorney" that "he was so angry about the ruling that he intended to grant the plaintiff's motion for judgment in the pending civil case because the defendant was represented by [the judge's] law firm."

In his defense, Judge Schiff said he ruled in favor of the plaintiff based solely on the facts of the case and not out of any revenge on the other judge.

That might have been so, the appellate court ruled, but it didn't matter in his discipline case. "Whether [he] actually decided the plaintiff's motion on the merits in that case as he contends is largely irrelevant to the charge because the harm inured when he indicated he would use his judicial powers to satisfy a personal vendetta, a classic instance in which an appearance of such impropriety is no less to be condemned than is the impropriety itself." And, because he "created the impression that he was using his judicial office to retaliate, and thus failed to avoid the appearance of impropriety and to conduct himself in a manner that promotes public confidence in the impartiality and integrity of the judiciary," the appeals court agreed that he should be removed from the bench.

◇

It's doubtful Texas Justice of the Peace Judge Lucy Leal ever heard of the 15th century English Court of the Star Chamber, which was favored by Henry VIII for doing his scandalous bidding. But, she acted like one. Judges of the juryless Star Chamber could act on a single complaint and detain and force testimony from people. Its harsh, arbitrary punishments included the pillory, whipping and mutilation.

Oh, Judge Lucy Leal didn't lash anyone to the public stocks or mutilate them. She just had two people illegally arrested, and then lied about it. In 2018 Judge Leal agreed to resign after the state Commission on Judicial Conduct investigated her. She had been on the bench since 2011 in La Pryor, a dusty town of 1,700 in Zavala County in southwest Texas.

Here is the folksy tale.

In May 2015 another Justice of the Peace, Judge Dagoberto Correa, called the county sheriff to complain that Gustavo Jimenez III had "improperly repossessed his truck." A Zavala County deputy sheriff investigated the complaint and after checking state DMV records learned that Jimenez had a lien on the vehicle. The deputy decided the affair was a "civil" matter, no crime had been committed, and filed a report. The deputy took no further action.

Two months later the judge in the dispute over the truck went to Judge Leal and "filed an unsworn complaint" that stated two words, "criminal trespass" without details or more information. Two days after that Judge Leal issued two arrest warrants for Gustavo Jimenez, one for "theft" and the other for "criminal trespass." Based "solely" on the complaint from Judge Correa, the warrant was issued without any additional evidence or information of probable cause for the arrest. Jimenez was then arrested by deputies, booked into jail and posted bail.

Months later in January 2016 Judge Correa called the sheriff's department to complain about a telephone conversation he had had with Joey Maldonado about an incident involving Maldonado's daughter who had been at a party. "Judge Correa alleged that Maldonado called his office and began using vulgar language," records showed. "The judge indicated that he wanted to file charges for terroristic threat against Maldonado."

However, a deputy investigated Judge Correa's complaint the same day, and concluded, "no criminal activity occurred" and filed a report. The deputy took no more action.

Apparently dissatisfied with the sheriff's handling of his complaint against Maldonado, the next day Judge Correa met with Judge Leal. According to records of the Texas judicial commission, Correa asked Judge Leal to issue an arrest warrant for Maldonado. Again, as in the first arrest, Judge Correa "did not file a sworn complaint or affidavit of probable cause, or indeed provide any documentation whatsoever (sworn or otherwise) to Judge Leal, in support of the request," records stated.

On that flimsy legal ground the judge issued her warrant. The arrest warrant signed by Judge Leal referenced "terroristic threat/public servant" of which Maldonado had been "accused by the written complaint, under oath, of Dagoberto Correa." As a result, Maldonado was arrested by deputies and was booked into jail where he spent seven hours before being released on bail.

After receiving a complaint of the unlawful arrests, the state commission launched an investigation, and in May 2017 a commission investigator interviewed Judge Leal under oath. The investigator had been tipped off by law enforcement that Judge Leal had spoken to Judge Correa by phone on her way to the commission interview. With this knowledge, he asked her when she had last talked to Judge Correa, and she answered that it was the "day before" at a court meeting. Pressing her, the investigator asked if her cellphone was seized what would its records show. Caught in her lie, the judge admitted that she had talked to Judge

Correa on her way to the interview with the commission investigator.

Related to the inquiry or not, less than a month later Judge Correa died from a self-inflicted gunshot.

After interviewing the deputy who had investigated Judge Correa's complaint against Gustavo Jimenez, III, the commission concluded: ". . . No one from law enforcement ever prepared an affidavit of probable cause for the arrest of Jimenez. Any arrest warrant in this matter was requested solely by Judge Correa. Justice of the Peace Lucy Leal never consulted with [the deputy] regarding the alleged facts of this case prior to issuing an arrest warrant for Mr. Jimenez." The commission's investigation turned up similar evidence in the arrest of Joey Maldonado, stating that "no one from law enforcement ever prepared an affidavit of probable cause for the arrest of Joey Maldonado. Any arrest warrant in this matter was requested solely by Judge Correa. Justice of the Peace Lucy Leal never consulted" the sheriff's office about "facts of this case prior to issuing an arrest warrant for Mr. Maldonado."

Early in the commission's investigation Judge Leal was asked to list the information she used to justify issuing the arrest warrants. In her response, let's just say she embellished it a bit: "Judge Dagoberto Correa came into my office to let me know about the incident and brought police reports and told me he wanted to file a formal complaint on both Gustavo Jimenez, III, and Joey Maldonado. After reading the reports and hearing his complaints, I felt there was probable cause to issue warrants."

Police reports?

She had no police reports.

Later after being pressed by an attorney for the commission on the "protocol" she used to issue arrest warrants, the judge waffled. "It is not my practice to issue an arrest warrant without an accompanying affidavit of probable cause, but when a person comes in to complain, especially when the complaint is very real and valid, there may be a need to act, BUT it is still my practice to inform all complainants to report and complain to the police." She dug the hole she was in even deeper. "While I use police officer's investigative reports for arrest warrants, as stated above, there are instances when I will issue the warrants due to the facts of the matter affirmed to by the affiant, and which meet the criteria for issuance of such warrants. In this case, if you will note, the alleged investigations took place the day prior to the issuance of warrants.

While, as the investigator states, no affidavits for probable cause were issued, this information was not provided to me at the time. By then, and based on the affiant, and thereafter any other information he provided to me, I issued these warrants. At this point in time, having looked at all the records, it is now my recollection I may not have used the police reports in these cases."

Judge Leal just acknowledged that "there may be a need to act" and order some poor possibly innocent scofflaw's arrest, without probably cause as required by the Fourth Amendment of the United States Constitution.

Thereafter, an attorney for the judge wrote to the commission, stating that the "single act of alleged misconduct, especially when she did not take this action intentionally, but perhaps misinformed" did not warrant her removal from office. The lawyer also later suggested that the local court system lacked "checks and balances that provide cover to overcome obstacles, such as the reporting officers having made the contact reports directly to her for proper determination instead of just letting things happen . . ."

It was cover your ass time.

Obviously it was the fault of the cops who somehow didn't read the judge's mind that she was going to arrest the two men. As might be predicted, at a formal hearing before the commission Judge Leal tried to place blame on the deputies. A lawyer for the commission asked her: "And judge, regarding all of this and your decision to issue the arrest warrant, are you placing any of the responsibility on this on the law-enforcement officers that investigated" the two cases.

Judge Leal: "Well . . . I felt like somebody from the sheriff's office could have contacted me [if] they felt that it was not – that didn't show there it was probable cause. And I never did hear from anybody from the sheriff's department."

What she meant was that once the two men were arrested by deputies the sheriff should have called her and told her the warrants were faulty. Come on man. A cop isn't going to call a judge and tell her she just ordered him to arrest someone unconstitutionally.

At this point, members of the Texas Commission on Judicial Conduct simply wanted Judge Leal to accept responsibility for the unconstitutional arrests, and it was the proverbial pulling of teeth.

"Regarding both of these instances, are you taking full responsibility for this? Or are you saying it was law enforcement? Or are you saying it was [Judge] Correa?" she was asked.

"Yes, I did take responsibility somewhere along the line, like I mentioned earlier, I feel like the sheriff's department, somebody from there, could have gone, you know, like . . . told me, you know, like, 'Hey, you know there's something missing here.' I mean, I just don't wanna blame 'em, for sure, but I feel like . . . somewhere along the line they failed me."

Commissioner: "So if I understand you correctly, judge, you're blaming in part the sheriff's department for your mistake."

Judge Leal: "Well, not entirely. But I just feel like . . . you know, they could have . . . said, 'I don't think there was actually probable cause.'"

Commissioner: "But isn't it up to you? Don't they rely on you? Didn't you fail them?"

Judge Leal: "Maybe."

Then, apparently frustrated by her prevarication, the commissioner said: "Why can't you just say, yes? Why can't you just accept that it's your fault . . . You signed the arrest warrant? . . . Why blame somebody else for your failure?"

Judge Leal: "I know I should. I mean . . . I guess I will take the blame because I did sign it."

◊

Judges also get into common scrapes. Like Circuit Judge Beatriz Santiago of Cook County, Illinois who was buying a house, and although she didn't intend to live there, she allegedly "attempted to and did deceive her mortgage lender by making several misrepresentations" in the loan documents that "caused her lender to believe she occupied" the house in Chicago. She was censured in 2016.

◊

When a group of high school students in Cook County, Illinois went to the courthouse for a tour, none of them thought it was to be arrested. That's what happened in the courtroom of Circuit Judge Glynn J. Elliott, Jr. in the late-1980s. During the tour the judge singled a student out and told him to approach the bench, which, obviously, the frightened kid did. The judge then "castigated" the boy for "creating a disturbance even though no disturbance had occurred," records of the judge's discipline case stated. The judge ordered the kid into custody. The student was taken to the judge's private office and "handcuffed" by a bailiff to a chair. Later, when the judge allowed the student to return to court he was publicly berated for the "manner in which he approached the bench." Again the student was taken to the judge's chambers and cuffed to the chair. Before the judge released him, the student was "required to apologize in open court."

◊

Irving, Texas Justice of the Peace Bill R. Lowery was booted from office in 1998 for one of worst racial slurs made off the bench in any discipline case. In May 1996 Judge Lowery pulled into a lot near the Dallas County Administration center where he had parked in the past without paying a fee. He was immediately approached by an African-American parking attendant who informed him the parking lot was under new management and he would have to pay three dollars to park. Refusing to pay, Judge Lowery said he'd move his car to a space reserved for county employees. The attendant responded if he parked there his car could be towed away. At that point the attendant asked the judge, who had shown him his identity badge, his name.

"Nigger, can't you fucking read?" the judge said.

At that point they went to the administrative office of the parking lot, where the judge "admitted" calling the black man a "nigger." The story made *The Dallas Morning News*, and the judge publicly apologized to the attendant, but denied using the racial slur.

A panel of special masters investigating the case agreed the judge had used the slur, and another – "black motherfucker" – at some point in the parking lot. In removing the judge from office for this incident and others, the Texas Supreme Court found the judge's words "abusive, indecent, profane or vulgar," and "used in a public place . . . tended to incite an immediate breach of the peace."

In his defense Judge Lowery argued that "evidence to support a finding that he used racial slurs" was insufficient, a defense discounted by the disciplining court. The judge also attempted other defenses, including that his comments were made as a private citizen and not on the bench, issues rejected because they had been argued and rejected in previous cases. It also did not help the judge's case that in 1996 he had been ordered to undergo additional judge's training and had tried to get another judge to vouch that he had completed the training when he had not done so. The other judge reported his misconduct to the commission.

Chapter Twelve

Years ago when the author was in the courthouse he was stopped by a high-ranking county judge who railed about the vast "power of the media." I had just written a story about a friend of his, a physician who had prescribed pain medication to a patient who had then died, ostensibly from the pain pills. The doctor was being investigated in connection with the woman's death, and the judge railed against me, declaring that I had ruined his friend's reputation. The judge said that the media had too much power. I rather laughed inside at his reasoning, and told him frankly that media power was peanuts compared the power of a judge in a capital case who can sentence a person to death.

Huffing off, he didn't like my answer.

My point was and still is judges have immense power. Most judges quickly learn how to leaven it appropriately and to cope temperately with it, and, to essentially control it. However, a few of them, and much to the determent of everyone around them, become overwhelmed and consumed by their state-given power. They just can't handle it, and become "little gods" high on the bench over everybody else in their courtrooms. Few things are scarier for a lawyer, a court worker or a member of the public who riles the ire of a judge and then feels his wrath.

Like this criminal defendant.

When Terry Lee Morris walked into the Texas courtroom in 2014 he had no idea he had been transformed back to the Spanish Inquisition. It wasn't the rack or the dreaded Judas chair, it was George Gallagher of Fort Worth District Court.

Mind you, as a career "kid diddler," Mr. Morris wasn't a sympathetic character, as he would be convicted at the trial and sentenced to 60 years in prison for child molestation. But, what the Texas Commission on Judicial Conduct found in 2021 was actions taken by the judge to inflict physical courtroom pain on Mr. Morris went too far, although they were too polite to say it resembled something from the hand of Marquis de Sade. An appeals court wasn't so shy and called the judge's actions in the trial "disturbing," and overturned the conviction and sentence of Mr. Morris.

The case revolved around the 15-year-old daughter of a woman Morris once dated. When he stopped seeing the mother, he contacted the girl online and "solicited and received nude" pictures of the her "that lewdly depicted her genitals."

Bailiffs who escorted the defendant to court on the first day of trial told the judge he was unruly and recommended a "stun belt" be put on his ankle to ensure that he did not act up, a suggestion the judge ordered. Texas law gave judges "sufficient discretion" to maintain "proper conduct" in courtrooms, especially during jury trials.

Stun belts used on prisoners are fastened to an ankle by four-inch wide elastic bands underneath pants. Powered by two nine-volt batteries which deliver shocks of about 50,000 volts for eight seconds, about the same as a police taser, stun belts can knock a person to the ground. Court records stated that "an electrical jolt of this magnitude causes temporary debilitating pain and may cause some wearers to suffer heartbeat irregularities or seizures." Especially people with "heart problems, epilepsy, or individuals using psychotropic medications." A police officer described what he felt during training when hit with a stun belt: "It is as if you had nine-inch nails and you tried to rip my sides out and then you put a heat lamp on me." In one training session a Texas officer died from "cardiac arrhythmia" after being hit by two 45,000 volt stun belt shocks.

According to court records, here is what happened, after the judge asked Morris how he pled.

Judge: "To this charge you may plead guilty or not guilty. What is your plea?"

Morris: "Sir, before I say that, I have the right to make a defense."

Judge: "The –"

Morris: "It was brought to my attention by the United States district court to do this. And before the court – for the information of the court, yesterday you gave this man orders to put a shock rag or a shock collar on my ankle to prevent me from saying anything in my defense. If it happens, it happens. But let me just say for the record –"

Judge: "No, wait just a minute."

Morris: " – lawsuit pending against this judge."

Judge: "Jury, go to the jury room."

Morris: "I have a lawsuit pending against this attorney. I've asked this judge to recuse himself off my case. It's in relation to the Ken Paxton case, Attorney General Ken Paxton. I've asked this attorney to recuse himself off my case. They both refused to. I have that right."

After the jury left the courtroom, Mr. Morris tried to continue his objections, and, according to the court of appeals, the judge "warned Morris about any further outbursts." When Morris persisted, the judge ordered the bailiff to "activate" the stun belt and shock him. He did, But it didn't stop Mr. Morris from talking, saying. "a defendant has a right to object."

The judge then said, "Mr. Morris, I am giving you one warning. You will not make any additional outbursts like that, because two things will happen. Number one, I will either remove you from the courtroom or I will use the shock belt on you."

Morris: "All right, sir."
Judge: "Now, are you going to follow the rules?"
Morris: "Sir, I've asked you to recuse yourself."
Judge: "Are you going to follow the rules?"
Morris: "I have a lawsuit pending against you."
Judge: "Hit him."

The bailiff activated the stun belt, shocking Mr. Morris.

The official transcript of the trial does not reflect Mr. Morris's reaction to the eight-second, 50,000-volt electric shock, in other words, whether he screamed or if he fell to the floor writhing in pain, although court records stated his allegation that the shocks "injured" and "scared" him. The shock having happened, the judge resumed questioning of Mr. Morris, according to the transcript.

Judge: "Are you going to behave?"
Morris: "I'm an MHMR [mental health patient] client."
Judge: "Are you going to behave?"
Morris: "I have a history of mental illness."
Judge: "Hit him again."

The bailiff shocked Mr. Morris.

At that point, Morris complained that the judge was "torturing" him, a mental health patient, and that he was on medication for mental health problems. "You're torturing an MHMR client. I have agoraphobia. I'm under medication . . . You're wrong for doing this."

Judge: "Are you going to behave?"
Morris: "I take 17 pills a day for my disability, my MHMR disability. You have no right to do this."
Judge: "Are you going to behave?"
Morris: "I have the right –"

Judge: "You have no right to disrespect the court."
Morris: "I have the right."
Judge: "I'm going to give you the option to do one of two things. You can either behave in the courtroom –"
Morris: "I don't have an attorney. I'm firing this man. I've told him to get off my case. And the defendant has a right to refuse counsel. I have the right to represent myself in this case, and I shall."
Judge: "All right. Let's talk about that . . . How far did you go in school?"
Morris: "Sir, that's beside the point. There's serious allegations that I have in the United States District Court against this [attorney]. No one wants to be represented by someone they have a lawsuit against. No one wants a judge to preside over their case who the lawsuit is against. No one wants to be tortured because they're an MHMR defendant prevented from saying anything in the court in front of the jury pertaining to any such cases such as the grand jury –"
Judge: "Mr. Morris, are you going to answer my question?"
Morris: "I've asked you, I've filed a motion asking –"
Judge: "Would you hit him again."

The bailiff stunned him, or as the appeals court would say later, "after electrocuting Morris," the judge asked him again if he was going to behave. When Morris "did not answer yes or no," the judge had him "physically moved from the court room." Once Morris was led away, and the jury was still out of the room, Judge Gallagher apparently realized that he had to "make a record" to justify his actions of hitting the defendant with repeated shocks.

Judge: "All right. For purposes of the record, before we go any further, the court would like to place into the record, when Mr. Morris began his statements in the presence of the jury and before I was able to send the jury back out, the defendant had gone from merely standing next to counsel to beginning to move to his right just a little bit towards the edge of the table and his agitation continued to increase. Once the jury . . . was outside of the courtroom and outside the presence of the jury, the record will adequately reflect that the defendant continually refused to talk – to answer the court's questions and his demeanor continued to escalate. Let the record reflect that within about five feet from where the defendant was standing there is an 87-inch electronic smart board that weighs over 200 pounds that is readily within reach of the defendant, that had he grabbed that board, could have brought it over to the counsel table to affect the safety of the lawyers . . . and the two prosecutors that would be siting within anywhere from three to five feet if he went the other way. It was based on the totality of his continuing escalation and his movements that the court ordered that the shock belt be initiated. It was done for the safety of the lawyers and all of the participants."

Mr. Morris stayed away from Judge Gallagher's court for most of the remainder of his trial. His attorney told the judge his client was "scared" of what would happen to him if he did. The 15-year-old girl testified, saying that Mr. Morris knew she was a minor and that in messages between them on Facebook he "turned the conversations sexual, and that she eventually sent him nude images of herself while she was underage," court records stated. Morris returned to the courtroom to testify at the phase of the proceeding in which the jury considered his sentence. His testimony was described as "rambling" in court records and he denied ever molesting any girls, although there was evidence he had in previous years.

While the federal government later investigated the case for civil rights violations, the government declined to bring any action against the judge. The state's Commission on Judicial Conduct wasn't so sanguine, although didn't slam the judge very hard, either. The discipline board issued what is called a "public warning" which is a reprimand against a judge. It is the commission's lightest penalty for inappropriate action on the bench. The commission included the judge's rationale for his actions in its report. ". . . Judge Gallagher explained he ordered the activation of the stun cuff because Mr. Morris began moving from behind the defense counsel table into the court well and posed a security threat to others in the courtroom. Judge Gallagher acknowledged the contemporaneous record of the proceeding does not reflect this fact but pointed to a statement he made later that day for purposes of the record which details the threat Mr. Morris posed at the time the stun cuff was activated. Judge Gallagher also submitted written statements from, and summaries of interviews with, seven individuals who were present in court that day, including Mr. Morris's attorney, all of whom supported Judge Gallagher's version of events."

The Texas appeals court that overturned Mr. Morris's conviction and ordered a new trial didn't pull punches when it came to the stun belt. It essentially said that the judge used the stun belt on Mr. Morris for reasons of maintaining courtroom "decorum" and not for security reasons, such as protecting courtroom employees. "When the trial judges of this state don their robes and ascend the bench each morning, those with criminal dockets are often confronted with defendants who are rude, disruptive, noncompliant, belligerent, and in some cases, even murderously violent. In the face of this reality, Texas trial judges shoulder another heavy burden: the burden to tame the chaos before them, impose order, and uphold the dignity of the justice system," wrote appellate court Judge Yvonne Rodriguez. ". . . But discretion has its limits." She added: "Because the trial transcript clearly shows that the trial judge, during a heated exchanged with the defendant outside the presence of the jury, ordered his bailiff to electrocute the defendant three times with a stun belt – not for legitimate security purposes, but solely as a show of the court's power as the defendant asked the court to stop "torturing" him – we harbor grave doubts as to whether Morris's trial comported with basic constitutional mandates. As such, we have no choice but to overturn Morris's conviction" due to Judge Gallagher's "improper use of the stun belt."

Clearly electrocuting Mr. Morris for belligerence was way out of order, and the trial's actual transcript reporting what was happening when it was happening shows that. There were easy alternatives. Wrote editorial writer Jacquielynn Floyd for the *Dallas Morning News* about the stun belt case: "Being a trial judge would probably be more agreeable work were it not for defendants like Terry Lee Morris – obnoxious, disruptive, bent on turning the courtroom into a reality TV free-for-all with himself as the star. This guy, as the saying goes, would have tested the patience of a saint. But a Tarrant County judge's fix for Morris's obstreperous behavior . . . is unimaginable: three powerful shocks with an electrified stun belt, administered by a bailiff at the judge's behest. That shut Morris up, all right – so much so that he cowered in his cell for the rest of his trial."

There was a simple, ready alternative to the electrocution Morris suffered. Ms. Floyd quoted another Texas judge as saying: "If I have a situation with a civil defendant being disruptive, I'll just remove him from the courtroom. It doesn't take but 10 minutes and a 16-year-old kid to set up a camera" for a remote feed from the courtroom. "The judge can resort to force to ensure courtroom safety – but it's usually left to a judicial power-of-personality to keep routine order," wrote newspaper columnist

Ms. Floyd. "A good judge doesn't need to deliver electric shocks to do it."

◊

Tip: don't leave your cell phone on when you walk into a courtroom, especially not if it's Judge Robert M. Restaino's, of the Niagara Falls City Court. For in 2005 after the judge heard a cell phone ring while his court was in session, he metaphorically went over the falls.

Even a member of the New York Commission on Judicial Conduct, in opposing the judge's removal from office, admitted he "simply snapped . . . and engaged in what can only be described as two hours of inexplicable madness." Like I said – splash, over the falls.

A judge since 1996, Judge Restaino handled domestic violence cases in a program requiring defendants to remain in court all day even after their individual case was heard. While defendants were free from custody, if they failed program requirements, such as not using drugs, they could be sentenced to jail.

At around nine in the morning in March 2005, the judge took the bench with a crowded calendar of cases and 70 people sitting and staring back at him in the gallery. The courtroom was also jammed with attorney and court personnel including security, and counselors in the domestic violence program. Outside it was humid and a cold 26 degrees.

For the first 45 minutes things went swimmingly, with the judge handling ten cases, releasing these defendants on their promise to return to court, and instructing them to remain as required.

Then a cell phone rang in the back of the courtroom.

"Now, whoever owns the instrument that is ringing, bring it to me now or everybody could take a week in jail," the judge said into the courtroom. "And please don't tell me I'm the only one that heard that." He asked a person in court if he had heard it. Unsatisfied with the response, Judge Restaino, then 48-years-old, said: "Everyone is going to jail; every single person is going to jail in this courtroom unless I get that instrument now. If anybody believes I'm kidding, ask some of the folks that have been here for a while. You are all going."

Despite threatened mass incarceration, nobody came forward with the offending device.

As a result, the judge told everybody to remain in court, and a security officer barred anyone from leaving. Before the incident, as is customary in courtrooms, attorneys were coming and going. The judge told security people to find the phone, and took a five-minute break. Afterward, he was informed the phone hadn't been found. At that point the judge asked the defendant who was nearest the bench when the phone rang whether he knew whose phone it was.

"No. I was up here," the guy said.

The judge instantly revoked the man's OR (recognizance release), set his bail at $1,500 and ordered him into custody. He did this knowing the man's cell phone wasn't the one that had rung. Afterwards, the judge proceeded, faster than the Tribunal Révolutionnaire in the French Revolution sent aristocrats to the guillotine, to call up each defendant in the room and ask if it had been his cell phone that rang. When a defendant said no, the judge revoked non-custody status, set bail, and ordered him into custody. By the time the legal carnage was through, he calmly ordered 46 defendants into custody, some of whom were on their first day of the program. Only one of the defendant had his attorney along. Despite protests from defendants, including one who had returned to court four times as promised and pleaded with the judge: "My little girl is coming home at 3 [p.m.] Can I be sanctioned next week so I can get my girl?" The judge ordered his custody anyway. (And, obviously, this guy wasn't about to pull out a cell phone and call someone to pick up the girl.)

It didn't matter the excuse. Defendants said they might lose their jobs if taken to jail, with one man pleading that he had just gotten a job "I love" and didn't have $1,000 for bail. Another defendant said "his mother was having surgery that day." All to no avail. The complete unfairness of the judge's en mass jailing wasn't lost on anyone, especially later when the New York judicial commission heard the defendants' pleas and protests and the sarcasm of the judge.

"This is not fair to the rest of us," a defendant had said.

"I know it isn't," said the judge, taking him into custody.

Said another: "I know this ain't right."

The judge: "You're right, it ain't right . . . at all."

The judge also stated that the person whose phone rang was being "selfish," and said, "that's really a shame and it isn't fair at all. Somebody completely doesn't care."

Another defendant said, "I don't see everybody going to jail for this, I really don't."

Said another: "It's a shame, everybody being penalized."

Another said out loud what they were all thinking. "I'm sorry I had to be here today."

"I'm sorry, too," the judge told him.

Then a pearl of wisdom from a defendant: "I think the more people you send to jail, [the] less likely [the] culprit is to come forward."

As you might expect, defendants also pleaded for the cell phone owner to reveal himself. None did. The judge compared their silence to a gangster film. "The other thing which is amazing here with this group, this is better than watching a mob movie," the judge said. "Everybody that comes to this microphone, and I got to tell you something, you're all pretty good, when you come up to this microphone, and if you saw somebody got shot or killed, you would say, 'I didn't see nothing, I heard shots.' And if a body dropped right in front of you, you would say that 'I didn't see a thing.'"

At one point in this judicial mayhem, while it didn't seem intended as self-introspection, Judge Restaino asked why a person could remain silent and let fellow human beings suffer. "This hurts me more than any of you, imagine because someone in this courtroom has no consideration for you, no consideration for me and just doesn't care." He also said: "This troubles me more than any of you people can understand. Because what I am really, really having a hard time with, that someone in this courtroom who is so self-absorbed, so concerned only for their own well-being, they kind of figure they're going to be able to establish the bail and it won't matter so screw all of the rest of you people. Some of you people may not be in the [same] economic situation this selfish person is in, and you have to start realizing amongst your own selves someone out there who is the typical reason we have this [program]; they put their interests above everybody else's. They don't care what happens to anybody."

Did he just say, "*they*" don't care about other people?

Some defendants were allowed the leave at the end of the day after being carted off to a holding tank. Some produced bail and were released, while others were taken to jail, where they would spend several hours in custody.

Stated a commission member: "In causing 46 individuals to be deprived of their liberty out of pique and frustration," the judge "abandoned his role as a reasonable, fair jurist and instead became a petty tyrant, abusing his judicial power and placing himself above the law he was sworn to administer. It is tragic that in a crowded courtroom, only the individual wearing judicial robes, symbolizing his exalted status and the power it conferred, seems to have been oblivious to the enormous injustice caused by his rash and reckless behavior."

Months after the New York commission removed the judge from his $114,000 job, the state's appeals court in Albany upheld the dismissal. But the judge didn't disappear. Practicing law after being removed from the judicial bench, he was elected to the Niagara Falls School Board. As an aside, his attorney daughter ran for the Niagara Falls City Court in 2014, but lost to the incumbent.

◇

Let's face it, courtrooms can be very intimidating places, even for attorneys. Years ago when I asked a few attorneys why they only practiced in state courts, the answer got me thinking. The honest ones said they were "scared to death" in federal court because federal judges wielded too much power. On a whim, they said only half facetiously, they "can hit you with contempt and cuff you."

Seminole County, Florida Court isn't the federal bench, but for regular folks thrown into the court system it became just as intimidating whenever "abusive" Judge John Sloop, 57, took the bench.

In 2006 the Florida Supreme Court booted him from his $137,000-a-year judgeship after an investigation by the state's Judicial Qualifications Commission. The Supreme Court called his case "among the most egregious examples we have seen of abuse of judicial authority."

In a nutshell, the judge ordered 11 people to jail when they were "inadvertently" directed to the wrong courtroom for their traffic tickets. Even when other judges informed him it was all a mistake, Judge Sloop kept the poor retches locked up for hours.

Can you imagine: you wake up in the morning at your suburban home, eat a breakfast of bacon and eggs, kiss your wife goodbye, drive to the courthouse to pay your traffic ticket, and bam, the next thing you're rotting in jail like a gangster.

Oh, you say it sounds like a nightmare you've had?

Judge Sloop had a history of nightmares. "This case marks the fourth occasion Judge Sloop has faced allegations of judicial misconduct," the judicial commission (JQC) stated in the jailing incident. "Judge Sloop first came to the JQC's attention early in his tenure as a county judge in Seminole County, where he has served since 1991. In his first year on the bench, he was investigated by the JQC for alleged misconduct in an eviction proceeding and for displaying a firearm in court. Those investigations concluded with private admonishments . . . In 2002, the JQC again investigated Judge Sloop, this time for alleged rude and abusive behavior." As a result, he was "warned" about "his temper" by the commission and by other judges.

The commission wrote the following about the thoughtless jailings. "On December 3rd, 2004, you (Judge Sloop) issued arrest warrants for approximately 11 traffic defendants who had not answered your docket call, but who were in fact, properly in an adjoining courtroom pursuant to their summonses or the direction of the judicial deputy sheriffs or bailiffs. You were informed of the circumstances, but nevertheless proceeded to have the arrest warrants carried out, and these defendants arrested, and you initially declined to release them. As a result, these traffic defendants remained in jail until their release was considered by another judge. You then revisited your arrest warrants."

The commission stated "Judge Sloop admitted this allegation."

The confusion was caused because the new Seminole County Courthouse had only recently been completed after several delays, and courthouse staffers weren't "certain" in which courtrooms each judge would sit. That's why the 11 people were sent to the wrong courtroom.

It was all an honest mistake, and probably harmless in all other courtrooms in the land.

Victims testified before the commission, and supported by a court videotape, said that after Judge Sloop recessed the morning session they were herded into his courtroom by officers who came from "all over the courthouse." Meanwhile, Judge Sloop left the courthouse and didn't return until afternoon.

Being booked into the slammer like a murder suspect was horrifying for these innocents. "They were handcuffed and chained . . . and transported to the jail where they were processed and strip searched," the commission reported. Originally, a dozen people had been busted. But a girl was quickly released when officers found out her young age. Victims were arrested before noon and weren't released from jail until nine at night, despite pleading with jailers, saying it was all a mistake. And then, they were released after another judge prepared the paperwork.

Earlier in the day Judge Sloop refused to release the 11 even though two other judges came to him and said these folks "had been present in the wrong courtroom and should not be arrested."

In his defense before the commission, Judge Sloop "repeatedly stated that he assumed that they would be immediately released and he denied having any idea that persons arrested under such circumstances would be strip searched in the jail facility." Such searches were required by jail staff.

The arrests happened on Friday. On Monday the county court's chief judge asked Judge Sloop why he had not solved the problem by simply walking back into his courtroom and taking care of it immediately. Judge Sloop responded that he did not understand why this was a "big deal."

For the judge his defense before the commission came down to his mental state. He said that since the incident he had undergone "anger management" therapy and "received a diagnosis ... for [adult] Attention Deficit Hyperactivity Disorder." He contended it contributed to his poor judgment.

A psychiatrist testifying in his behalf before the discipline commission said that people with this condition are "easily distracted, impulsive, and have a low frustration tolerance, all of which could have contributed" to his "poor decision-making." A psychologist who had given the judge personality tests also testified. She said Judge Sloop probably had adult Attention Deficit Disorder but she didn't believe it played a role in his misconduct. She said the judge had "a control feature to his anger."

When all was said and done, the state's Supreme Court decided that John Sloop wasn't a man they wanted on their courts, and dismissed him from the bench. Ronald Parilla, who was arrested that day, agreed to talk to the local newspaper about the firing. "He got what he deserved," he was quoted as saying. "I think the Supreme Court sent a clear message to other judges: they're not going to tolerate any other black-robe power trips."

◊

When a bully's in the school yard, watch out, and stay out of his way. When the bully's on the bench and you've been hauled into court, you're toast. Especially if you're female and in the courtroom of Donald R. Roberts, justice of the Malone Village Court in Franklin County, N.Y.

Here's a guy who called "protective orders" to stop wives from being beaten to a pulp by violent husbands "not worth anything" and "just a piece of paper."

In the mid-1990s he refused to grant a protective order to a woman whose husband had "knocked her to the floor, kicked her in the stomach [and] choked her." The same battered woman called the cops a month after she was choked and kicked by her husband and asked police to remove him from the house. Police informed her they couldn't take him away because there was no protective order in force.

When prosecutors implored the judge to grant protective orders for battered wives, the judge, referring to the letter about protective orders from the district attorney, told his court clerk "in a serious tone": "Every woman needs a good pounding now and then."

This incident and many others in which the judge bullied women were the reason the New York State Commission on Judicial Conduct fired Judge Roberts, stating, in non-soufflé-speak: "The record depicts a biased, mean-spirited and bullying judge who, in a number of cases, abandoned his proper role as a neutral and detached magistrate."

Complaints against him included having a welfare mother arrested for not paying her fine after failing to pay cab fare of $1.50. The judge fined her $90, and she promised to pay $20 every two weeks. When the first payment came due, she only had $5 in her purse to pay. The judge had her arrested and brought to his chambers. "He loudly and angrily told her that he had about 300 people who owed fines to the court and that he was going to make 'an example' of her." The women cried, and the judge sentenced her to 89 days in jail.

Only one of the complaints brought before the commission involved a male, all others involved women. In its ruling to fire the judge the commission never called him a misogynist. By highlighting his comment that "every woman needs a good pounding now and then," it didn't have to.

◇

In sifting through pages of discipline records, once in a while a case came along that made the reader want to slap the offending judge up the side of the head, and gladly accept punishment for assault. Discipline of Judge M. John Steensland, Jr. of Alabama is one of them. In all, this bench bully was charged with 60 ethical violations, including on a "number of occasions" asking "victims" of domestic violence "what they had done to cause the abuse."

While the district judge in Houston County, Alabama was censured by the state judicial discipline commission for acts of what must be called "bullying," it was his treatment of a female soldier who had returned from Iraq, suffering post-traumatic stress disorder that screamed loudest, and was most offensive. The woman had been issued a speeding ticket and she was the first defendant to appear that day in 2010 on Judge Steensland's traffic court docket. She entered a plea of not guilty and asked for a trial. At that point evidence was heard and the judge found her guilty of speeding, and sentenced her to 10 days in jail.

Afterward she was handcuffed and moved into a chair along the wall at the front of the courtroom. At that point, she would later testify before the state discipline body, she told the judge that "she was a veteran of the Iraq war, that she had been injured while serving in Iraq, and that she suffered from post-traumatic stress disorder. Because of her injuries and her disorder, [she] explained, she could not endure being handcuffed."

Despite this, the judge left her handcuffed for the next two hours, during which, she told the judicial commission, "she was crying and shaking, and, at one point, it appeared as though she was about to hyperventilate." Court personnel tried to calm her by saying she "would not actually be going to jail," that apparently it was some kind of scare tactic. To add insult to his bullying of the Iraq war veteran, Judge Steensland made an example of her. "According to testimony from a number of witnesses, as other defendants came forward at the session of court to enter their pleas in traffic cases, Judge Steensland would ask whether they wanted to plead guilty or 'end up' like [the soldier] No other defendant requested a trial during the traffic-case docket that day."

Once all traffic cases were handled the judge set aside the soldier's jail sentence and ordered her to pay a fine. But, the damage, as they say, was done. She and four other women who said the judge used profanity and seemed angry during the session filed complaints against him.

During the commission's investigation, Judge Steensland sent in his retirement letter in May 2010, which included a sentence, which after reading the final verdict of the commission a year later, was comical: ". . . Any request, whether now or in the future, that I return to active duty status, or exercise any judicial authority, is hereby declined."

In its verdict the commission stated: "Judge Steensland [is] publicly censured [and] this court also prohibits M. John Steensland, Jr., from ever serving as a judge in any case in any court in Alabama or from exercising any judicial authority in any manner whether now or in the future."

In light of his thoughtless treatment of the Iraq war veteran in his courtroom that day, (15 charges against the judge stemmed from his actions in her speeding ticket case), it was interesting that a resume posted on a web site for the former judge, with his photo, listed his academic accomplishments such as having a degree in civil engineering as well as in law, and mentions his service as a judge from 1989 until retirement, but it doesn't list military service. In Alabama, of all places, military service is something to be especially proud of.

◊

The slang interjection OK meaning "all right" has been around since 1839 when in New York it was part of a language fad in which abbreviations were used for common phrases, including "KG" for "no go" and "NC" for "enough said." OK gained public usage and credibility in the 1840 re-election campaign of President Martin Van Buren whose nickname was "Old Kinderhook" or "OK" because he was born in Kinderhook, N.Y.

Anyways, "OK" or spelled out "okay" has stuck around in common English speech for more than a century. That is unless you walked into the courtroom of Queens New York Judge Terrence C. O'Connor.

In March of 2018 the state's Commission on Judicial Conduct had had enough of his crap and kicked his butt off the bench.

What did he do?

It seemed the judge, son of a former Queens district attorney, never used the adverb "OK" in speech himself. Because when two lawyers "absent-mindedly" repeated the word "okay" when witnesses answered their questions, the judge punished the linguistic sin by eliminating the testimony from the official court record. To add judicial injury, the judge dismissed the cases for lack of evidence.

In a shame court of baboons, it'd have gone like this:
Lawyer: "So, sir, what did you see?"
Witness: "I saw Bobby pull a gun and kill Mr. Jones."
Lawyer: "Okay."

Judge: "You said okay . . . you're leading the witness so I'm striking the testimony from the record."

Berating attorneys for informal speech in a formal setting wasn't the real reason he was booted from his cushy $193,500 judgeship. The Judicial Conduct people also said Judge O'Connor failed to cooperate in the commission's investigation.

The New York Post reported that following a hearing on March 7th, 2017 in which the judge refused to testify under oath, "two [commission] staffers heard O'Connor fume, 'This place is a fucking clown show.'"

"Judges are obliged to cooperate with official disciplinary inquiries into their behavior," the commission said in a statement. "Failing to cooperate, and acting in a manner intended to thwart an ethics inquiry, is itself misconduct, often more serious than the underlying behavior. Judge O'Connor was removed from office for his intransigence." As is often the case, the judge was involved in a previous discipline case in 2013 in which he was censured for his conduct.

◊

No other way to describe it. Judge Sandra J. Holien wasn't judge material, or as Iowa's Supreme Court put it in firing her in 2000 – "We believe [she] is simply and unalterably unsuited to be a judge."

Her courtroom from hell certainly had its ridiculousness: she held court sessions in her private office without defendants' attorneys or even jailers for protection in violation of open court rulings by the United States Supreme Court and state criminal procedures. The judge told a clerk to post a sign on the public access door of her courtroom that stated, "Do Not Enter Courtroom When Court is in Session," on a day when guilty pleas and sentencings were taking place. When people came into her courtroom, the judge asked them "why they were there." Around the courthouse there was an "unwritten rule" to not enter her courtroom during a hearing. Generally such "stay out" signs go up only for court hearings involving juveniles and during a trial when a judge is reading "jury instructions" to jurors. Otherwise, U.S. Supreme Court precedents say courts are open.

The judge also caused havoc with the courtroom docket by using her own system of keeping track of cases. Inexplicitly in handling the court's calendar, she haphazardly scheduled 80 trials on the same day. The whole state listed only 53 judges.

In the end, District Judge Holien, then about 50 years old, was investigated for being a cantankerous and obnoxious cog in the wheels of the state judicial bureaucracy. "Judge Holien's frequent conflicts with almost all of the people with whom she came in contact," the state's high court stated in its removal order. "These included the chief judge, the other judges of the Second Judicial District, the district court administrator, several court reporters (although at least two apparently had no problems), court attendants, clerk's office employees, peace officers, domestic violence personnel, department of corrections employees, attorneys and the public. The depth and breadth of her hostilities must have touched every aspect of her judicial services in Marshall County. She has been like the proverbial bull in a china shop."

When such bulls make life unbearable for a bureaucracy they get slaughtered. The bureaucrat playbook has two chapters. The first talks about self-preservation; the second, getting along.

Remarkably, vividly showing the number of people in the Marshalltown, Iowa justice system who this Mrs. Scrooge had bah-humbugged, 84 witnesses came forward to testify at the Commission on Judicial Qualifications discipline hearing, which lasted eight full days. More than likely this is still a national record.

Stories of being nasty on a daily basis to nearly everybody she spoke with cram the official report to overflowing. Court stenographers quit because of her tirades (she returned one stenographer's Christmas gift), and it got so bad none of the stenographers would agree to type the record in her court.

A female judge testified that Judge Holien "hung" up on her when she called her. After that time, the judge testified, "It didn't matter what time of day I would call, she never answered the phone again when I called her."

A court administrator who said when he tried to speak to the judge about her courtroom practices that were causing near chaos for court clerks, she told him to telephone her attorney in Minnesota if he wanted to discuss it. Think about it. What do you think would happen to you if you worked for a private business and another employee came to you to talk about a work issue, and you told her to call your attorney to talk about it? Buddy, you'd be in the unemployment line the next day.

The judge was one kooky bird.

In dealing with law enforcement things really got strange. "When peace officers brought prisoners to court [the judge] would make rude and embarrassing remarks to the officers," the commission stated. "Several times she asked the officers why they were spying on her. Judge Holien's attitude became so hostile toward peace officers that in August of 1997 the chief jailer wrote a letter to her asking her to conduct herself in a respectful way when doing initial appearances in the county jail. When [her] treatment of peace officers continued to be rude and intemperate, the Marshalltown Police Department complained to the court administrator. The court administrator contacted Judge Holien, who refused to respond."

Accusing the cops of "spying" on her (she had also said the court administrator was spying on her) tended to show paranoia. It was something the Iowa Commission on Judicial Qualifications considered because it had psychiatrists testify at her discipline hearing. "To a layperson looking at the facts of this case, it might appear the [judge] has a form of mental illness, perhaps paranoia," the Supreme Court wrote in its removal order. "However, neither psychiatrist who examined her in connection with this proceeding has made a diagnosis of mental illness."

The court called her "volatile, often angry [and] unwilling to yield even though it was clear she was wrong. She adamantly refused to follow the rules of criminal procedure and the statutory provisions for an open court. She made people fearful of offending her, fearful of working with or for her, or even being in her court. From 1994 until . . . 1999, hostility and chaos were her trademarks. Civility toward fellow judges, court employees, attorneys, and the public – traits that should be valued by all judges – were almost totally lacking. In fact, her job performance was the antithesis of a judge's role as envisioned by our Code of Judicial Conduct."

The Supreme Court ordered her removed if she did not quit, and Judge Holien resigned.

She opposed the order on technical issues, which the state high court rejected, and sought a program of behavior modification under the watchful eye of a tutor. "We believe [she] is simply and unalterably unsuited to be a judge and no attempts at behavior modification are going to change that significantly. She simply should not be a judge."

It wasn't that this graduate of the University of Minnesota Law School was incompetent. It seemed that she just didn't like other people.

Eight years after her resignation, an Iowa newspaper lamented the fact that other professions such as teachers, police officers and elderly care nurses go through background checks before being hired – even strip club owners are subject to an "extensive back ground check – but not district court judges in Iowa. The case of Judge Holien was cited as an example in the story.

◊

Under an Illinois Supreme Court rule "upper-level law students" can perform "specified legal services" of a licensed attorney.

Around 1999 Jackson County, Illinois Judge William G. Schwartz was proud when his stepson decided to follow in his footsteps and attend Southern Illinois University School of Law. The judge also "sought the advice and assistance of certain law school faculty members and administrators with respect to his stepson's application." However, in July of 2000 his stepson was denied admission to the school.

"Immediately following his stepson's rejection," the judge "banned" all law students from appearing alone in his courtroom by implementing a state law, requiring an advisory attorney to be with them. But, because Carbondale, Jackson County's most populous city, is the home of Southern Illinois University School of Law, the ban affected "only" its law students. Illinois Courts Commission contended that the judge's action was either "in retaliation for the rejection of his stepson's application to the law school, or created the appearance that it was." Fairly defenseless to the accusation, the judge moved to settle the case and was reprimanded in 2001.

◊

Even when judges try to do good, they get slammed by their state discipline masters for it. Alabama's Judicial Inquiry Commission filed a complaint against Circuit Judge Marvin Wayne Wiggins in 2016, and all he did was try to save lives. In 2015 the judge handled what was called a "pay-due" docket in which defendants who owed fines to the court were supposed to pay their fines. However, many defendants that day didn't bring cash with them. Just so happened the judge had helped arrange to have the local blood bank's mobile collection van parked outside. The judge announced from the bench: "For your consideration, there's a blood drive outside and if you do not have any money and you don't want to go to jail, as an option to pay it [your fine], you can give blood today . . . So . . . consider giving blood today and bring your receipt back or the sheriff has enough handcuffs for those who do not have money." In all 47 people from Judge Wiggins's courtroom donated blood – that's almost six gallons of the lifesaving stuff.

Yep, the discipline commission thought it judicial misconduct. "Judge Wiggins's conduct regarding the incarceration of criminal defendants and his conduct in threatening to incarcerate those defendants who did not have any money unless they gave blood were so coercive as to be reprehensible and inexcusable," the commission stated. In his defense the judge said he never intended to jail anyone who didn't donate blood, and in fact, didn't have any defendants placed in custody for not paying fines. However, he agreed that his remarks were "inappropriate and could lead a reasonable person to believe he or she would be ordered to jail for failure to pay court-assessed fines and costs if he or she did not donate blood." Also in the judge's defense, his lawyer said that Alabama judges are under pressure to collect fines. The "pay-due" session was in Perry County.

The state's high court censured the judge, who had been on the bench since 1999, and whose Fourth Judicial Circuit Court handled matters from Bibb, Dallas, Hale, Perry and Wilcox counties.

Chapter Thirteen

Witnesses told the state's judge watchdog commission that his chambers reminded them of "my teenager's bedroom." The problem with a judge having a messy courtroom and office is he can lose more than a pair of dirty socks. And, that's what happened to Riverside County, California Superior Court Judge Robert G. Spitzer, who probably should have listened better when told to clean up his room as a kid.

After the trial in a small claims case, the "file" went "missing" in the courtroom clutter. As a result the verdict was finally recorded nearly six years later when the judge was forced to hold a new trial, and record the verdict. During this time, 1996 to 2002, furthermore, the judge was paid nearly 40 paychecks from his $150,000 annual salary in violation of state law because the small claims case had not been finalized for so many years.

For Robert Spitzer, a former star in the Riverside County District Attorney's Office appointed judge in 1990, it was only the beginning of a thick sticky-wicket of problems with the California Judicial Performance Commission, which booted him off the bench in 2007. And according to State Bar of California records, the UCLA grad and University of Southern California Law School graduate was no longer eligible to practice law in the state. He was originally admitted to practice in 1975.

His sloppy housekeeping preceded him to the courthouse. "Judge Spitzer has been plagued by organizational issues since the beginning of his career in the district attorney's office," the state commission stated in a report on its investigation. "Numerous witnesses, including (California) Justice Douglas Miller, the former presiding judge, and . . . Judge Spitzer's longtime courtroom clerk, testified that the judge's courtroom and chambers were in shambles . . . Files and loose documents were strewn about without any discernable organization. As a result, court records were routinely lost or misplaced."

Of course, this prompted attorneys and litigants to repeatedly call the courthouse, asking about the status of their cases being handled by Judge Spitzer. The paper disaster zone got so bad that in 2001 the court's presiding judge ordered his courtroom and office cleaned up and an inventory of pending cases taken. Other judges took up the slack generated by the judge's slapdash habits.

Around 2003, the commission sent Judge Spitzer a letter, saying that he faced discipline if he didn't clean up his act. The case was dropped when, in December of that year, the judge appeared before the commission, and "assured [it] that he had no cases under submission for more than 90 days, that the problem had not re-occurred since February or March of that year, and that he had set up procedures to avoid a repetition of this problem." Four years later in its 2007 report, the commission stated, "In fact, the evidence . . . establishes that these assurances were false."

Even while the judge spoke to the commission in 2003 he had at least two tardy cases, the commission stated. Remarkably, he brought the judgment of an important case with him to the commission hearing in 2003, and even after he returned to his office he still didn't have it immediately finalized in county records.

In fact, it was this case of egregious delay that might have pissed off commissioners most, among his other tardy cases. That's because in this case Judge Spitzer's inaction probably cost a litigant his appeal. According to commission records Judge Spitzer ruled on the case in July 2003 but didn't "process" it until the following June. It was an important lawsuit involving a city and a regional government agency. Worse yet, when the regional agency later filed an appeal of Judge Spitzer's ruling, the appellate court "dismissed" the appeal because it was "untimely because over thirteen months had elapsed since entry of judgment." Stated the judicial commission: The litigant's "appeal was dismissed as untimely as a result of the judge's delay in processing the judgment. By allowing judicial orders to sit unprocessed in his cluttered chambers for months, Judge Spitzer showed a complete indifference to the rights of litigants and his judicial responsibilities."

The commission called his "practice of signing orders and not sending them to be entered . . . inexplicable and amounts to a dereliction of duty."

For Judge Spitzer having a messy courtroom and office might have spared him from the most serious of eight charges leveled against him by the Judicial Performance Commission in 2006 – allegedly "backdating" his judicial orders. Judge Spitzer testified before the commission and said it was his practice to sign orders and place them somewhere in his cluttered chambers or courtroom rather than giving them to his clerk to be processed. The commission found "it is credible that if Judge Spitzer signed an order and did not put it out for processing it could get lost" in his "extremely disorganized" office. "It is plausible signed orders were misplaced," the commission stated. In other words, the "backdating" allegation was unproved, and in fact wasn't considered in his dismissal from office. Although the commission's records do not go deeper into the issue, it is assumed that backdating would have been one way to show there were no delays in rulings, which would mean paycheck affidavits were true because there were no cases pending longer than three months.

(When I first read the commission's report, it reminded me of stories I wrote as a daily newspaper reporter. The first was about money apparently stolen from a hotel owned by a city in which financial records were so screwed up it was impossible to say for sure whether money was missing. The second was about a public charity that allegedly made improper interest-free loans to key employees. When I confronted the charity's director, he plopped boxes of financial records on a table and gave me five minutes to examine them and show him any wrongdoing. Records were in such disarray I couldn't make hide nor hair of them.)

The commission stated that "Judge Spitzer's chronic state of disorganization and gross neglect of court records" and "his dysfunctional practices . . . raise serious concerns regarding his fitness to hold judicial office." Let that be a lesson to you judges out there. Before you leave for the day, tidy up your desk!

Because he had such long delays in finalizing some cases, the commission essentially accused Judge Spitzer of failing to do his job. "Litigants and the public have a right to expect judges to take action on matters assigned to them in an expeditious and efficient manner. A judge's failure to act deprives litigants of resolution of their disputes and grievances through the court system," the commission stated.

A deeper look shows that Judge Spitzer wasn't lazy, he was preoccupied. An experienced prosecutor who had many criminal trials to his credit, the judge valued holding trials and in his own words was diligent "in focusing on cases currently before him" rather than on cases already heard.

A member of the commission hit on another reason for the judge's less than staller ability to tie up judicial loose ends. It appears, the member said, "to some degree" the judge was "escaping to trial" where he was most comfortable as a judge. Even the judge himself suggested he was more backlogged than other judges because he presides over more trials, and "therefore did not have time to handle submitted matters and administrative tasks." Stated the commission in its report: "We do not disagree . . . that Judge Spitzer is a hard-working judge . . . We concur with the (examiners) that Judge Spitzer's failure to give his other judicial responsibilities his prompt attention added insult to existing disadvantage and did nothing to improve public confidence in an increasingly inaccessible system of civil justice." In the words of a fellow judge, "Judge Spitzer was in a state of denial for a long time that he wasn't able to control his caseload."

Then there was his finger-pointing. In his testimony before the commission's examiners, Judge Spitzer suggested that his clerk let signed orders sit unprocessed on her desk for significant periods of time, a claim refuted by his clerk. In his oral presentation before the commission, "Judge Spitzer implied that court staff shared responsibility for his delays and missing documents because they refused to come into his cluttered chambers and because they failed to locate files and documents he had misplaced. He also blamed staff for failing to bring inquiries about cases to his attention, a claim contradicted by the testimony of court staff." The commission wasn't buying. "We emphatically reject any implication that staff were at fault," it stated. "Judge Spitzer, not his staff, was responsible for his misconduct. Judge Spitzer attempted to deflect responsibility for his six-year delay in deciding [the small claims case] by testifying he had decided the matter but simply failed to sign the order, a claim we . . . have rejected. He also took the position that he was not responsible for deciding matters under submission after he was transferred to a criminal [courtroom] assignment, despite receiving e-mails from his presiding judge informing him he was still responsible for civil matters under submission . . . By allowing judicial orders to sit unprocessed in his cluttered chambers for months, Judge Spitzer showed a complete indifference to the rights of litigants and his judicial responsibilities."

In his finger-pointing, the judge blamed delay in one of the cases on his clerk whom he said had been on vacation. "Judge Spitzer testified that the signed document in [one case] sat on [the clerk's] workstation for months waiting to be processed." However, the clerk and the clerk who filled in for her while she was on vacation denied it. His clerk "testified that she kept up-to-date in processing documents because she did not have enough work to do during that time," commission records showed.

The commission found that during 2003 and 2004, "Judge Spitzer failed to cooperate with his presiding judge's repeated inquiries regarding the status of the cases and directives to resolve all outstanding matters." And, "rather than cooperating with his presiding judge, who made repeated attempts to get Judge Spitzer to resolve delayed matters, Judge Spitzer resented being 'micro-managed.' As a result . . . Judge Spitzer became passive-aggressive and actually ignored some of the directions he received from [the presiding judge] . . . The failure to cooperate with the presiding judge was foolish and unhelpful, since the presiding judge was seeking to assist him." Finally, the presiding judge spoke in language Judge Spitzer understood. The court's presiding judge sent Judge Spitzer an e-mail, telling him that he would not get his paycheck because of the backlog. In relative short order, the cases were processed by Judge Spitzer.

Money, apparently spoke loudly.

In the end, the filing false salary affidavits probably lost Judge Spitzer his job.

Please allow a brief digression, though a relevant one. Years ago in covering the courts I got to know a judge name George C. Grover. The late Riverside County Superior Court judge was among the friendliest, nicest, and most jovial and kind-hearted person I ever met. He was also smart. A graduate of USC Law School, he was an expert in the complex area of water law and won a state Supreme Court case that helped provide Los Angeles its water needs. He served as president of the California Public Utilities Commission before becoming a judge. But most of all I remember his honesty, which is why I mention him here. Judge Grover's integrity was so intense it sometimes cost him his judicial paycheck. Under California's Constitution, judges are expected to decide cases within 90 days after being submitted to them. Judges are prohibited from receiving their salaries when they have undecided matters under submission for more than three months. To be paid, the judge must sign an affidavit affirming he has no "overdue" cases. It is a way to keep the court system's backlog at a minimum and assure as much as possible that justice is speedy. Judge Grover often admitted to me that he wasn't being paid because he had cases older than 90 days, and in fact, it was this reason which was most often cited by attorneys who had voted him the "worst" judge in Riverside County in the mid-eighties. In other words, they weren't lambasting him because of ill judicial temper or poor legal knowledge. Attorneys practicing before him thought he was too slow in making judicial decisions, which, of course, adversely affected their own paychecks. Still, George Grover didn't cheat. Each month he would righteously inform state court administrators that he was tardy with his rulings and, thereby, would not collect his paycheck. More judges on the California courts should have George Grover's honesty. Commission records show that many judges have been disciplined for filing false salary affidavits, like Judge Robert Spitzer.

Walking with an air of arrogance, Spitzer, in his seventies, was the kind of man who regaled at how well he had done on his college SATs. He had risen to supervisor in the Riverside DA's Office. After his appointment to the municipal court in Riverside, the courts consolidated and he became a judge of the county's more powerful Superior Court, handling civil and criminal cases. If truth be known, however, he never really enjoyed the civil law side of being a judge. Nevertheless his legal scholarship was never in question. "Based on the testimony of Riverside County judges and lawyers, the (commission) found that Judge Spitzer has a reputation as a knowledgeable and honest judge," the commission stated. "We do not question Judge Spitzer's intelligence or knowledge of the law. Nor do we doubt that his character witnesses believe Judge Spitzer to be a man of integrity . . . ."

Harvard University's Business School analyzes monumental blunders by corporations and outlines them in instructional materials to teach MBA students how not to make the same mistakes. Details of the discipline case against Judge Spitzer, while more than a decade old, provide a good primer on what not to do as a trial jurist. In the summer of 2006 he was "charged" by the Commission on Judicial Performance with eight counts of judicial misconduct, ranging from "failing to dispose of matters promptly," to improperly communicating with a witness and "executing false salary affidavits in four cases." On the latter allegation in four instances Judge Spitzer submitted "false" statements, saying his backlog was up to date, thereby allowing him to collect his paycheck. From a public purview perspective the worst violation of his ethics was falsifying pay records. "He signed salary affidavits . . . declaring that he had no matters pending for more than 90 days after submission, although he had been informed he had such matters," the commission stated. "Submitting false salary affidavits, even if recklessly rather than knowingly, was willful misconduct . . . A judge who executes a salary affidavit affirming he or she has no overdue rulings should take care to ensure that the statement is true when it is made. It is unjudicial and damaging to the public esteem for judicial office for a judge to submit false statements to obtain salary to which the judge is not then entitled." It is taxpayers' cash after all. It was never proved that Judge Spitzer "knowingly" filed false pay statements. Before the commission, he "denied ever knowingly signing false salary affidavits." And, in its investigation the commission's examiners "found the evidence did not clearly and convincingly prove Judge Spitzer knowingly signed false salary affidavits." In its final report, the commission agreed with investigators, stating, "We defer to this finding."

Judge Spitzer wasn't Clyde Barrow. He was more like your absentminded uncle. To show his honesty, he told the commission "there were occasions over the years when he did not sign salary affidavits because he knew he had matters under submission for more than 90 days." He provided no details, however, and didn't say any of these involved the four cases charged against him. The commission stated: "Judge Spitzer signed false salary affidavits with a reckless disregard for the truth in those instances where the evidence clearly and convincingly proves he continued to execute salary affidavits after being informed he had delayed matters pending." Commission records showed many other judges have been accused of, and disciplined for, accepting pay when they had cases pending longer than 90 days.

Judge Spitzer made more blunders. At first he failed to respond to the disciplinary commission when asked to do so. Later, as written above, he pointed the blame-finger at others and gave testimony to the commission that members didn't believe. He should have known nothing pisses off the state Supreme Court as much as a lowly Superior Court judge thumbing his nose at the court's watchdog commission, and then telling perceived fibs. In a previous case, the California Supreme Court had strongly denounced a judge who lied to the commission. "There are few judicial actions in our view that provide greater justification for removal from office than the action of a judge in deliberately providing false information to the commission in the course of its investigation into charges of willful misconduct on the part of the judge," was the court's non-sugar-coating of it.

The commission itself also showed displeasure at "Judge Spitzer's willingness to impugn the credibility of two district attorneys and [a witness] by implying they falsely testified concerning material facts in these proceedings." Blasting the judge's credibility, the commission snarled: "The lack of candor we have observed in these proceedings is fundamentally at odds with the role of a judge who is sworn to uphold the law."

Another serious allegation in the misconduct case involved what the law calls ex-parte communications, or, having a litigant or his attorney discuss a case with a judge without the opposing side being present.

It's a long-held judicial no-no.

Judge Spitzer had presided over the trial of a drunken driver who killed a boy and was charged with second-degree murder by the district attorney. Judge Spitzer thought the jury should be allowed to consider the alternative of gross vehicular manslaughter as well as murder. But the district attorney's office declined, which meant the jury had two choices, either guilty of second-degree murder or not guilty. At the end of the trial the jury voted eleven to one in favor of second-degree murder, which amounted to a hung jury. The result was the judge declared a mistrial. As a matter of law the judge's suggestion was reasonable and would have given the jury an alternative crime to convict the driver of. But, if there's a law-and-order DA in office, he's probably not going to give the impression that he is soft on crime by allowing manslaughter to get in the way of a good murder conviction.

At the end of the drunken driver's trial, with the prosecutor and defense attorney in attendance, "Judge Spitzer addressed several members of the [dead boy's] family who were present in the courtroom," said the commission's account of what happened. "He told them the case should be settled with a plea to vehicular manslaughter and even suggested he would dismiss the murder charge if a second jury did not reach a verdict." His unwelcomed remarks likely pissed off the prosecutor and delighted the defense. However, what the judge did next was bone-headed in the extreme. During a recess he spotted the mother of the dead boy, Kathleen Kavanagh in the courthouse hallway. She had arrived late to court and Judge Spitzer invited her into his chambers for a chat – without prosecutor or defense attorney – amounting to an ex parte communication. The office door was closed, and according to Judge Spitzer, he only informed her of what he had stated in open court earlier. After hearing testimony from the mother and others, the commission observed "the judge's comments to Ms. Kavanagh went beyond what he said in open court . . . He read her sections of the Penal Code, explained the difference between second-degree murder and manslaughter, and told her it would be difficult for the prosecution to prove murder." The mother later told the discipline commission she felt intimidated by the judge who told her: "Look, basically the charge should have never been murder in any degree; it was a crime that should only have held a manslaughter charge . . . [the defendant] did not intentionally plan to kill your son, with all due respect, Ms. Kavanagh, for you and your son it was an accident." She said that Judge Spitzer told her the drunken driver faced a "substantial amount of time" if convicted of manslaughter. The mother testified that she replied: "Well, my son isn't never getting to come home; so why should he [the defendant] ever get to come home?" Then, according to the commission, the judge "suggested" that she "try to influence the deputy district attorney to charge the defendant with manslaughter so there would not have to be a second trial." She said the judge "warned" he would have to dismiss the murder charge if a second jury did not reach a verdict. Kathleen Kavanagh also told the commission that Judge Spitzer showed an arrogant side, and of being on a bit of a power-trip. "This is my house; and when you get your house, you can do things your way," she said he told her. "And this is my house, and we're going to do things my way."

Judge Spitzer told commission officials that he tried to "comfort" the mother. Far from perceiving Judge Spitzer's comments as comforting, Ms. Kavanagh testified that she "took it as he was intimidating me." In addition, the judge said he invited the mother into his chambers to "provide her with the same information he had given those who appeared in court that day."

In the course of the commission's investigation Judge Spitzer admitted his comments to Ms. Kavanagh "gave the appearance he was trying to influence her to consent to a reduction of the murder," the commission stated. With disgust it added: "Attempting to convince a mother whose child was killed by a drunk driver that her child's death was unintentional by reference to Penal Codes, legal terminology, and sentence calculations reflects an alarming lack of sensitivity in addition to being extraordinarily inappropriate and unjudicial." In a court session after the trial "Judge Spitzer continued to pressure the deputy district attorney for a manslaughter disposition. He told the deputy district attorney and the defense attorney he had a conversation with Ms. Kavanagh and his impression was she was 'not hostile' to a manslaughter plea bargain." As the commission concluded, Judge Spitzer "abandoned his role as a neutral arbiter and became embroiled," wherein a judge "surrenders the role of impartial factfinder, and joins the fray."

After his actions in the first trial, Judge Spitzer was disqualified by the prosecutor from hearing the second trial. Presided over by another judge, the drunken driver was convicted of second-degree murder in the second trial. But the case obviously left a bitter taste in the mouths of prosecutors in the judge's former office. Because for a time afterwards, the district attorney "disqualified" Judge Spitzer from hearing all felony cases.

The commission doubted Judge Spitzer would ever change his stripes and clean up his act. Summing up, the commission stated: "A pattern of misconduct consisting of delays, indecision, signing false salary affidavits, ex parte communication, embroilment, and failure to cooperate with his presiding judge and the Commission on Judicial Performance inevitably lowered public esteem for the judiciary. His indifference toward his obligation to promptly and efficiently decide matters had an adverse impact on the litigants who appeared before him and his fellow judges. A judge who is not competent to handle a civil calendar and who has a history of embroilment which at various times has resulted in his being disqualified from hearing criminal cases does not serve the public and cannot remain on the bench," the commission stated, in recommending that the state's high court boot Judge Spitzer from office.

◊

The whole courthouse run by Judge Scott Sulley of the Maricopa, Arizona Municipal and Justice Courts was something akin to a county landfill. A jurist since 2003, Judge Sulley was removed from office in 2014 by the state's Supreme Court because the two courts he administered were in "total disarray," with checks for fines left unopened in envelopes and case files stacked up in random piles. A 2010 audit of the court found "deficiencies specifically in handling of cash payments" in the courts. Another audit three years later found that the judge wasn't depositing "defensive driving school" checks from a driving program in the court's account. It was discovered that $112,000 which should have been put in the court's account wasn't deposited. About $66,000 of the money was in opened and unopened envelopes sent in by people who had appeared in court. "Evidence of theft was discovered," auditors stated, but the general disarray of court records made it impossible to figure out how much money was actually missing. In 2014 the state Supreme Court ordered the small courthouse taken over, and put a Superior Court judge in charge of administration. The Supreme Court suspended Judge Sulley from his court duties, although he continued to collect his pay. Auditors found the municipal and justice courts in a mess, with "files stacked in random locations." Files from the municipal court were "comingled" with files from the justice court and "randomly strewn" about. Orders weren't entered in the court's index, making finding records difficult. Auditors learned from court employees that Judge Sulley would not let them seek outside help with questions, and the commission later alleged that the judge did this so outsiders wouldn't discover his mismanagement. Employees also contended he treated them harshly and dressed them down with members of the public present. Helping to prove these claims was the fact that during a 12-month span the courts had 10 clerks quit within three months of hire.

The saga of Judge Scott Sulley did not have a happy ending. After his suspension from the bench the judge's friends told the local newspaper that he went into seclusion. "Everything he went through had such a devastating effect on him," an acquaintance said. "Once that happened, I didn't see him very often. He really disconnected and kind of disappeared." In 2017 the former judge drove himself to the hospital for an undisclosed illness, where he fell into a coma. Less than a month later family members ordered him taken off life-support. Friends remembered him as a "good man" and hoped he would not be remembered for the court fiasco.

Chapter Fourteen

During the height of the Covid-19 pandemic in 2020, courts in cities like Los Angeles closed, people weren't being called for jury duty and trials were postponed. Each state court system made changes and closed courthouses, restricted access and postponed trials and permitted video-conferences for attorneys' oral arguments. Non-case related activities were dumped. Federal courts in Alabama postponed all trials and California state courts shut down until May 1st. 2020. Ohio courts closed until June and grand jury proceedings went dark. Declaring a judicial state of emergency the Georgia Supreme Court warned "all attorneys, parties and other visitors to stay away from the court if they have a fever or symptoms of respiratory illness or if they have been exposed to anyone diagnosed with Covid-19." In a word the judicial system was in a state of disarray. So, it was bound to happen. Two judges in Tennessee got reprimanded publicly by the Board of Judicial Conduct for virus-related incidents in their courtrooms.

Judge Jere Ledsinger of Manchester, Tennessee, greeted people on July 16th, 2020 and pointed out that they were required to wear protective masks in his courtroom. The court was jammed with criminal defendants, among them African-Americans, when Judge Ledsinger said: "The grand wizards of our Supreme Court said we have to wear these masks."

For those words he was snitched him off to the state's judge discipline body.

The judge told the Board of Judicial Conduct that his remark wasn't done to disparage anyone. He said it was his way to "soften any resistance by those present in the courtroom of wearing a mask, as we have had negative feedback to this [Tennessee Supreme Court] mandate."

Actually, his intent was correct, and had he said the high court's "pooh-bahs" had mandated masks he mightn't have put himself in jeopardy. But his reference to the hooded Ku Klux Klan went many steps too far. Stated the ethics board: "Comments such as the ones involved here, even if made off-the-cuff and with no intent to be offensive, reflect an ethical lapse that undermines public confidence that our judges are unbiased in fact and in appearance."

On the other hand, Hohenwald, Tennessee Judge Michael E. Hinson's discipline was meted out by the conduct board for failing to acknowledge pandemic restrictions in his courtroom. He got kicked with a reprimand because, according to the board, he failed to "limit the number of persons in [his] courtroom, and [had] not enforced social distancing requirements" laid down by the state Supreme Court during the pandemic. Added the board: "To the contrary, your courtroom has . . . been filled to capacity . . . to the point of members of the public having to stand shoulder-to-shoulder along the wall because all the seats are taken."

What a namby-pamby discipline case.

The discipline board acknowledged the judge presided in a "small" courtroom and he was trying to "avoid a backlog of cases." Any lawyer, member of the public or newspaper reporter who has been in a "large" courtroom when a judge is handling criminal arraignments, for example, has had to stand "shoulder-to-shoulder" against a wall because all courtroom seats were occupied.

The judge agreed he was wrong in not following the Covid-19 dictates, and said he would comply in the future.

◊

Los Angeles County Municipal Court Judge Alfonso D. Hermo spent 30 unblemished years on the bench and made one mistake, trying to help a friend keep his job. It began on a humdrum, 70-degree day in a routine legal case in his placid Whittier, California courtroom. Like he had done hundreds of times in the past three decades Judge Hermo called the ho-hum misdemeanor case of a man driving with a suspended license, four other minor charges and a violation of probation. When the defendant didn't show, the judge did his usual practice of signing a failure-to-appear arrest warrant for him. The case, however, was about to get complicated, very.

That afternoon the man came to court, and without an attorney, the judge re-called the arrest warrant and told the man to take a seat in the jury section of the courtroom until he set the man's bail, which would be $25,000. The judge's bailiff for 24 years, a deputy sheriff and friend of the judge showed the man where to sit down in the jury section of the court. The judge took a break and left the bench. At some point the man wised up, and realized he couldn't raise bail, and was about to be carted off to the hoosegow. In a panic the man jumped from the jury box and ran from the courtroom. Giving chase, the man was too fast for the bailiff and ran out the courthouse door.

The bailiff returned to the judge's office with the bad news. The judge immediately issued a new arrest warrant for the man, setting total bail at $175,000. Judge Hermo noted in the man's file: "Defendant ran out of the courtroom." It would amount to smoking-gun evidence later. The bailiff didn't report the escape to his supervisors at the sheriff's department. Instead he lied, saying Judge Hermo released the man from custody on his written promise to return to court in the future, a so-called "own recognizance" release. But, the bailiff faced a dilemma. The man's eventual arrest on the $175,000-bail warrant would expose his fib. He went to the judge and they talked privately in chambers. The bailiff said he would be "suspended without pay" three weeks if his bosses learned the man had escaped while in his custody.

Judge Hermo judge immediately took pity on him and Hero recalled the warrant. He then changed court records to show the defendant has been given an "OR" release, which matched the bailiff's false account of what had happened. The judge then had his court clerk alert the district attorney's office and the public defender that the man's bail had been changed to OR.

"You took these actions to help [your bailiff] avoid being suspended without pay for allowing [the] escape," the commission said later of Judge Hermo. "You understood at the time that [your bailiff] was supporting a family and had numerous debts."

So what did this dubious "good deed" get him?

Indicted.

Once the little scheme that seemed so innocent got out a county grand jury indicted the judge and bailiff for felony "conspiracy to obstruct justice" in 1999, about a year after the man's escape. The indictment listed all of the steps the judge took in changing court records to reflect the bailiff's lie. A few months later both the judge and bailiff owned up to their "criminal" actions and pleaded "no contest" in court, which is the legal equivalent of guilty. Both sentenced to "unsupervised" probation, which meant they didn't have to report each month to a probation officer, they were fined $1,000 each and ordered to perform 40 hours of volunteer work. Of course, tarnish to the judge's reputation was his worst sentence. He soon retired.

Following completion of the "criminal" cases, the state Commission on Judicial Performance had to take its pound of flesh. For his actions, the commission ruled that because the judge had retired the worst punishment it could slam him with was barring him from making money by filling-in for other judges on vacation. That is what they did in a public censure of the judge, all for trying to help a friend.

◊

Called to war, North Carolina does its part in spades. In a relatively small population of 10 million in North Carolina, roughly 200,000 residents are members of the United States military. Through military operations such as the Army's Fort Bragg and Camp Lejeune of the U.S. Marine Corps, one in ten jobs is linked to the military, which pumps a massive $66 billion into the state's economy each year. Given the significance of the military on North Carolina's economic health, and the vaunted place in America's collective heart for members of our military, it was surprising to find a judicial misconduct case of a judge who essentially denied a soldier due process under U.S. law which protect soldiers overseas.

The discipline case against Judge Brenda G. Branch of the General Court of Justice wasn't one of a jurist intentionally trying to harm an Army sergeant who was stationed in Korea and couldn't come back to North Carolina to defend his interest in a divorce and child custody matter. It was more of a big, bruising public relations black eye for the state's judiciary, and sent the wrong message to a very vibrant group in North Carolina's economic fabric.

As well the underlying court case wasn't a complicated one. After an Army sergeant's wife sued for divorce and for custody, the sergeant who was stationed in Korea wrote the judge a letter, dated July 2012, saying because he was overseas "his military service precluded him from participating in court proceedings" until April of the following year, a delay of about nine months. He also astutely pointed out that "legal counsel informs me that federal law requires a stay of proceedings for a minimum of 90 days for service members on active duty" and cited federal law, which supersedes state law." The sergeant had gotten his legal advice from a Judge Adjutant General officer stationed in Korea. Adding some legal weight to his assertion that he couldn't just get on a flight and come back to North Carolina, the sergeant's commanding officer wrote to the judge, stating that the sergeant's mission in Korea was "essential" and that federal law required the judge to postpone the sergeant's appearance in her North Carolina courtroom.

It seemed pretty cut and dried: U.S. law protecting due process rights of members of the military, serving overseas required some kind of delay in the divorce action in the judge's Halifax County Family Court. As the North Carolina Supreme Court ruled later in the case, U.S. Service member's Civil Relief Act of 2003, or SCRA, "states in plain language that, if it appears that defendant is in military service, the court may not enter a default judgment against the absent member until after the court appoints an attorney to represent defendant."

Meanwhile, the divorcing wife's attorney, eager to get on with the case, asked the judge for an order "seeking further information from" the soldier "concerning his status under the SCRA" and sought to deny the soldier's request to postpone the divorce until April 2013.

During a hearing on the wife's attorney's request, Judge Branch sought "supporting documents" on the "stay" order and allowed the attorney to "present arguments and evidence challenging the validity of defendant's claim for a stay." At this hearing, nobody represented the soldier, and the judge didn't appoint a lawyer for him.

In her defense, the judge told the state's Judicial Standards Commission that the sergeant's letter and the letter from his commanding officer both mentioned they were citing "advice of counsel" and this was the reason she didn't appoint a lawyer for the soldier to appear for him at the hearing on the "stay" order. Her argument was weak, and later the state Supreme Court discarded it by saying neither letter sent from Korea by the soldier or the commanding officer listed the name or address of an attorney, nor say that an attorney licensed to practice in North Carolina would represent the soldier.

At the hearing, the wife's attorney gave the judge "an undated, uncited publication" titled, "Crossing the Military Minefield: A Judge's Guide to Military Divorce in North Carolina," which discussed ways "that a judge could deny a serviceman a stay, when so requested, by finding that the serviceman did not show 'good faith and diligence' when responding to a court action." The attorney might well have handed the judge a recipe on how to make baked beans because the publication itself carried no citable legal weight in court, lacking North Carolina or federal case law upon which she could base a ruling.

Stated the state Supreme Court: "Here, [the soldier] was not properly served with any motion or objection from [his wife's attorney], had no notice of her objections to his request for a stay, and was not provided with the documents [the attorney] presented to [the judge]." The high court also wrote, in a disclosure that didn't look good for the judge, that she had "used" the publication in her "consideration" for her eventual order to deny the soldier's request for postponement of the divorce because he was deployed overseas. In September 2012 the judge declared that the letter from the soldier and from his commanding officer were "insufficient" to order postponement of the case, and set a deadline for October 1st, for the soldier to respond. The sergeant didn't get the letter which stated the judge's intent to let the case go forward until less than a week before the deadline. On November 5th, the judge formally denied the soldier's stay, citing "a lack of good faith and due diligence" as outlined in the publication on how "a judge could deny a serviceman a stay." Her order stated that the soldier's requested stay was "a willful and direct intention to maneuver and prolong the case at the [soldier's] will for as long as the [soldier] saw fit without regard to the [wife]."

In the next few months, while the soldier remained in Korea, doing his duty for his country, Judge Branch "entered default judgments" against the sergeant, without his being represented in court, essentially granting everything the wife had sought in the divorce. A default happens when a defendant in a civil case doesn't plead or otherwise defend himself.

The Supreme Court stated that the judge cooperated in the investigation and agreed to be reprimanded. The court also found that her misconduct wasn't the result of an intent to harm the soldier's case, and that she believed she was "acting within the scope of her discretion and that she was acting to preserve the integrity of the court." The court stated that her "misconduct appears to have resulted from insufficient inquiry into her obligations under the Service member's Civil Relief Act of 2003, her insufficiently-based conclusion that [the soldier] had legal representation, and from an inappropriate reliance on legal arguments advanced by one party that [the judge] did not sufficiently research for herself." The court went on to say that "the [judge] has a good reputation in her community," concluding, "the actions identified by the commission as misconduct . . .

appear to be isolated and do not form any sort of recurring pattern of misconduct." It said the judge "openly" admitted error.

When the soldier finally got home he hired an attorney to represent him in the divorce that already had been granted by default. The North Carolina Supreme Court wasn't too upset with Judge Branch because about a year after the reprimand, it appointed her as new chief judge of a merged judicial district. In the news story about the appointment the sergeant's divorce case wasn't mentioned.

◊

Judge Rex Stacey of the District Court in Minnesota was publicly reprimanded 2016 for making "accusatory, hostile, and discourteous comments" during a court appearance of a mother of two children who sought court protection from her former husband. "You need counseling badly, because your kids are suffering," the judge told the woman, according to board records. "Not because of him [the father]. Because of you . . . Because you don't see the truth in things. I don't believe your children are afraid of their father. I think they're afraid of you." Some people might say the judge was simply telling it how he thought it, but the discipline board said there was no evidence that the woman's children were afraid of her. The board said that Judge Stacey's discourteous comments did not serve any legitimate purpose and caused the woman to believe that he was biased against her. It wasn't the first time the judge had been punished by the board. In 2014 during a divorce case, the judge told an attorney who was questioning a witness at the time, "I'll be right back. Just continue without me." He walked out. Returning later, the judge said, "I've never done that before. It felt good."

◊

Sometimes a judge says what everybody's thinking, and gets popped for it. That's what happened to Solano County, California Superior Court Judge Daniel J. Healy, who was publicly admonished for his utterances. In 2013, handling legally routine divorce and child custody cases, he ruled in a case involving a mother who allegedly drove drunk in the middle of the night with her child in the car. In an effort to "get to the bottom of what happened" that night, the judge let the mother tell her story but not until he told both parents: "I don't think either of you understand the beat-down that is coming, because this child deserves a thousand times better than all of this drama."

At a hearing set later, Judge Healy told the couple what he really thought of them both. "I think that I do not have any evidence in front of me rising to the level of any chronic abuse of anything or rises to a level regarding drugs or alcohol," he said. "I just think, to be honest with you, sometimes people are just rotten, and they can't respect other people. Everything's drama. It's like they're trying out for 'Jersey Shore' [a reality TV show with fairly disgusting characters]. You guys just both strike me as rotten. Maybe what I should do is have [child protective services] save your child from both of you because you are both rotten." Later the mother tried to convince the judge that she wasn't lying about what happened in the drunk driving. Responded Judge Healy, "Okay. Why don't you prove to me that you recognize what a train wreck you are, and then maybe we'll be somewhere?" He then called her a "liar," adding, "I don't know why you think you deserve anything [but] a cell door closing behind you."

Who knows. They probably were rotten parents. Sometimes you just have to say it. The Commission on Judicial Performance disagreed, and publicly admonished the judge for his remarks.

Other remarks by the judge are worthy of note.

Another child-custody matter Judge Healy presided over concerned a father's "vulgar and threatening text messages" to his ex-wife about visitation. One message stated, "Bitch, trust me, bitch, I'm not having it." The judge told the father that his conduct was unacceptable, and that he was talking "like some Ghetto whatever." He then told the father he was "stupid and thuggish." When the father said his neighbors knew him "as a person who would not allow harm to his children," Judge Healy asked the man "if he talked to his neighbors like he had talked" to his former wife in the messages. "Do you call your neighbors' wives bitches and hoes, all that?"

In a separate family law case he referred to the father as "morbidly obese and at risk of dying any time."

The judge didn't like the "attitude" of a mother who appeared in his courtroom in a case involving her daughter, and he expressed how he viewed the woman. "So, just an observation. This is the first time I've seen you, but if you are exposing your daughter to one-fifth of the attitude I'm getting from you right now, you might as well have her start walking the streets as a hooker, because that's the life you're going to subject her to when you treat her like this, when you flash this attitude like this."

In his defense before the state commission the judge "argued that blunt and evocative language is sometimes necessary to compel litigants to gain awareness of their circumstances, the harm that they are causing their children, and the importance of respect and cooperation."

In admonishing him, the commission stated: "Referring to litigants as rotten and stupid and thuggish, and telling litigants their child might as well start walking the streets as a hooker is the antithesis of imparting the importance of respect."

◊

The Board of Judicial Conduct in Tennessee reprimanded Judge Casey Stokes in January 2023 for calling a litigant a "tough guy" in court. Sounding more like a dude in a bar arguing with another dude over a spilled beer than a judge on the exulted bench, Judge Stokes seemingly challenged the litigant to a fist-fight. Referring to the judge as "your" in the quotation, the board contended the judge told the litigant: "If somebody called [your] grandfather an SOB, we would be in more than a cuss fight, we would be in a fist fight, and probably to the death."

Talk about being a tough guy.

The judge told the discipline board that the litigant had "interrupted" him and was "being rude toward the opposing party" in court.

The board reminded Judge Stokes that he had gotten a "warning" in the past about his "lack of self-control" and using "intemperate" words in court.

The board said judges must maintain their self-control even when litigants don't. Use of "overly harsh" words by a judge can give the impression he is biased against a litigant. "Regardless of how rude or disrespectful a participant in a legal proceeding may be, the judge cannot reciprocate," the board stated.

◊

Sometimes, not often, in reading details of judicial punishments you find one where a judge got a raw deal. In one such case, and at first blush, Orange County, California Superior Court Judge Pamela Lee Iles doesn't come across as a sympathetic character.

A judge for 25 years when she retired in 2008, she had an experienced past with the Commission on Judicial Performance, which had issued her four disciplinary letters over the years. One of these in 1997 for telling a criminal defendant that he would violate *his* probation if *his victim* contacted *him*. Obviously a novel approach.

Nonetheless, in a case involving an Iraqi man in 2002, Judge Iles showed heart and courage for an immigrant before "Sanctuary City" was ever a rallying cry for groups on the right and left to engage in political battle. The judge approved an unusual plea bargain proposed by the defendant and his attorney and accepted by the prosecution in a case involving Abbas Alhusainy, who was charged with "making criminal threats, child abuse causing great bodily harm, and assault with a deadly weapon arising from a domestic violence incident."

The plea deal was unusual if not illegal because it called for the defendant to plead guilty and not be sentenced if he left California and didn't return. The agreement stated that if he came back he would be arrested and sent to prison for up to seven years.

Judge Iles ordered the defendant to cooperate with the public defender's office, which later took him to Los Angeles International Airport for a flight to Detroit, where he had family which had offered to help him.

You must be asking, "what the hell is going on here?"

Four years after the plea deal was found to be unconditional by an appellate court, the discipline commission launched an investigation and asked Judge Iles why in the world she had agreed to such a strange plea bargain. For her, she said, it came down to a case of life or death. She explained she approved the deal because of the defendant's immigrant status. He would have been deported back to Iraq if she had sentenced him. By not sentencing him, it kept him out of the clutches of the old Immigration and Naturalization Service.

Here's the nub of it from commission records.

"Judge Iles stated that she was advised that there was an outstanding death warrant for the defendant in Iraq, and she was assured by counsel that deportation would result in torture and likely execution, which was never subject to dispute . . . It was the reason defendant's counsel proposed the plea bargain, and the reason that Judge Iles felt the plea bargain could be accepted. She stressed that the defendant voluntarily agreed to the plea bargain. Judge Iles stated that she was unwilling to leave the defendant's family in danger of further violence, or allow him to have assaulted them with impunity, but was unaware of any alternative that would have avoided the 'very real specter of torture or death following deportation.'" She told the commission that he was unlikely to harm anyone in Michigan because the "only people likely to be harmed by him were his wife and children," and sending him away protected them.

It was unlikely that she would have sentenced him to the maximum, and she said she was unwilling to sentence him and then have him tortured and executed in Iraq.

She believed the plea bargain was an appropriate solution under the circumstances.

So what did the judicial commission do?

It voted to publicly admonished Judge Iles for violating the judicial ethics code by not being "faithful to the law" and complying with legal precedents. As far back as 1953 the courts had established that "dumping criminals in other states" was against public policy.

Cases were pretty clear, saying that so-called "banishment" would "tend to incite dissension, provoke retaliation, and disturb that fundamental equality of political rights among the several states which is the basis of the Union itself." And stated another case: "To permit one state to dump its convict criminals into another is not in the interests of safety and welfare; therefore, the punishment by banishment to another state is prohibited by public policy."

What happened in the case of this crusading judge is she listened to her heart instead of her head.

◊

Arizona Superior Court Judge Steven Conn was preparing to sentence a defendant in a criminal case when he received a letter from the victim, a woman, who wrote that she opposed sending the defendant to jail. On the day of sentencing the woman arrived in the courtroom and the judge didn't "verify" whether the victim was present. During the sentencing hearing, however, he mentioned her, calling her an "idiot," and questioned her motivations for seeking no jail time for the defendant. The Arizona Commission on Judicial Conduct said that the judge's "comments about and characterizations of the victim" were misconduct. He was reprimanded in 2013.

◊

In the 1980s I wrote extensively about a male nurse who murdered elderly people in hospitals by injecting them with lethal drugs. Upon the man's conviction for a dozen murders, the judge who sentenced him said his crimes were particularly heinous because his victims were the most vulnerable of society, the elderly. Old people had suffered heart attacks and came to the hospital to be saved. Instead, he murdered them. When I read three separate cases involving judges who committed crimes against elderly people in New York and in California, I thought of the day I sat in the courtroom and heard the judge sentence the nurse to death. What would he have thought of his New York and California brethren who had preyed on the old?

The New York case is particularly disturbing because the victim was not only an elderly woman but she was also suffering from dementia and could not care for herself. The judge, Laura D. Stiggins, Justice of the Dansville Town Court of Steuben County, was convicted of two misdemeanors of "physically abusing a mentally incompetent patient" in 1998 at a nursing home where she worked as a licensed practical nurse. While working as an LVN at the Livingston County Campus Skilled Nursing Facility, a residential health care facility in Mount Morris, the judge threw the old woman who could not care for herself into the arm of a "Geri-Chair," a movable seat with sides on it. The fall caused a fractured rib. A jury convicted the nurse, who also sat as a judge, of third-degree assault – endangering the welfare of an incompetent person. She was sentenced to probation for three years. Afterward, New York's judicial discipline commission filed a complaint against the judge, saying her crime "demonstrates her lack of fitness for judicial office."

Even off the bench, as she was when she worked at the nursing home, the commission stated that "a judge remains clothed figuratively with his black robe of office devolving upon him standards of conduct more stringent than those acceptable for others . . . By physically abusing a mentally incompetent patient . . . [the judge] engaged in conduct that is unacceptable by any standard . . . [and] is intolerable in one who holds a position of public trust." With such harsh words, it was no surprise the commission voted to boot her from the bench in 2000.

The first California case involved a different kind of crime. Grabbing onto an elderly couple's multimillion estate, and allegedly milking it.

Before becoming an official at the courthouse in Oakland, Alameda County Superior Court Judge Paul D. Seeman, who graduated in1979 from the state's top law school, the University of California's Boalt Hall in Berkeley, practiced law in the San Francisco Bay area. In 1991 he served as a referee in the Alameda County Juvenile Court and by 2004 was named a court commissioner, handling regular court cases, and played a role in developing a dependency drug court. A Democrat, he was named a full-time Superior Court judge by Republican Governor Arnold Schwarzenegger in 2009, the same year he won a prestigious award as California Juvenile Court Judge of the Year. He seemed the unlikeliest of jurists to run afoul of the law.

Unfortunately for Judge Seeman, while still an attorney in 1998, he had met an elderly couple – an 89-year-old man and 85-year-old woman – who lived across the street from him in the ritzy Berkeley Hills neighborhood. They had been forced out of their home after authorities ruled it uninhabitable because of hoarding. Neighborly attorney Mr. Seeman offered to represent them and help get them back into their house.

The couple had no children, and none of their relatives lived nearby. In 1999, Mr. Seeman was allowed into the couple's home where he discovered stock certificates which he learned were worth one million dollars. The attorney continued to handle the couple's financial affairs. In 2004 was appointed a court commissioner and five years later he was appointed to the Superior Court judgeship. During all of these years he continued to handle financial affairs for the couple until the husband's death, and for the wife until 2010.

California Commission on Judicial Performance records stated that "in June 2004, when [the woman was 91 years old, [her] stock brokerage account was changed from an account for which Mr. Seeman had power of attorney to an account naming him as the pay-upon-death beneficiary." As such, upon her death, Judge Seeman "would have obtained sole ownership of the account, which was worth approximately $2,000,000." In addition, "Mr. Seeman's name was added to two of [her] bank accounts, one with $200,000 in it and the other containing about $250,000." Again, upon her death these accounts would have gone to the judge. He also got the woman to give him a $250,000 "signature" loan.

Although Judge Seeman "managed" the woman's life savings for about a decade, she proved not to be as senile as he might have thought. At some point in 2007 she hired another attorney to look into her finances, and the lawyer told Judge Seeman to remove his name from her accounts. The judge failed to do so.

However, sometime later Berkeley police began looking into the case, and after a drawn-out white-collar crime investigation, the cops arrested Judge Seeman in his chambers at the courthouse in Oakland in 2012. The judge was charged with 30 felonies in the case. He pleaded no contest, the legal equivalent of guilty to felony elderly abuse and was sentenced to probation for five years. The judge resigned in March 2013 before he was booted off the court by the state commission, which showing forethought, got him to agree to be disbarred and prevented from practicing law in California.

◇

The second California case involving the elderly was in Riverside County. Superior Court Judge William H. Sullivan was a man of large stature, and by all accounts had a personality tending to the quiet and docile side. A little too docile. Because under his watch in the 1990s of running the county's conservatorship court, where assets of elderly people who could not care for themselves were supposed to be protected, a slick conservatorship business owner stole money from infirm folks whose conservatorships Judge Sullivan had approved.

Black's Law Dictionary defines "conservator" as someone "appointed by court to manage" the estate of "incompetent, protected persons." Few conservatorship scandals ever bastardized the definition more than this one. For instance, a 95-year-old woman placed in the care of the crooked conservator started with an estate of $300,000. In five years it was worth $10,000. Where'd the money go? For two years the crooked conservator paid $170,000 for "home care" to a company she owned. Astoundingly the insurance company that bonded the conservator was on the hook in 34 claims for up to $3.2 million. A prosecutor called the case "worse than grave robbing" because victims were "at the end of their lives . . . and most vulnerable." By the time the dust settled, the crooked conservator and her attorney were convicted and sentenced to long stretches in prison.

There were warning signs. Not only did families of elderly people under county conservatorships complain about missing money, jewelry and antiques, court employees and even the court's own examiner complained to Judge Sullivan about problems. When a complaint came in, the docile judge asked the crooked conservator and she always had a pat response. Rarely did the judge demand documentation to back up her denials. In some cases the judge ordered her to refund money she had "padded" as expenses for her services.

Essentially his watchdog role was toothless. Perhaps the judge didn't want to rock the boat too hard because he had his own little secrets to hide.

According to Commission on Judicial Performance records, Judge Sullivan was secretly handling "trust" accounts for affluent people who had given him control over their financial assets when he was practicing law. Judicial ethics prohibit a judge from handling trusts outside his own family.

It was a sweet deal. "Between 1990 and 1994, [Judge Sullivan] loaned himself $186,000" from a trust fund at a stock and bond brokerage "by writing checks from himself as trustee to himself as an individual." Records showed he repaid the loans later. The judge also carried on a lucrative business of buying and selling deeds of trust between various trust accounts he managed, and pocketing fees from transactions. He also committed judicial misconduct when he failed to report the transactions on his required financial disclosure forms, which judges must file annually.

These actions were sufficient to have him investigated by the state commission and possibly removed from office for unethical conduct. What sucked him into the overall conservatorship scandal, however, was a private investigation by an advocacy group for older people. After family members became frustrated that their complaints about the crooked conservator fell on deaf ears of county officials, including the district attorney's office, they asked the private Northern California advocacy group to take a look. An attorney for the group went to the Riverside courthouse and photocopied thousands of pages of probate records. The documents revealed the depth and scale of the massive scandal, which ignited a belated but vigorous investigation by Riverside law enforcement. But the records also showed that the judge had purchased a house in the affluent Canyon Crest neighborhood of the city from an elderly man who was under a conservatorship presided over by Judge Sullivan. His unethical behavior had taken a step up. The deal represented a real sleight of hand by the judge. In 1992 he signed an order authorizing sale of the man's house, and despite the obvious conflict of interest, he entered into a sales agreement to purchase the two-bedroom home. As required by law, a notice of trustee sale of the house was published in the newspaper for three weeks in June, stating that the house would be sold, and bidders should state their interest. However, to short-circuit bidding, the judge ordered the date of the sale changed, which in effect, denied others to bid on the property that he had agreed to buy. After buying the man's house, the judge continued to preside over his court conservatorship.

Once the overall conservatorship scandal was exposed, and the case was properly investigated by the district attorney's office, Judge Sullivan retired in 1999. But his purchase of the house was included in a misdemeanor case against him. The judge pleaded guilty and was fined about $25,000. At the conclusion of its own investigation, which cited the house purchase as well as many other unethical acts, the judicial commission barred him from ever sitting as a judge in the state. A judge since 1987 and a graduate of Stanford University Law School in 1955, Judge Sullivan died six years after retiring.

Responsibility for the massive conservatorship scandal cannot be laid on Judge Sullivan, when it was the wicked work of a crooked conservator and attorney. Yet, there's little doubt it spun out of control because of his lax oversight. Also sharing blame was the probate court's status as a courthouse stepchild, to the point of disinterest by judges in charge of all court departments. The opinion seemed to be, it's only probate – wills and conservatorships – the dead and the old. Who cares? Demonstrating this is the fact that the final order confirming sale of the Riverside house to Judge Sullivan was signed by *another* judge.

◊

Hey, the judge had a business to run. He owned two rental houses in Southern California, in La Habra and Whittier, and somebody had to collect the rents. So he let his clerk and bailiff do it, during court hours. Tenants stopped by and handed over rent checks. In return, the staff provided a receipt.

Come on, it was as smooth as a well-run courtroom.

The Commission on Judicial Performance – those capitalist haters – didn't like how Orange County, California Superior Court Judge John M. Watson used government workers for his private real estate dealings. The commission publicly admonished him in 2006, saying his "use of court staff, court resources and the court facilities for his personal real estate business was improper." Look at all of what the clerk had done for the boss. "The clerk received and returned telephone calls from tenants and relayed messages between the judge and the tenants about matters such as inspections and repairs. She made calls to various businesses and the Los Angeles Housing Authority in connection with the judge's properties, and occasionally sent and received faxes from the Realtors who leased the La Habra property for the judge... [She] prepared 40 letters and legal notices in connection with his real estate business, including tenancy termination notices." And, she "performed these tasks whenever the judge requested, in the courtroom during the workday."

That's a dedicated employee!

◇

A travelling judge in Maine had a tough job, and the state's Supreme Judicial Court admitted it in 1986. "We recognize that a judge at large, while traveling throughout the state, must function under many difficulties, including a heavy caseload and inadequate physical facilities." Still, the court ruled that District Court Judge at Large Ronald L. Kellam should not have mistreated people the way he did in his courtroom. By today's standards of rudeness the judge's discourteous comments to litigants who came into his court without attorneys were tame. To a husband who sought a protective order from his wife because she made death threats against him, Judge Kellam shot back: "You're here, aren't you? She didn't kill you yet." To a wife seeking the same kind of order from the judge to keep her abusive husband away from her, the judge told her he couldn't change history. "He hasn't changed since he met you, why did you marry him? Why do you want me to do something about it now?"

Citing the state's ethics code for judges which required them to be "patient, dignified, and courteous to litigants, jurors, witnesses, and others with whom he deals in his official capacity," Maine's Supreme Judicial Court ruled that the judge's rudeness was severe enough to warrant a censure and suspension from duties for 20 days and loss of $3,500 in salary.

◇

Los Angeles County Court Commissioner Alan Friedenthal had an interesting way to describe himself in court one day. Commissioners rule on some court cases just like judges. In talking in court about someone who was afraid of coming to his courtroom, he said, "I don't know why she's refused to come. She's told [another judge] she's afraid of me, which I think is hysterical, this pudgy little judicial officer she's afraid of... Tell her I have been defanged, and I no longer have rabies."

◇

New Jersey Municipal Court Judge Steven Brister was suspended for a month without pay in September of 2021 for preaching from the "pulpit." When a man who had been arrested for repeated bashings of his wife appeared before the judge in February 2019, Judge Brister "noted that the defendant had multiple domestic violence matters," and said: "I'm going to tell you what I tell a lot of people with this same charge. Because all of these charges are the same. We, as men, and I can speak to you as a man [be]cause I am a man as well. We get frustrated with the women human beings because we try to straighten out a creation [be]cause they was created with a curve. But we as men, we think we [are] above creation and we can straighten it out. No matter how much you try, or how you try to straighten out that curve, you can never do it. We get frustrated and then but, in our frustration you can't come at them like you['re] Mike Tyson and they're in the ring like they're Leon Spinks. You can't do it. You can't punch, you can't hit. At best, you treat [them] as if you're holding a feather, just to let them know you're the man and you're in control. But in each of these five complaints it said you went at them like Mike Tyson."

After a complaint was filed against the judge, the state's judicial misconduct commission told him that his "reference to women and the manner in which men should treat them was inappropriate, disparaging to women and had the potential to create the appearance of a gender bias in violation" of the New Jersey Code of Judicial Conduct. Obviously curious, commissioners asked the judge what he meant by saying women were "created with a curve"?

To this Judge Brister responded: ". . . When I was young, I was [an] altar boy . . . So if you believe in a creation from a higher power, then that curve is the creation of the woman [Eve] with the curve of the rib of Adam."

Oh, Lord! The judge used a biblical reference from the bench – clearly anathema to the separation of church and state crowd. The commission stated: "Respondent [the judge] assimilated his personal religious beliefs into his judicial role and demonstrated an inability to conform his conduct to the high standards" of the New Jersey courts.

Judge Brister freely admitted that he "did mistakenly assimilate his personal religious beliefs into his judicial role and failed to conform his conduct to the high standards of conduct expected of judges." In a settlement of the discipline case, he agreed to seek online education on bias, and watched videos with titles like, "Sexual Harassment in the Practice of Law," "A Bad Day in Black Robes," and "Maintaining A Bias-Free Court Room." Judge Brister also met with another judge for additional anti-bias training and that judge stressed that "it is vital for the future that [Judge Brister] omit extraneous, irrelevant references to religious beliefs and practices, irrelevant comments about human sexuality and other comments that may have any tendency to demonstrate bias."

◊

If anybody doubts that judges must be careful in what they say and how they act when *not* on the job, ask Texas Judge Jeremy Warren, a judge since 2011. Coaching his 12-year-old son's Little League team, Judge Warren didn't like the refereeing in a tournament game in September 2016 in Houston. Like a fan in the stands, or a father deeply into his child's sports, the judge expressed it.

He did not like a game-ending call by the umpire at home plate, in which the ump said the judge's player tried to take the catcher out with a "malicious swing, like he tried to hit him." The call ended the tournament for the judge's baseball team, and it stirred a shouting-match. Judge Warren gave his best impersonation of old-time Yankees Manager Billy Martin, famous for in-game skirmishes with umps. "You suck," the judge shouted, calling the ump an "asshole," "bastard" and "racist." He didn't forget to call the guy's future of wearing the blue into question, either, telling him he "will never umpire again . . . ever."

The judge claimed the ump called him a liar. "You're the liar," the judge retorted. "Bring it [to] . . . Angleton, Texas County Court Number Three." With that statement the judge let everybody in earshot know he was a jurist. His hot-headedness had probably already trod on his judicial ethics, yet when he revealed his official position, he assured it.

Of course there were plenty of nosy cellphones at hand to record the heckling and a local television station got the juicy sound bites. The judge apologized to the team, stating that "they should never see an adult act like that. I didn't set a good example for them." He also said he "regretted" his heckling of the ump.

The judge knew his apology wasn't the end of it. As required he reported the incident to the Texas judicial conduct group, which later issued a "warning" and ordered him to get "education" to help avoid such bad behavior. The commission stated that his argument with the umpire "cast public discredit upon the judiciary." It also stated that he "injected" his position of being a judge into the situation for his own interests.

Arguing that his actions did not bring "discredit" on the court, the judge unsuccessfully fought the public rebuke and said the incident in no way changed how he conducted himself on the bench (not the baseball bench). He said he had always been fair and "will continue to be."

In a little ironic footnote on the game, film showed that the ump's call of a "malicious swing" at home plate was erroneous. The sponsor of the baseball tournament ruled that the man wouldn't umpire again.

Justice?

◊

Baseball played a role in another judicial discipline case, this in California.

Damn the verdict, this is the playoffs!

The judge didn't say that, but might have thought it.

On October 4th, 2004 he read the boringly complicated instructions to the jury in a double-murder case, and the case went to the jury. It was a complicated one, involving a 2002 drunk driving accident in which the defendant's girlfriend and unborn baby had perished.

The following morning the judge arrived at the courthouse in Riverside, California. It was October 5th, a big day in Southern California baseball. The first game of the American League Division Series, pitting Major League Baseball's L.A. Angels of Anaheim against the Boston Red Sox of slugger David Ortiz. Maybe Angels Vladimir Guerrero, a future Hall-of-Famer would crush one out of Big A stadium, which was just down the freeway in Orange County.

Around late-morning Riverside County Superior Court Judge Paul E. Zellerbach left court and headed to the ball park, which would rock later with 44,600 fans. Thoughtfully, he arranged to have another judge answer questions jurors might have during deliberations.

Unexpectedly, around 2:30 in the afternoon, about an hour and a half after the first pitch (maybe enough time for a mustard dog and brewsky), jurors announced reaching a verdict. His courtroom clerk immediately tried to reach the judge on his cellphone but had to leave a message about the verdict when he didn't answer. Smartly, she then called another judge and asked if he would take the verdict. He said, of course. The clerk called the attorneys in the case and told them to come to court for reading of the verdict at 3:30 p.m., "in order to allow them sufficient time to have the defendant's and victim's families present for the verdict."

All seemed orderly, and you've got to admire the bright initiative of the courtroom clerk. But even the best laid plans go awry. The judge returned his clerk's call, and when she told him she had arranged to have another judge – who had worked with Judge Zellerbach in the district attorney's office – Judge Zellerbach "said that he wanted to do so himself, and instructed his clerk to tell the attorneys to return to court the next morning, October 6th." It was the playoffs, after all.

The clerk who must have been a bit beside herself called the attorneys and told them of the judge's decision. Despite her call, the attorneys came to court and asked the clerk to call Judge Zellerbach again because they wished to "have the verdict taken that day." Stuck in the middle, the clerk called the judge again at the baseball stadium and he repeated that he "did not want another judge to take the verdict, and that he would take the verdict himself the next day." That ended it, and by the way the game also ended at about 4:15 p.m., after three hours of play. (Angel Guerrero had a home run in the series.)

Judge Zellerbach took the verdict the morning.

It didn't set well with the Commission on Judicial Performance. In 2006 the commission issued a public reprimand of the judge for not giving his judicial duties "precedence" over the baseball game.

In his defense the judge said he went to the game without arranging for another judge to take the verdict "because he did not think the jury would return with a verdict that day, given the complicated issues in the trial." The commission noted that the judge had nearly three decades as a judge and prosecutor and "must have known that it is not possible to predict how long a jury will deliberate, irrespective of how complicated the issues or how long the trial." The commission stated that the judge admitted as much when he appeared before the commission. Judge Zellerbach also asserted that he instructed his clerk to put the case over until the next day, rather than allowing another judge to take the verdict, "because he was concerned about complicated legal issues in the case and as related to the possible verdict." To this assertion, the commission shot back: "Given the asserted complexity of the legal issues, Judge Zellerbach should not have gone to the baseball game while the jury was deliberating." The commission said the judge "acknowledged the correctness of this conclusion" as well.

But, didn't the commission understand it was the playoffs? This was what might have pissed off the six commission members who voted for a public reprimand, calling his actions a "serious dereliction of judicial duty." Its report concluded: "Judge Zellerbach jeopardized the verdict in a double homicide case and imposed hardship and additional stress on jurors, the families of the victim and the defendant, and on counsel and the defendant."

The verdict? The defendant was convicted of two counts of second-degree murder and later sentenced to prison for 15 years to life. And the Angles lost the October 5th game, 9-3, and went on to lose the series to Boston. And what about Superfan Zellerbach? He'd go on to be elected district attorney of Riverside County, and attend many more ballgames.

Afterword

I don't have to tell you that there's some pretty strange ducks sitting on judicial benches, or, for that matter, who served until they got the boot by their respective watchdog commissions. That said, as I pointed out in the introduction, judges who violate ethics rules are the exception and not the rule, just as the criminals in America's prisons do not reflect the attitudes, beliefs and character of the majority of Americans. A guy pulling in $50,000 a year isn't going to like me saying that a state judge making $175,000 a year is not being paid enough. The fact is judges could make much more money working as attorneys in the private sector. In researching this book I discovered some Florida judges made only $137,000 a year. Pharmaceutical salesmen can make more. Chief Justice of the U.S. Supreme Court John Roberts has said that judges aren't paid enough, which goes against the opinion of many economists and others, including philosopher Plato, who argued the pay of public servants should be low to discourage men of selfish motivations from seeking office, a view prevalent today. For comparison, I knew an attorney in the 1980s who made $400,000 a year handling DUI cases, a field of easy and settled law. He never had to crack a law book. At the same time I reported on a grueling trial lasting months, involving a toxic waste dump and the EPA's Superfund. The case was full of extremely complicated, and unsettled issues of law. The judge who ruled on these head-throbbing issues was paid little more than a quarter of the salary of the DUI lawyer and, in my opinion, was brighter by a factor of four. Administering justice is also dangerous. Judges have been shot by courthouse stalkers, including in Steubenville, Ohio, in which a judge was shot and wounded outside the courthouse by a man who was involved in a wrongful death lawsuit being handled by the judge. The judge's bailiff shot and killed the assailant, and the judge also fired shots back, proving anew that many jurists believe they need concealed weapons for protection and do.

I first became acquainted with workings of the California Commission on Judicial Performance in the early 1970s. I chuckled at the antics of some judges who had been slapped by the commission. In the ensuring years I saw significant changes in the breadth and detail of complaint information released to the public. In its early years the commission was stingier than Scrooge in disclosing details of a judge's misconduct. When it did, the information was scraped and sanitized with a metal brush. Here's an example. This is the full report of a case in 1971, in which the judge received a serious censure: "During a conversation in his chambers concerning the disposition of criminal charges pending in his court [the judge] referred to the victim of the alleged crimes in an insulting and inexcusable manner and on a later date made certain intemperate comments in open court in connection with the same case." We're never told what the judge's comments were. The full public report on the misconduct was 323 words. Obviously the dearth of detail was supposed to protect the judge from embarrassment, and the poor bewildered public was left to imagine what the judge's "insulting" words had been. In 1995, state voters rebelled and changed the California Constitution and transformed the judicial discipline commission into a formidable judicial policeman. Today the California commission releases detailed information on a judge's misconduct which can amount to thousands of words, and contain details to make a sailor blush. After reading this book you know what I mean.

Here is where this is going.

The federal court system was 20 years behind California in establishing the Judicial Conduct and Disability Act of 1980, and in 2006, a blue-ribbon panel of federal judges led by Associate Justice Stephen Breyer of the U.S. Supreme Court was asked to study the success or failure of the act which spells out rules for handling misconduct complaints against federal judges. In particular, the review looked at 700 complaints that weren't investigated by the federal courts. Essentially the group found no problems in handling or dismissing complaints, although it reported that too many so-called "high profile" complaints had slipped through the cracks, and recommended remedies. A far less scientific but much more on-point study was done in 2018 by a CNN investigative team. Reporters reviewed 5,000 federal court discipline orders, from 2006 to 2017. Reporters found records "rarely [gave] the name of the judge who was the subject of the complaint or the specifics of the grievance asserted." CNN concluded: "The vast majority of the orders issued were only one or two pages and comprised of boilerplate procedural language." In other words, if there's widespread sexual harassment behind the thick doors of the federal bench we're purposely blinded to it.

Long before iconic TV entertainer Bill Cosby dreamed of a Spanish fly, sex scandals have plagued state courts and the judges who preside over them. This book clearly illustrates it. At the federal level, however, other than Anita Hill accusing her former employer, then-Supreme Court nominee, conservative Clarence Thomas of sexual harassment in 1991, the only racy matter to hit the U.S. Supreme Court – as far as we know – has been sober, elderly justices watching X-rated movies to decide pornography cases. Federal courts have been largely free of publicity about sexual harassment, seemingly by design, if the CNN review of records is to be believed. Except for the abrupt retirement of Judge Alex Kozinski of the 9th Circuit Court of Appeals, which was described earlier, U.S. courts have kept sex problems completely robed.

Which raises this point. The federal court system should reform the way it publicly reports complaints against its judges. Naming names and citing facts is the backbone of every courtroom in the land. The U.S. Supreme Court should look to its own precedents. In particular, a media case known by the shorthand, *PE II* (1984), in which the court ruled that just because a juror might be embarrassed to answer a question about rape in open court it was insufficient reason to close a courtroom to the press and public during jury selection. By extension, if it is all right to expose a regular citizen to possible embarrassment in court, it is also all right to expose a federal judge to embarrassment by releasing his name and the full details of complaints against him.

The federal courts are so far behind the states in complaint full-disclosure that it edges towards self-protectionism. Change is always messy. Because, as a national study on judicial discipline by Cynthia Gray and the State Justice Institute found ". . . part of the purpose of judicial discipline is to deter other judges and to reassure the public that the judiciary does not tolerate judicial misconduct." Ms. Gray added, "decisions" on discipline should "be available on a web site." Federal reformers should look to states such as California, New York, Michigan, Illinois and Texas for ideas of reform. That doesn't mean states have entirely clean hands when it comes to punishing – or not punishing – judges for misconduct. The Reuters news service conducted an investigation of state discipline commissions published online in 2020, and declared: "In the past dozen years, state and local judges have repeatedly escaped public accountability for misdeeds that have victimized thousands. Nine of 10 kept their jobs, a Reuters investigation found – including an Alabama judge who unlawfully jailed hundreds of poor people, many of them black, over traffic fines." The report went on to say, that "Reuters identified and reviewed 1,509 cases from the last dozen years – 2008 through 2019 – in which judges resigned, retired or were publicly disciplined following accusations of misconduct." While the news agency didn't do this calculation, in breaking the numbers down in cases in which judges were both punished and their misdeeds were made public a troublesome trend developed: such discipline cases amounted to little more than two per year per commission when based on 52 judicial commissions, including Washington, D.C.'s own and that of Puerto Rico. That's a dismal statistic. Many states still do not release details of misconduct by judges, and the Reuters report went on to say that "reporters identified another 3,613 cases from 2008 through 2018 in which states disciplined wayward judges but kept hidden from the public key details of their offenses – including the identities of the judges themselves." In the first in a series of stories, amounting to more than 6,500 words, the news agency named less than a dozen judges who were investigated and punished by commissions. "All told," reported Reuters, "9 of every 10 judges were allowed to return to the bench after they were sanctioned for misconduct." The news agency also provided a reasonable explanation for the "9 of 10" statistic, quoting a New York University law professor. "Although punishment short of removal from the bench is appropriate for most misconduct cases, Stephen Gillers said, the public 'would be appalled at some of the lenient treatment judges get' for substantial transgressions."

End

www.ingramcontent.com/pod-product-compliance
Lightning Source LLC
Chambersburg PA
CBHW020631220526
45464CB00001B/100